An Investigation Into the Nature of Consciousness and Form

An Investigation Into the Nature of Consciousness and Form

Mechanistic And Nonmechanistic Science

Richard L. Thompson

MOTILAL BANARSIDASS PUBLISHERS
PRIVATE LIMITED • DELHI

First Indian Editon: Delhi, ***2007***
Earlier published by the Bhaktivedanta Book Trust
with the title ***Mechanistic and Nonmechanistic Science***
(formerly published by Bala Books)

ISBN: 978-81-208-1920-7

MOTILAL BANARSIDASS
41 U.A. Bungalow Road, Jawahar Nagar, Delhi 110 007
8 Mahalaxmi Chamber, 22 Bhulabhai Desai Road, Mumbai 400 026
203 Royapettah High Road, Mylapore, Chennai 600 004
236, 9th Main III Block, Jayanagar, Bangalore 560 011
Sanas Plaza, 1302 Baji Rao Road, Pune 411 002
8 Camac Street, Kolkata 700 017
Ashok Rajpath, Patna 800 004
Chowk, Varanasi 221 001

PRINTED IN INDIA

BY JAINENDRA PRAKASH JAIN AT SHRI JAINENDRA PRESS,
A-45 NARAINA, PHASE-I, NEW DELHI 110 028
AND PUBLISHED BY NARENDRA PRAKASH JAIN FOR
MOTILAL BANARSIDASS PUBLISHERS PRIVATE LIMITED,
BUNGALOW ROAD, DELHI 110 007

Dedicated to

His Divine Grace
A.C. Bhaktivedanta Swami Prabhupāda

om ajñāna-timirāndhasya jñānāñjana-śalākayā
cakṣur unmīlitaṁ yena tasmai śrī-gurave namaḥ

Contents

PART III. CONCLUSION

Introduction

In an article on the theory of evolution, the biologist John Maynard Smith declared, "The individual is simply a device constructed by the genes to ensure the production of more genes like themselves."[1] This statement conveys in a nutshell what modern science has to say about the meaning of human life. It tells us that the individual person is nothing more than a machine composed of material elements. This machine has come into being only because it and the other machines in its ancestral line happened to be effective at self-duplication in their particular environmental circumstances. All of this machine's attributes—including its thoughts and feelings, its abilities, and its hopes and desires—are meaningful only insofar as they contribute to the propagation of the machine's genetic blueprint. And this is meaningless in any ultimate sense, for the genes themselves are nothing but inanimate molecules.

Smith's statement is by no means exaggerated or atypical. It is a straightforward expression of the conclusions of conventional evolutionary theory. Moreover, if we generalize this statement by allowing it to refer not just to genes as we know them but to any possible system of physical self-reproduction, then the statement follows as an unavoidable corollary of the mechanistic world view of modern science.

The term "mechanistic" refers to the theoretical system of modern physics, which is based on measurement and calculation. Loosely speaking, the fundamental premise of physics is that all phenomena are produced by an underlying stuff called matter. Physicists have developed a number of different theoretical descriptions of matter, and they have still to agree on a final theory. Yet all of their theories share the following two features:

(1) Matter can be represented by numbers that correspond directly or indirectly to experimentally measurable properties.

(2) The behavior of matter can be described by mathematical expressions called the "laws of nature."

The world view of modern physics is essentially mathematical, and to a person steeped in this way of seeing things, the mathematical abstractions of physical theories (such as orbitals, waves, and particles) seem more real than the tangible phenomena they are used to describe.

Today, research in nearly every scientific field revolves around the mechanistic premise that all phenomena are due to matter acting in accord with the laws of nature. In biology this premise implies that living organisms are combinations of material elements, and that they must have arisen from earlier states of matter by purely physical processes. Since the goal of mechanistic theorization is to explain as much as possible by the natural laws, scientists hypothesize that life developed from matter that existed originally in a disorganized, nonliving form. This hypothesis has been systematically elaborated, first in the Darwinian theory of evolution, and then in the theory of molecular evolution. The first of these theories deals with the origin of higher species from single-celled organisms, and the second tries to account for the origin of the first living cells from simple chemical compounds in a "primordial soup."

In psychology the mechanistic premise implies that mind is merely a name for certain patterns of electrochemical interaction in the brain. This means that psychological terms such as "purpose" or "meaning" correspond to nothing more than patterns of behavior that arose as evolutionary adaptations. The mechanistic premise implies that it is pointless to seek an absolute sense for such terms or to apply them on a universal scale, for the universe as a whole consists of nothing but an inexorable flux of physical actions and reactions. Persons are thus reduced to mere subpatterns of an inherently meaningless universal pattern.

Although many scientists assert that the mechanistic approach of modern science is correct, many also admit that it leaves them with a feeling of dissatisfaction. Thus the physicist Steven Weinberg winds up his account of the big bang theory by describing human beings as the "more-or-less farcical outcome of a chain of accidents reaching back to the first three minutes," and he concludes that only the quest for knowledge by physicists like himself "lifts human life above the level of farce, and gives it some of the grace of tragedy."[2] The bitterness and disappointment in this conclusion can also be seen in Bertrand Russell's declaration that, because the mechanistic world view has become so solidly established, "only on the firm foundation of unyielding despair can the soul's habitation henceforth be safely built."[3]

The mechanistic world vision tends to create in sensitive individuals such a sense of existential despair. It denies the very existence of an absolute dimension of higher purpose that seems essential for the satisfaction of the inner self. Of course, some people may argue that if we have no purpose in an absolute sense, we can create our own purpose. Yet this answer, too, is not satisfying, for if we contemplate such manufactured "purpose" from the mechanistic viewpoint, we see it dissolve into nothing but a meaningless juxtaposition of physiochemical events.

The mechanistic world view also exerts a powerful influence on human social relationships. The peaceful conduct of day-to-day affairs depends on people's adherence to certain laws and standards of behavior. These depend on systems of moral and ethical values that ultimately cannot be imposed by force, but must be accepted by inner conviction. Yet mechanistic theories can provide no compelling justification for any system of social values, and they exclude any attempted justification that draws on nonmechanistic concepts.

A list of higher human qualities might include such items as charity, self-control, nonviolence, truthfulness, freedom from anger, compassion, freedom from greed, modesty, cleanliness, and forgiveness. Such qualities are certainly conducive to the well-being of human society, but on what basis can people be induced to value them? Some evolutionists have tried to use the principle of natural selection, or "survival of the fittest," to explain higher modes of behavior as convoluted Machiavellian tactics designed (in an unconscious, mechanistic sense) to further the goal of widely disseminating one's genes.[4] Thus far, these arguments have been vague and unconvincing. Yet even if a convincing case could be made, it seems this kind of reasoning would not induce people to cultivate higher qualities and moral principles. Indeed, by creating a sense of cynicism, it might likely have the opposite effect.

Actually, the mechanistic principles cannot support any line of reasoning about how people should behave. The mechanistic philosophy implies that you will simply do whatever your bodily chemistry drives you to do. This philosophy denies the very idea of the self as a responsible agent with free will, and thus it also renders meaningless the idea of moral choice.

In the past, people derived their values and their sense of meaning and purpose in life from traditional, nonmechanistic religious systems. Today this is still going on, but many people have become convinced that religion is inferior to science. Mechanistic science has become widely accepted as the only source of genuine knowledge about the world, and as the domain of science has been extended, the authority of the traditional religions has been steadily eroded. Yet religion remains the only source of values and conceptions of higher purpose. As a result, many people find themselves in a painful situation: It seems that they can acquire rational knowledge only at the price of being cast adrift on a trackless sea of fundamental meaninglessness.

Mechanistic science provides a dynamic method of acquiring more and more verifiable knowledge about the world, and it has been impressive because of its prodigious power to explain and manipulate material phenomena. In contrast, religion seems to depend on the blind acceptance of rigid, unverifiable doctrines, many of which have been discredited by modern scientific theories. The world views of the traditional religions are fundamentally incompatible with the world view of modern science, and as the latter vision has gained widespread acceptance, traditional religious conceptions have come to seem more and more antiquated and unrealistic. For these reasons the credibility of the traditional religions has steadily declined, and this decline has been accelerated by the corruption, inequity, and insincerity that have been prominent in many religious establishments. It has also been aided by the tendency toward compromise, unbridled speculation, and downright concoction, which has produced a bewildering welter of conflicting religious sects and philosophies.

With the eclipse of religion and its replacement by the mechanistic philosophy of modern science, human society has been precipitated into a moral and spiritual crisis. If the mechanistic world view is indeed valid, then it is hard to see how a satisfactory solution of this crisis can be achieved. In that case all we can do is try to live with the conscious awareness that life has no intrinsic purpose—or else plunge willfully into delusion and try to live in a divided house of faith and reason.

Yet there is evidence that the mechanistic world view does not represent the whole truth. In this book I show on the basis of logic and ordinary evidence that the prevailing theories of physics and biology have serious defects which can be traced to shortcomings in their underlying mechanistic framework. This negative conclusion suggests that the spiritual crisis of modern society might be relieved if we could find a truly scientific system of spiritual knowledge that extends and partly supersedes the current theories of science. I try to make a positive contribution by introducing such a nonmechanistic alternative to the mechanistic world view. This system of knowledge must satisfy the following four criteria:

First, since mechanistic theories have nothing to say about purpose and personal values, this system must be nonmechanistic. A scientific theory can be briefly defined as a logically consistent system of statements that can often be verified by objective observations, and that do not conflict with observation. All of the important theories of modern science can be translated, at least in principle, entirely into mechanistic terms. In other words, they can be expressed in the form of statements about measurements and calculations. Yet there is no reason to suppose that a valid scientific theory has to be mechanistic. Nonmechanistic scientific theories are possible, and to establish a sound foundation for spiritual knowledge we must seek such a theory.

The second criterion is that our system must attribute some dimension of absolute reality to personality. Unless there is some sense in which personality is built into the nature of things, it is not possible to formulate a satisfactory definition of ultimate purpose. Also, in the absence of some conception of the individual as an actual being endowed with free will, there is no meaning to moral and ethical values.

In this connection I should note that there are some nonmechanistic philosophies—including Buddhism and the monistic philosophies of India and China—which hold that personality is essentially unreal. Recently there have been some attempts to reconcile these philosophies with the mechanistic theories of modern physics.[5] However, these efforts do not achieve the goal that I have in mind. The problem is that in their treatment of personality, these philosophies are indeed in harmony with the mechanistic world view. They also accept personal existence to be meaningless, and their aim is to relieve the anxieties of personal life by bringing the individual to the realization that he fundamentally does not exist.

The third criterion is that the new system must disagree with the existing theories of modern science to some extent. Some people entertain the hope of finding a system of spiritual knowledge that harmonizes with the existing scientific theories. I propose that this hope is unrealistic. The first two criteria are necessary for an adequate spiritual science, and they cannot be reconciled with a universal mechanistic system. Yet this does not mean that the search for a scientifically valid spiritual system is futile. If we closely examine modern science, we can see that in its pretensions to universality it has deviated seriously from its observational foundations, and has fallen into error.

In this book I will discuss two major areas in which any adequate system of spiritual knowledge must clash with the theories of modern science. Both turn out to be areas in which scientists have made unjustifiable extrapolations of physical theories in an effort to create a universal world picture. Both are also areas in which a careful examination of theory and observational evidence shows that the existing scientific picture is seriously deficient.

Biology is the first of these areas of unjustifiable extrapolation. Modern biology is founded on the premise that life can be understood *completely* in terms of chemistry and physics. No one would deny that many features of living organisms can be adequately explained by physiochemical models, and it is reasonable to anticipate that our physiochemical understanding of biological processes will be greatly extended in the future. Yet no one thus far has even come close to giving a complete physiochemical analysis of any living organism.

In modern biology the view that life cannot be fully described by physical theory is called vitalism. The attitude of many biologists towards vitalism is illustrated by the remark, written in a standard biology textbook, that "those today who may still be prompted to fill gaps in scientific knowledge with vitalism must be prepared to have red faces tomorrow."[6] It is true that many vitalistic theories of the past have been faulty, and have been disproven by later scientific findings. Nevertheless, such negative evidence does not prove that life can be fully explained without recourse to nonphysical principles, and the blustering tone often used by scientists who make such assertions betrays the weakness of their position. In this book I will argue that life cannot, in fact, be understood without the introduction of principles that are not merely nonphysical as we presently understand this term, but are strictly nonmechanistic.

The field of evolutionary theory is the second area of unjustifiable extrapolation that I will consider. During the Darwin centennial celebration Sir Julian Huxley declared, "The evolution of life is no longer a theory; it is a fact and the basis of all our thinking."[7] It is certainly true that a theory of evolution is an essential ingredient in any universal mechanistic system. Yet here again, the aggressive tone with which Huxley and others affirm the present theory of evolution betrays an underlying lack of convincing proof. In this book I will argue that the theory of evolution is not actually supported by the factual evidence of biology and natural history, and I will also show that there are fundamental theoretical impediments confronting any attempt to construct a mechanistic account of the origin of life.

The work of criticizing existing scientific theories is essentially negative, and its purpose is to clear the way for a positive alternative to the mechanistic world view. But how can we arrive at such an alternative? This question brings us to the fourth criterion for a scientific system of spiritual knowledge. If such a system is indeed to provide ultimate standards of personal meaning, then it must make reference to information that relates to persons and that is built into the very nature of things. In other words, the system must have recourse to some universal source of personal direction.

If such a source exists and is accessible to human beings, it stands to reason that other people may have known about it in the past. Indeed, it makes little sense to suppose that a genuine source of absolute personal guidance would remain unknown to human beings throughout history, only to be revealed at the present time. This consideration greatly simplifies the task of finding a genuine spiritual science. Instead of having to invent such a science from scratch, we should search for it among the many philosophical and religious systems of the past and present. Our problem becomes one of recognition rather than one of creation.

A genuine system of spiritual knowledge should have all the characteristics of a scientific theory. It should provide a logically consistent description of reality, and it should entail procedures which can be used to verify important features of this description. The system should be in agreement with existing mechanistic theories insofar as they are valid, but it may be expected to clash with many elements of the modern scientific world view that rest on unsound speculation and extrapolation. Most importantly, the system should contain practical methods of obtaining absolute information about the ultimate meaning and purpose of life.

In this book I will try to make a positive contribution by describing such a system of spiritual knowledge. This means that I shall introduce a specific system of theory and practice that has been expressed in a particular language and handed down in a particular cultural tradition. Since a practical science must exist in concrete form, it is not possible for me to avoid these details. Nonetheless, my concern is with general principles that are universally applicable. My purpose is to demonstrate the possibility of a scientific system of spiritual knowledge by describing an actual example of such a system. I do not want to pass judgement on other systems or become embroiled in any kind of sectarian controversy.

I shall describe the system of *bhakti-yoga* that is expounded in the *Bhagavad-gītā,*[8] the *Bhāgavata Purāṇa,*[9] and other Sanskrit literatures of India. *Bhakti-yoga* is the technical name for the philosophy and practical methodology of a living religious tradition called Vaiṣṇavism. The system of *bhakti-yoga* has been taught by many prominent Indian spiritual teachers, or *ācāryas,* including Rāmānuja (A.D. 1017–1137), Madhva (A.D. 1239–1319), and Caitanya Mahāprabhu (A.D. 1486–1534).[10] I have personally learned about *bhakti-yoga* from His Divine Grace A.C. Bhaktivedanta Swami Prabhupāda, and my presentation of this system is based on his teachings.

The first eight chapters of this book are devoted to a critique of modern scientific theories and the parallel introduction of basic elements of the theoretical system of *bhakti-yoga.* In the ninth chapter I show how these elements provide the theoretical framework for a practical process of obtaining absolute personal knowledge. The analysis of current mechanistic theories is intended to reveal some of their deficiencies, and to show the need for some kind of nonmechanistic alternative. This analysis does not prove that the system of *bhakti-yoga* is the only possible alternative, but it does show that this system is a reasonable candidate. The validity of *bhakti-yoga* can be demonstrated conclusively only by means of the practical observational process of *bhakti-yoga* itself, and this is discussed in the ninth chapter.

My discussion of modern scientific theories rests entirely on logic, the evidence of ordinary experience, and evidence reported in technical journals and other conventional sources of scientific information. Under the heading of ordinary experience I include the evidence provided by our normal awareness of subjective consciousness. As I will argue in detail later on, except for our direct experience of consciousness, all of these forms of evidence can be translated into mathematical language, and thus they are all mechanistic. Conscious awareness, however, defies representation in mathematical terms, and thus it is a truly nonmechanistic feature of our normal experience.

It is not possible to base a nonmechanistic theory entirely on mechanistic evidence—that is, on patterns of correlation in numerical data. So if nonmechanistic entities and properties are to play more than a vague speculative role in a theory, some means must be available for directly observing them. It is significant, then, that our consciousness, or our inner power of observation, is of a nonmechanistic character, even though we normally use it to make observations that can be represented in numerical form.

The nonmechanistic system of *bhakti-yoga* is, in fact, based on the principle that the scope of our conscious awareness can be greatly extended. According to the philosophy of the *Bhagavad-gītā,* conscious personality is the irreducible basis of reality. There are two principle types of conscious being: the one universal Supreme Person, or *puruṣottama,* and the innumerable localized conscious selves, or *jīvātmās.* Just as electrons interact with an electric field according to certain natural laws, so the *jīvātmās* interact in a natural way with the *puruṣottama,* the all-pervading conscious being. *Bhakti-yoga* is concerned primarily with the practical study of this interaction through direct conscious realization, and thus *bhakti-yoga* can be thought of as a kind of physics of higher consciousness.

In physics the interaction between an electron and an electric field can be studied by certain experimental procedures that take advantage of the principles of electromagnetic theory. Similarly, the interaction between the individual self and the Supreme Self can be directly studied by exacting procedures that take advantage of the properties of these entities. The ultimate goal of these procedures is to elevate the consciousness of the individual *jīvātmā* so that he can reciprocate with the Absolute Person on a direct, personal level. Once this is accomplished, the person attains incontrovertible knowledge of the nature and meaning of his own existence.

In the first part of this book, I discuss the nature of individual consciousness and introduce the concept of the *jīvātmā.* There is material on the subject of artificial intelligence, the classical theories of the mind-body relationship, and the mind-body theory of Karl Popper. There is also an imaginary dialogue in the style of Galileo on consciousness and the role of the observer in quantum mechanics. I argue that consciousness is objectively real, that the contents of consciousness can be correlated only in a very indirect way with the physiochemical states of the brain, and that consciousness cannot be explained in mechanistic terms. Some nonmechanistic explanation is required, and I propose that the concept of the *jīvātmā* provides a simple explanation that is consistent with known facts.

In the second part I discuss the origin of complex form. In their attempts to arrive at a universal picture of reality, scientists and philosophers have always been faced with the problem of how to find unity and harmony in a world of variegated complex forms. I explore this problem in Chapters 5 and 6, which deal with chance, the laws of physics, and the origin of higher life forms. Chapter 5 is devoted to an analysis of evolutionary processes by means of information theory. There I argue that in a mechanistic theory of the origin of life, unity can be attained only by the sacrifice of completeness, and therefore no satisfactory theory of this kind is possible. I arrive at a similar conclusion in Chapter 6 by using nontechnical arguments about the nature of chance. But I go on to show that a unified theory of the origin of life is possible if we introduce the concept of the all-pervading superconscious being, as understood in the philosophy of *bhakti-yoga.*

Chapters 7 and 8 contain a nontechnical discussion of two types of natural forms—the abstract forms of artistic and mathematical ideas, and the physical forms of living organisms. Chapter 7 deals with the origin of ideas and focuses on the phenomenon of inspiration, in which fully developed ideas appear suddenly and unexpectedly in the mind. I use this phenomenon as the starting point for a discussion of the interaction between the *jīvātmā* and the Supreme Person.

Chapter 8 deals with the conventional neo-Darwinian theory of evolution, and includes a brief analysis of its historical role as a replacement for the idea of divine creation. I argue that this theory has never been given a substantial scientific foundation, and that the idea of creation by an absolute intelligent being still provides the most reasonable explanation for the origin of biological form. This is in accordance with the philosophy of *bhakti-yoga,* which holds that all manifestations of form are generated by the Supreme Person.

The concluding chapter contains a brief outline of the practical observational process of *bhakti-yoga.* This process takes advantage of the fundamental principles introduced in the first two parts of this book, and it is the only way of giving a tangible demonstration of the validity of these principles. I argue that this process is truly scientific, and that it shares with modern science such features as a theoretical system, necessary and sufficient conditions for the success of experiments, and independent evaluation and confirmation of results by a community of experts. The process of *bhakti-yoga* is also regulated by a theory of knowledge that strictly rules out unjustifiable speculation and extrapolation, and in this respect *bhakti-yoga* is methodologically superior to modern science. *Bhakti-yoga* also goes beyond modern science by providing the individual with practical methods of developing higher cognitive powers that lie dormant in the conscious self.

I will end this introduction by making a brief observation about the level of technical difficulty of the material in this book. Since the book deals with some highly controversial issues, I have felt it necessary to present certain important arguments on a rigorous technical level. At the same time I have wanted to make the book accessible to the general reader, and so I have tried to present as much of the material as possible in an undemanding style.

As a guide to the reader I have marked the more technical sections with asterisks in the table of contents. To fully follow these sections, the reader will need some familiarity with mathematics and physics. Nonetheless, the arguments they contain are essentially simple, and the general reader may find it worthwhile to skim these sections without worrying too much about the technical details.

Notes

1. Smith, "The Limitations of Evolutionary Theory," p. 239.
2. Weinberg, *The First Three Minutes,* p. 144.
3. Russell, "A Free Man's Worship," p. 41.
4. Wilson, *On Human Nature.*
5. Capra, *The Tao of Physics,* and Zukav, *The Dancing Wu Li Masters.*
6. Weisz, *Elements of Biology,* p. 10.
7. Tax and Callender, eds., *Evolution After Darwin,* p. 111.
8. A.C. Bhaktivedanta Swami Prabhupāda, *Bhagavad-gītā As It Is.*
9. A.C. Bhaktivedanta Swami Prabhupāda, *Śrīmad-Bhāgavatam.*
10. Satsvarūpa Dāsa Gosvāmī, *Readings in Vedic Literature,* pp. 50–53.

PART I

CONSCIOUSNESS

Chapter 1

Searching Past the Mechanics Of Perception

The life sciences are now dominated by the idea that life can be completely understood within the framework of chemistry and physics. Those who subscribe to this viewpoint say that we can explain all features of life—from the metabolic functioning of cells up to the mental phenomena of thinking, feeling, and willing—as the consequences of underlying chemical processes. This viewpoint has become so pervasive that it is generally presented in biology courses as the only valid understanding of life. Thus, in textbook after textbook we read that "life means chemical and physical organization,"[1] and that "all of the phenomena of life are governed by, and can be explained in terms of, chemical and physical principles."[2]

Yet despite the popularity of this view, we can point to at least one feature of life—the phenomenon of conscious awareness—that is not amenable to a molecular explanation. The basic phenomenon of conscious awareness is the most immediate aspect of our experience, and it is automatically presupposed in all our sensations, feelings, and thought processes. Yet even though consciousness certainly exists and is of central importance to our lives, the current theoretical framework of biological and physical science cannot even refer to consciousness, much less explain it.

To see this, let us examine the process of conscious perception through the eyes of modern science. Our examination will take us through several levels of successively increasing detail, and at each level we will try to ascertain whether our scientific picture of reality sheds any light on the nature of consciousness.

First let us consider a man observing a physical object—in this case, a thermometer. Figure 1 depicts the operation of the man's sense of sight on the grossest biological level. The process of perception begins when light reflected from the thermometer is focused on the retina of the man's eye, forming an inverted image. This light induces chemical changes in certain retinal cells, and these cells consequently stimulate adjacent nerve cells to transmit electrical impulses. These cells in turn stimulate activity in other

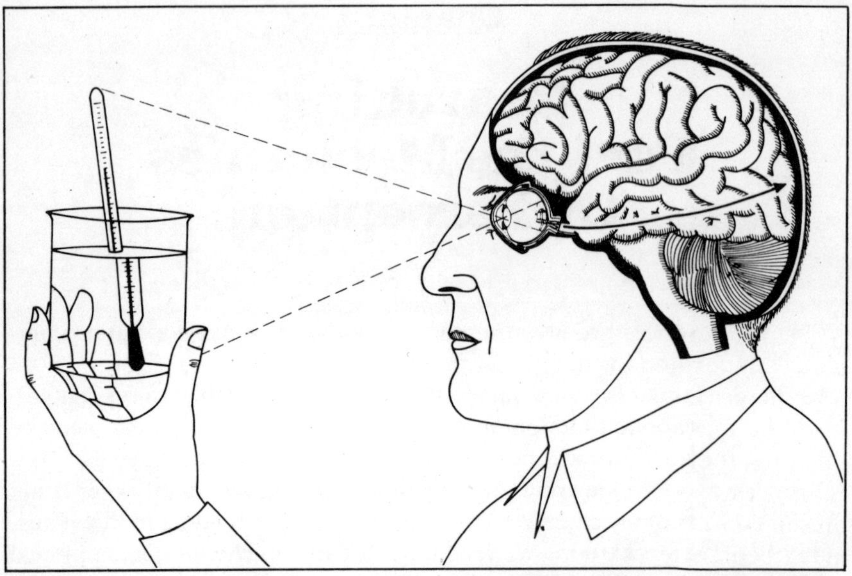

Figure 1. The process of perception begins when light from an object enters the eye and is focused on the retina. This light stimulates a series of neurochemical reactions that ultimately reach the brain as a systematic pattern of pulses. These in turn give rise to an exceedingly complex set of electrochemical reactions within the brain itself. By studying these processes we may learn a great deal about human behavior. But will such studies enable us to understand the nature of conscious perception?

nerve cells, and a systematic pattern of pulses is transmitted down the optic nerve. The image of the thermometer is now encoded in this pattern of pulses.

When these pulses reach the brain, a very complicated response occurs, involving many electrochemical actions and reactions. Although scientists at present do not know the details of this brain activity, they are nonetheless in substantial agreement about the basic phenomena involved. When the impulses streaming down the optic nerve reach the brain, they modify the overall pattern of chemical concentrations and electrical potentials maintained by the brain's vast network of nerve cells. This pattern is believed to represent in coded form the specific content of the man's thoughts and sensory impressions. As time passes, the physiochemical transformations of this pattern give rise to sequences of electrical impulses that emerge from the brain along various motor nerves, and these impulses in turn evoke corresponding sequences of muscular contractions. These organized contractions constitute the man's gross external behavior, which may include spoken reports of his sensations, such as "I am seeing a thermometer."

At this point in our investigation, we can understand how descriptions of this kind may, at least in principle, shed light on a person's external behavioral responses to environmental stimuli. We can easily imagine constructing a machine involving photocells and electronic circuitry that would respond to a red light by playing a tape recording of the statement "I am seeing a red light." On a more sophisticated level, we can visualize a computer that will analyze the images produced by a television camera and generate spoken statements identifying various objects. Thus although we are grossly ignorant of the actual physical transformations occuring in the brain, we can at least conceive of the possibility that these may correspond to processes of symbol manipulation analogous to those that take place in computers. We can therefore imagine that the man's statement, "I am seeing a thermometer," is generated by a computational process physically embodied in the electrochemical activity of the nerve cells in the brain.

But all this tells us nothing about the man's conscious perceptions. Our description of the image formed on the retina of the man's eye says nothing about the conscious perception of that image, nor do scientists suppose that conscious perception takes place at this point. Likewise, the statements that light-sensitive cells in the retina have been stimulated and that sequences of nerve impulses have been induced convey nothing at all about the actual subjective experience of seeing the thermometer.

Many scientists feel that conscious perception must take place in the brain. Yet our description of the brain, even if elaborated in the greatest possible detail, would consist of nothing more than a list of statements about the electrochemical states of brain cells. Such statements might have some bearing on patterns of behavior, but they cannot explain consciousness, because they do not even refer to it.

At this point one may argue that since consciousness is subjective, we cannot use the word *consciousness* in scientific statements describing objective reality. One might point out that while we can observe a man's behavior and measure the physical states of his brain, we could not possibly find any measurable evidence of his so-called consciousness. According to this idea, the man's statements about his conscious perceptions are simply electrochemical phenomena that require physical explanation, but to say that consciousness exists in any real sense is meaningless.

Each of us can refute this argument by considering the matter in this

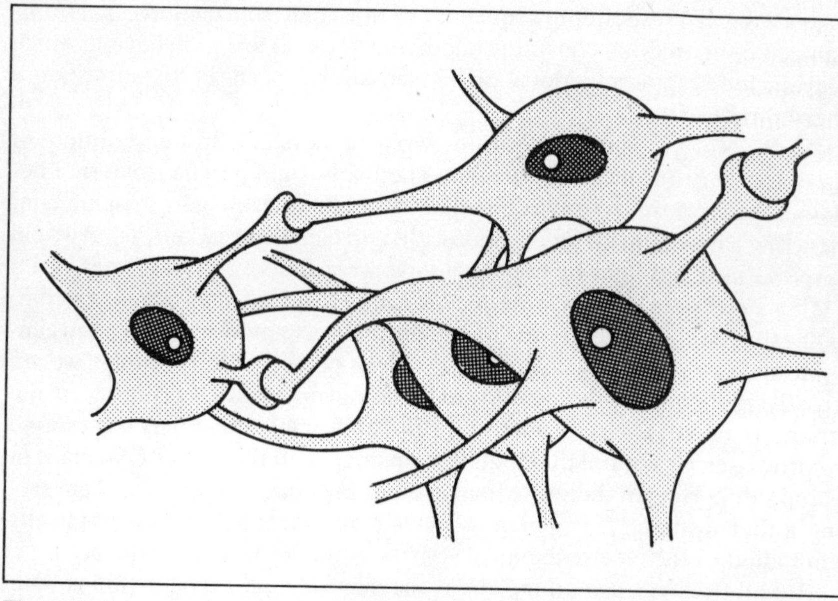

Figure 2. Can patterns of neural excitation account for the conscious experience of seeing?

way: The reality of my own conscious perceptions is certainly undeniable, and my understanding of all other aspects of reality depends on this basic fact. Thus I know by direct perception that consciousness exists in me, and it is also perfectly justifiable to suppose that other beings like me have similar conscious experiences. There is no need to embrace the futile and absurd viewpoint of solipsism, which holds that I am the only conscious being and that all others occupy a lesser status as mere automatons. Consciousness, therefore, exists as a feature of objective reality, and any scientific account of reality that fails to explain it is incomplete.

If consciousness exists but the level of biological description we have thus far considered does not refer to it, then how can we understand consciousness in terms of our existing scientific world view? The mere assertion that neural impulses "generate" consciousness does not constitute an explanation, for it offers no conception of any connection between impulses and our conscious perceptions. Our only recourse is to examine the structures and processes of the brain more closely, with the hope that a deeper understanding of their nature will reveal such a connection.

Figure 2 presents a closer view of some of the neurons in the brain, and

Figure 3 depicts some of the minute structures which constitute the internal machinery of neurons, and of cells in general. When we examine living cells closely, we find many intricate structures known as organelles. Just as we can describe the functions of the gross body in terms of the combined actions of its many component cells, so in principle we can describe the functions of the cells in terms of these subcellular components. Yet this does not help us in our attempt to understand consciousness, for it merely leads to a more complicated account of bodily behavior. As before, there is no reference to the conscious experience of seeing.

Let us go deeper. What is the essential nature of the cellular organelles? As we earlier pointed out, the nearly unanimous opinion of modern biochemists is that one can understand all biological structures as combinations of molecules, and all biological processes as the consequences of

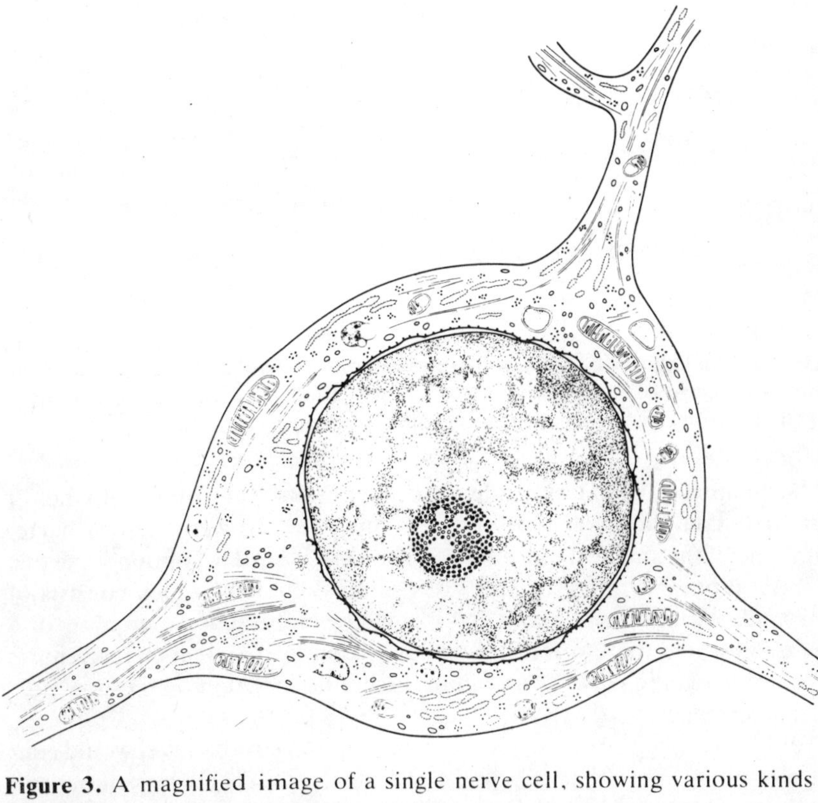

Figure 3. A magnified image of a single nerve cell, showing various kinds of organelles.

molecular interactions. Figure 4 depicts the three-dimensional structure of a globular protein, one of the many kinds of complex molecules found in the body. Organic chemistry describes the structure of such molecules in terms of three-dimensional arrangements of atoms, and molecular interactions in terms of the formation and dissolution of chemical bonds, or interatomic links.

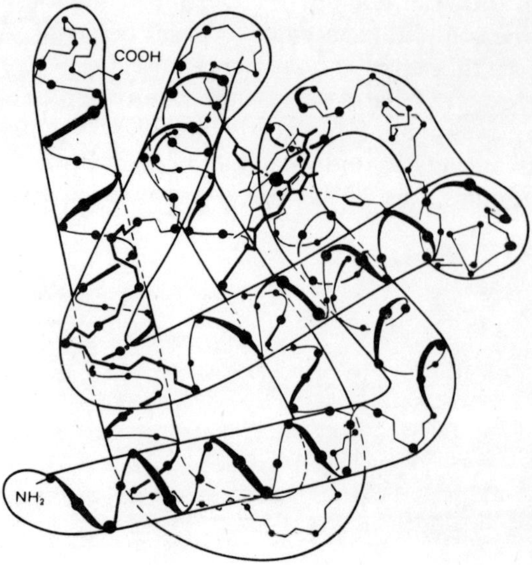

Figure 4. The three-dimensional structure of myoglobin, a large biological molecule. Can knowledge of the configurations of such molecules convey anything about the nature of our conscious awareness? [Redrawn with permission from R.E. Dickerson, "X-ray Analysis and Protein Structure," p. 634.]

Biochemists have found that living cells contain many different kinds of extremely complex molecules. For example, the *Escherichia coli* bacterium, one of the simplest unicellular organisms, is said to contain some two to three thousand different kinds of proteins, each of which consists of thousands of individual atoms.[3] A complete molecular description of a single cell would therefore be enormously complex, and, in fact, scientists have not yet come close to providing such a description, even for the *E. coli* bacterium.

Yet however complex it might be, a description on this level would consist of nothing more than a long list of statements about the making and breaking of chemical bonds. Such a list could give us no greater insight into the nature of consciousness than any of the higher-order descriptions we have considered thus far. In fact, lists describing patterns of bonds and lists describing trains of nerve impulses are equivalent, in the sense that both say nothing about conscious experience.

Can we find the insight we are seeking by taking a closer look at the atomic structure of molecules? In Figure 5 we see a diagram representing

Figure 5. An electron density map showing the structure of one of the helical segments of the myoglobin molecule. [Redrawn with permission from R.E. Dickerson, "X-ray Analysis and Protein Structure," p. 639.]

the spatial distribution of electrons within an organic molecule. Those who subscribe to the modern scientific world view claim that we can completely understand atoms and molecules in terms of the interactions of subatomic particles such as protons, neutrons, and electrons.

The branch of science that deals with these interactions is known as quantum mechanics, and it describes subatomic phenomena in terms of mathematical equations, such as the one depicted in Figure 6(a). Although diagrams such as Figure 6(b) can depict some features of the solutions to these equations, their solutions are generally impossible to represent pictorially. We might wonder, therefore, whether some deep insight into the abstract mysteries of these fundamental physical equations might finally enable us to grasp the nature of consciousness.

Unfortunately, however, this hope must meet with disappointment. If we study the essential nature of these mathematical equations, we find that they amount to nothing more than codified rules for the manipulation

(a) $H\Psi = i\hbar \frac{\partial \Psi}{\partial t}$

(b)

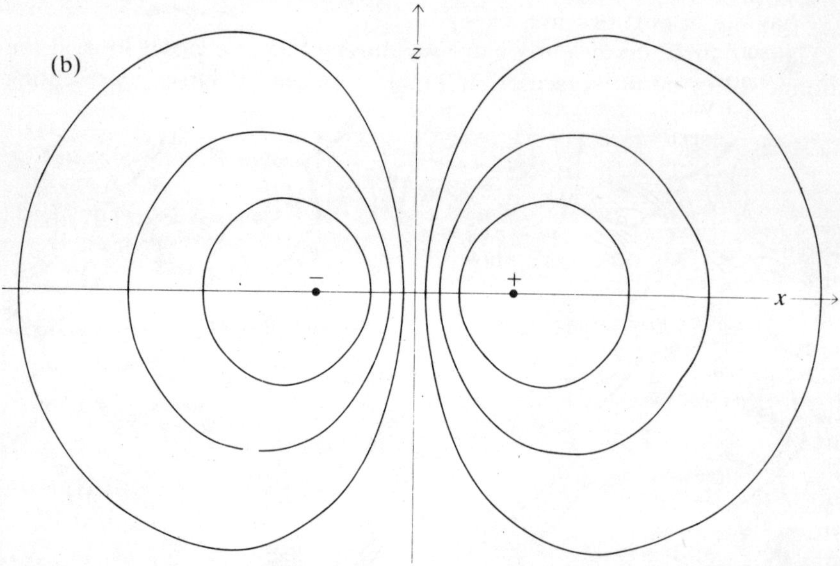

Figure 6. A quantum mechanical diagram describing the electronic structure of a single hydrogen atom is depicted in (b). These structures are deduced from equations such as the one shown in (a).

of symbols. Such symbols, in turn, are simply marks drawn from a finite alphabet. They may be represented by the internal states of an electronic computer or by marks on a piece of paper, but they are essentially arbitrary.

Thus Figure 7 gives us a glimpse of the ultimate appearance of a fundamental quantum mechanical description of nature when reduced to its elemental constituent terms. In this figure the alphabet of marks consists of 0,1,2, . . . ,9,A,B,C, . . . ,F, and the rules for their manipulation are expressed in terms of the internal language of a particular computer. These rules simply describe certain ways of rearranging patterns of marks to create new patterns. Finally, in Figure 8, we reach the end of our investigation of the scientific world view. Here we find both patterns of marks and the rules for their manipulation encoded as strings of ones and zeros.

At this point we meet with final frustration in our effort to understand consciousness in terms of modern scientific conceptions. At each stage of our investigation we have been confronted with a set of symbols that refer to repeating patterns in the stream of events we observe with our external

4A00	DD21004B	00130	4A11	DD7E02	00180	4A20	DD7701	00230
4A04	FD21104B	00140	4A14	FD8E01	00190	4A23	DD7E00	00240
4A08	DD7E03	00150	4A17	DD7702	00200	4A26	FD8E00	00250
4A0B	FD8603	00160	4A1A	DD7E01	00210	4A29	DD7700	00260
4A0E	DD7703	00170	4A1D	FD8E02	00220	4A2C	C32C4A	00270

Figure 7. The reduction of mathematical equations to fundamental rules for symbol manipulation. Can consciousness be defined in terms of combinations of such rules?

senses. Thus we began our investigation by describing a man with symbols like *retina* and *optic nerve,* which refer to observable features of gross anatomy. Now we have ended up with an abstract description in which our symbols refer to mathematical constructs, or even to elementary rules for manipulating arbitrary marks on paper. At each successive level of examination, our symbols failed to refer to consciousness, and, if anything, the symbols on each successive level seemed *more* unrelated to the world of our subjective experience than those on the level above it.

How, then, are we to understand consciousness? Although we know by direct perception that consciousness exists, we have seen that the methodology of modern science does not allow us even to refer to consciousness, and thus this methodology cannot reveal anything about it. Of course, some measurable physiological phenomena may be correlated more or less closely with the contents of a person's consciousness, but a detailed account of these phenomena does not have anything to say about con-

1011011010100110000001110101011111110010011
10100011100111000101100100010000111101001
00011011010100010110101111001010100011111
10010000100101010101100011110100011101010
00000000100110100101010010100111111010110

Figure 8. The ultimate reduction of scientific description to patterns of marks—in this case ones and zeros—that correspond directly or indirectly to the outcomes of physical measurements. Although consciousness is the primary feature of our existence, by its very nature it eludes description in these terms.

sciousness itself. When contemplating records of measurements made on another person, we have no real need to bring in the concept of consciousness at all, and indeed, the entire science of behavioral psychology is dedicated to the principle that people can be fully described without reference to consciousness. Our only basis for inferring the presence of consciousness from quantifiable features of another person is that we find such features associated with consciousness in ourselves, and by analogy we assume that this is true of others also.

Now, we have used the term "consciousness" to refer to the reality of our personal experience of sensations, thoughts, and feelings. We have emphasized that while these experiences are certainly subjective, they are nonetheless factual and are therefore part of the total reality of the world. We should note that while this fact has gone essentially unrecognized in the prevailing world view of modern science, many scientists and philosophers have pointed it out from time to time. For example, the physicist Eugene Wigner has argued that "there are two kinds of reality or existence: the existence of my consciousness and the reality or existence of everything else. This latter reality is not absolute but only relative."[4] Wigner is observing that external, measurable phenomena are known to him only by virtue of his consciousness, and thus consciousness is, if anything, more real than these phenomena.

Another well-known scientist who has recognized the reality of conscious experience is Thomas Huxley. After noting that the materialistic philosophers of his day attributed all phenomena to matter and force, Huxley wrote that "it seems to me pretty plain that there is a third thing in the universe, to wit, consciousness, which . . . I cannot see to be matter or force, or any conceivable modification of either."[5] Huxley held that consciousness must be an objective feature of universal reality that is somehow associated with the bodies of individual persons, but that does not fall within the categories of matter and energy. He proposed that consciousness is an "epiphenomenon"—a wholly nonmaterial phenomenon that is somehow generated by certain material interactions, but that does not affect them in turn.

According to Huxley's idea, consciousness is real but can only be perceived privately. Each person's consciousness is a causal dead end that is influenced by material processes in the brain, but cannot influence any conceivable material measuring apparatus. Furthermore, although consciousness is self-referential and must somehow act on itself to perceive itself, there is no provision in Huxley's scheme for the consciousness of one individual to directly influence that of another. If Huxley is correct, we cannot possibly learn more about consciousness than we already know. The consciousness of each person must remain the sole perceiver of itself, and the passive observer of the physiochemical processes of the body—processes over which it has no influence, even when the body is writing essays on the nonphysical nature of consciousness.

We would like to suggest that while Huxley was correct in pointing out that consciousness is something distinct from matter, his conception of consciousness as an epiphenomenon is too restrictive. In this chapter we would like to outline an alternative model in which consciousness is granted attributes enabling us to directly study it as a nonphysical, nonquantifiable feature of reality. Our sources of information for this model are the *Bhagavad-gītā* and other literatures from the Vedic tradition of India.[6] From these sources we will draw a few basic points about the nature of consciousness that can be thought of as axioms for our model. Here our objective will not be to prove the truth of the model, but rather, to gain some idea of what may possibly be true. As we shall see, however, our axioms will provide hints as to how the model can be investigated. As is true with any scientific theory, it is only by the positive results of such investigation that the value of the model can be established.

In our model we postulate that the consciousness of each person is due to the presence of a distinct nonphysical entity called the self, or *jīvātmā*. Some of the attributes of the *jīvātmā* are summarized in the following list:

1. The *jīvātmā* is the elementary unit of consciousness.
2. There are innumerable *jīvātmās,* and they can be neither created nor destroyed.
3. All *jīvātmās* are qualitatively equal.
4. The *jīvātmās* are not numerically describable, although they can exhibit quantifiable attributes such as position in space.
5. The *jīvātmās* obey higher-order psychological laws involving qualities and modes of activity that are not amenable to mathematical formulation.
6. The *jīvātmās* do not interact with matter according to the known laws of physics, such as the law of gravity or the laws of electromagnetism.
7. The *jīvātmās* possess self-reflective conscious awareness, and they possess innate senses capable of perceiving both matter and other conscious entities.

8. The *jīvātmās* tend to be associated with material bodies, but they are not dependent on matter and are fully capable of functioning without material connections.

The first of these axioms introduces the self as an irreducible, natural entity analogous to the idealized fundamental particles that physicists have sought as the basis of matter. The essential idea here is that consciousness is an inherent feature of reality and not merely a name for certain physio-chemical processes. Axiom 2 indicates the individualized nature of consciousness, although this axiom is, of course, too strong to be proven by the mere existence of such individuality. Although similarly difficult to prove, Axiom 3 provides the basis for a philosophy of universal equality by declaring the innermost selves of all sentient beings to be equal.

Axioms 4 and 5 express the basic conclusion we deduced from our analysis of the process of perception. Consciousness involves qualities and attributes, such as the color red, that cannot be numerically described, and thus the *jīvātmā,* or elementary unit of consciousness, also cannot be numerically described. Since the days of Newton, many scientists have been greatly inspired by the idea that all significant features of reality can be represented by patterns of numbers. Yet this idea is simply a convenient working hypothesis and not a necessary truth. Here we would like to introduce the idea that the world may contain many qualities, features, and entities that cannot be discussed quantitatively. We should stress, however, that a numerically indescribable entity may have some quantifiable features, as indicated in Axiom 4. By "numerically indescribable" we only mean that all attempted numerical descriptions must be significantly incomplete. We do not mean that they cannot apply at all.

Axioms 6, 7, and 8 give us a hint as to how our model of the self can be practically investigated. The essential ingredient for such an investigation is provided by Axiom 7, which states that the *jīvātmā* is equipped with its own innate senses. In our analysis of the process of perception, we studied the material sense of vision, and saw how information depicting an observed object eventually became represented in the brain in the form of nerve impulses. We were never able, however, to explain how such patterns of pulses give rise to the conscious perception of the object.

In our model this is explained by postulating that the *jīvātmā* possesses its own senses, but is using them only to pick up information provided by the sensory machinery of the body. The situation of the embodied *jīvātmā* can be compared with that of a person flying an airplane through dense clouds on instruments. In that situation the person can obtain only a very limited picture of his surroundings from devices such as the radar screen and the altimeter, even though he still possesses his normal senses and, in fact, is using them to observe these instruments.

Since the sensory apparatus of the body is composed of matter, this apparatus can provide information only about configurations of material energy and their transformations. This information may be used to make indirect inferences about the *jīvātmā* itself, but cannot directly reveal anything about it. Yet Axiom 7 opens up the possibility that the *jīvātmā* may be able to directly obtain information about other *jīvātmās* by using the full power of its own natural senses. If this could be done, the perception of consciousness would not be a strictly subjective affair. A group of persons who could perceive one another with awakened senses as conscious beings, could discuss and study consciousness with the same objectivity that scientists now bring to bear on the study of inanimate matter.

In this chapter our purpose is only to indicate the possibility of such a direct study of consciousness. Practical methods of carrying out such a study will be discussed in Chapter 9. Here we will close by noting an interesting feature of one of these methods—the method of *bhakti-yoga,* which is described in Sanskrit literatures such as the *Bhakti-rasāmṛta-sindhu* of Śrīla Rūpa Gosvāmī.[7] This method involves the chanting of *mantras* such as

Hare Kṛṣṇa, Hare Kṛṣṇa, Kṛṣṇa Kṛṣṇa, Hare Hare
Hare Rāma, Hare Rāma, Rāma Rāma, Hare Hare.

According to the system of *bhakti-yoga,* such chanting can purify the *jīvātmā* of the effects of involvement with matter, and thereby awaken the *jīvātmā's* natural sensory capacities. The interesting feature of this chanting is that the practitioners of *bhakti-yoga* understand the words *Hare, Kṛṣṇa,* and *Rāma* to be symbols with an absolute meaning lying outside the realm of numerical describability.

In the quantitative science of physics, we encounter numbers that are ostensibly absolute. For example, the fine structure constant, $\hbar c/e^2 = 137$, is believed by some physicists to represent an absolute, unchangeable feature of reality.[8] Now, we can reason that in a direct approach to the study of consciousness, it would be necessary to employ concepts, and even symbols, which are more than mere patterns of marks, but which possess a numerically indescribable dimension. To be fully appreciated, such symbols would have to be directly perceived by the senses of the *jīvātmā,* and not merely processed through the sensory apparatus of the body. It is therefore interesting to note that the system of *bhakti-yoga* makes use of absolute symbols of this kind—symbols that could be referred to as transcendental constants of nature.

Notes

1. Elliot and Ray, *Biology,* p. 67.
2. Villee and Dethier, *Biological Principles and Processes,* p. 12.
3. Watson, *Molecular Biology of the Gene,* p. 69.
4. Wigner, "Two Kinds of Reality," p. 251.
5. Huxley, *Essays on Some Controverted Questions,* p. 220.
6. A.C. Bhaktivedanta Swami Prabhupāda, *Bhagavad-gītā As It Is.*
7. A.C. Bhaktivedanta Swami Prabhupāda, *The Nectar of Devotion.*
8. Dirac, "The Evolution of the Physicist's Picture of Nature," pp. 48–49.

Chapter 2

Thinking Machines And Psychophysical Parallelism

Science fiction writers often try to solve the problems of old age and death by taking advantage of the idea that a human being is essentially a complex machine. In a typical scene, doctors and technicians scan the head of the dying Samuel Jones with a "cerebroscope," a highly sensitive instrument that records in full detail the synaptic connections of the neurons in his brain. A computer then systematically transforms this information into a computer program that faithfully simulates that brain's particular pattern of internal activity.

When this program is run on a suitable computer, the actual personality of Mr. Jones seems to come to life through the medium of the machine. "I've escaped death!" the computer exults through its electronic phoneme generator. Scanning about the room with stereoscopically mounted TV cameras, the computerized "Mr. Jones" appears somewhat disoriented in his new embodiment. But when interviewed by old friends, "he" displays Mr. Jones's personal traits in complete detail. In the story, Mr. Jones lives again in the form of the computer. Now his only problem is figuring out how to avoid being erased from the computer's memory.

Although this story may seem fantastic, some of the most influential thinkers in the world of modern science take very seriously the basic principles behind it. In fact, researchers in the life sciences now almost universally assume that a living being is nothing more than a highly complex machine built from molecular components. In the fields of philosophy and psychology, this assumption leads to the inevitable conclusion that the mind involves nothing more than the biophysical functioning of the brain. According to this viewpoint, we can define in entirely mechanistic terms the words we normally apply to human personality—words like *consciousness, perception, meaning, purpose,* and *intelligence.*

Along with this line of thinking have always gone idle speculations about the construction of machines that can exhibit these traits of personality.

But now things have gone beyond mere speculation. The advent of modern electronic computers has given us a new field of scientific investigation dedicated to actually building such machines. This is the field of artificial intelligence research, or "cognitive engineering," in which scientists proceed on the assumption that digital computers of sufficient speed and complexity can in fact produce all aspects of conscious personality. Thus we learn in the 1979 M.I.T. college catalogue that cognitive engineering involves an approach to the subjects of mind and intelligence which is "quite different from that of philosophers and psychologists, in that the cognitive engineer tries to produce intelligence."[1]

In this chapter we shall examine the question of whether it is possible for a machine to possess a conscious self that perceives itself as seer and doer. Our thesis will be that while computers may in principle generate complex sequences of behavior comparable to those produced by human beings, computers cannot possess conscious awareness without the intervention of principles of nature higher than those known to modern science. Ironically, we can base strong arguments in support of this thesis on some of the very concepts that form the foundation of artificial intelligence research. As far as computers are concerned, the most reasonable inference we can draw from these arguments is that computers cannot be conscious. When applied to the machine of the human brain, these arguments support a nonmechanistic understanding of the conscious self.

2.1 How a Computer Works

We shall proceed by raising some questions about a hypothetical computer that possesses intelligence and conscious self-awareness on a human level. This computer need not duplicate the mind of a particular human being such as the Mr. Jones of our story, although this is also an interesting possibility to consider. We will simply assume that it experiences an awareness of thoughts, feelings, and sensory perceptions that is comparable to our own.

First, let us briefly examine the internal organization of our sentient computer. Since it belongs to the species of digital computers, it consists of an information storehouse, or "memory," an apparatus called the central processing unit, or CPU, and various devices for the exchange of information with the environment.

The memory is simply a passive medium used for recording large amounts of information in the form of numbers. A typical computer memory can be visualized as a series of labeled boxes, each of which can store a number. Some of these boxes normally contain numerically coded instructions that specify the program of activity of the computer. Others contain data of various kinds, and still others are used to store the intermediate steps of calculations. These numbers can be represented physically in the memory as patterns of charges on microminiature capacitors, patterns of magnetization on arrays of small magnets, and in many other ways.

The central processing unit performs all of the computer's active operations. It is capable of performing a fixed number of simple operations of symbol manipulation. These operations typically include the following steps: First, a coded instruction identifying the operation to be performed is obtained from a specified location or "address" in the memory. According to this instruction, other data may also be obtained from the memory. Then the operation itself is performed. This may involve reading a number into the memory from an external device (input), or transmitting a number from the memory to such a device (output). It may involve the transformation of a number according to some simple rule, or the shifting of a number from one memory location to another. Finally, the operation will always involve the selection of a memory address where the next coded instruction is to be sought.

The activity of the computer consists of nothing more than the repetition of steps of this kind, one after another. The specific operations to be executed are specified by the instruction codes stored in the passive memory record. The function of the CPU is simply to carry them out sequentially. Like the memory, the CPU can be constructed physically out of many different kinds of components, ranging from microminiature semiconductor junctions to electromechanical relays. The functioning of the CPU is determined only by the logical arrangement of these components, and not by their particular physical constitution.

The operation of a computer can be understood most easily by considering a simple example. Figure 1 illustrates a program of computer instructions for calculating the square root of a number.[2] The thirteen numbered statements correspond to the list of coded instructions stored in the computer's memory, but here they are written out in English for clarity. There are also five boxes labeled (1) through (5) that correspond to areas in the memory intended for the storage of data and intermediate computational steps. To simulate the operation of the computer, begin by placing a number, such as 9, in box (1). Then simply follow the instructions one at a time. When you have completed the last instruction, the square root of your original number will be contained in box (2). In an actual computer, each of these instructions would be carried out by the CPU. They illustrate the kind of elementary operations used by present-day computers (although

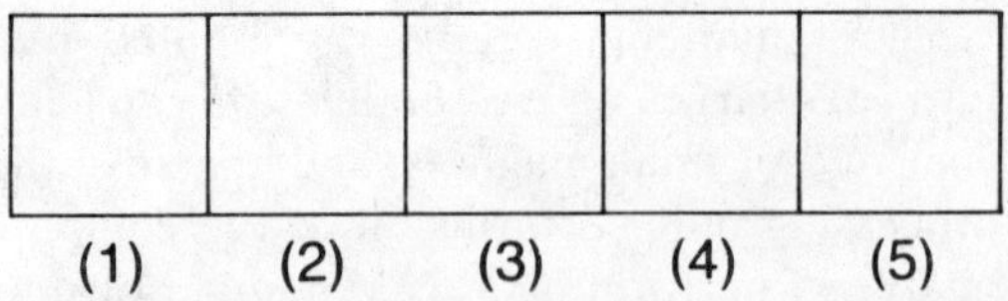

1. Write 0 in box (2).
2. Increment (2).
3. Write 0 in box (3).
4. Copy the number in (2) into box (4).
5. If box (4) contains 0, go to step 12.
6. Decrement (4).
7. Copy the number in (2) into box (5).
8. If box (5) contains 0, go to step 5.
9. Decrement (5).
10. Increment (3).
11. Go to step 8.
12. If the number in (3) is not greater than the number in (1), go to step 2.
13. Decrement (2).

Figure 1. Computer program for computing the square root of a number. To simulate the operation of the computer, place the number in box (1) and follow the instructions, starting with step 1. When step 13 is completed, the square root of the number (rounded down to an integer) will be in box (2). (In these instructions, "increment a number" means to add 1 to it, and "decrement a number" means to subtract 1 from it.)

they do not correspond exactly to those of any particular computer).

It may seem that the method of finding a square root given in this example is both cumbersome and obscure, but it is typical of how computers operate. The practical applicability of computers is in fact based on the observation that every fixed scheme of computation that has ever been formulated can be reduced to a list of simple operations of the kind used in the example. This observation was made by a number of mathematicians in the 1930s and 1940s, and is commonly referred to as Church's thesis.[3] It implies that, in principle, any scheme of symbol manipulation that can be precisely defined can be carried out by a digital computer of the modern type.

At this point, let us consider our hypothetical sentient computer. According to the exponents of artificial intelligence, the intricate behavior characteristic of a human being can be completely described as a highly complex scheme of symbol manipulation. By Church's thesis this scheme can be broken down into a program of instructions comparable with our example in Figure 1. The only difference is that this program will be exceedingly long and complex, and may run to millions of steps. Of course, up until now no one has even come close to actually producing a formal symbolic description of human behavior. However, for the sake of argument, let us suppose that such a description could be written and expressed as a computer program.

Let us suppose that a highly complex program of this kind is being executed by a computer, and let us see what we can understand about the computer's possible states of consciousness. When such a program is being executed, the computer's CPU will be carrying out only one instruction at any given time, and the millions of instructions comprising the rest of the program will exist only as an inactive record in the computer's "memory." Now, intuitively it seems doubtful that a mere inactive record could have anything to do with consciousness. Where, then, does the consciousness of the computer reside? The CPU at any given moment is simply performing some elementary operation, such as, "Copy the number in box (1687002) into box (9994563)." In what way can this be correlated with the conscious perception of thoughts and feelings?

2.2 Artificial Intelligence and Hierarchies of Function

The researchers of artificial intelligence have a definite answer to this question that is based on the idea of levels of organization in a computer program. To illustrate what is meant by levels of organization, we shall once again consider the simple computer program of Figure 1. Then we shall apply this concept to the program of our sentient computer and see what light it can shed on the relation between consciousness and the computer's internal physical states.

Although the square root program of Figure 1 may appear to be a formless list of instructions, it actually possesses a definite structure that is outlined in Figure 2. This structure consists of four levels of organization. On the highest level, the function of the program is described in a single sentence that uses the symbol "square root." On the next level, the meaning of this symbol is defined by a description of the method used to find square roots in the program. This description makes use of the symbol "squared," which is similarly defined on the next level down in terms of another symbol "sum." Finally, the symbol "sum" is defined on the lowest level in terms of the combination of elementary operations that is actually used to compute sums in the program. Although we have used English sentences in Figure 2 for the sake of clarity, the description on each level should use only symbols for elementary operations, or higher-order symbols defined on the next level down.

These graded symbolic descriptions actually define the program in the sense that if we begin with level 1, and expand each higher-order symbol we encounter in terms of its definition on a lower level, we will wind up writing the list of elementary operations in Figure 1. The descriptions are useful in that they provide an intelligible account of what is happening in the program. Thus, on one level we can say that numbers are being squared, on another level that they are being added, and on yet another that they are being incremented and decremented. However, the levels of organization of the program are only abstract properties of the list of operations given in Figure 1. When the program is being executed by a computer, these levels do not exist in any real sense, and only the elementary operations in the list are actually being carried out by the computer.

In fact, we can even go further and point out that this last statement is not strictly true. Actually, what we call the elementary operations are themselves symbols, such as *Increment (3),* that refer to abstract properties of the underlying machinery of the computer. When the computer is operating, all that is really happening within it are certain transformations of matter and energy which follow a pattern determined by the computer's physical structure.

In general, any computer program that performs some complex task can be resolved into a similar hierarchy of levels of description. Researchers in

1. Find the *square root* of X.
2. The square root of X is one less than the first number Y with Y *squared* greater than X.
3. Y squared is the *sum* of Y copies of Y.
4. The sum of Y and another number is the result of incrementing that number Y times.

Figure 2. Levels of organization of the program in Figure 1. The program in Figure 1 can be analyzed in terms of a hierarchy of abstract levels. The level of elementary operations is at the bottom, and each higher level makes use of symbols (such as *squared*) that are defined on the level beneath it.

the field of artificial intelligence generally visualize their projected "intelligent" or "sentient" programs in terms of a hierarchy similar to the following: On the bottom level the program is described in terms of elementary operations. Then come several successive levels in which mathematical procedures of greater and greater intricacy and sophistication are defined. After this comes a level in which symbols are defined that refer to basic constituents of thoughts, feelings, and sensory perceptions. This is followed by a series of levels involving more and more sophisticated mental features, culminating in the level of the ego, or self.[4]

Here, then, is how the relation between computer operations and consciousness is understood by these researchers: Consciousness is associated with the higher levels of operation of a "sentient" program—levels on which symbolic transformations take place that directly correspond to higher sensory processes and the transformations of thoughts. In contrast, the lower levels are not associated with consciousness. Their structure can be changed without affecting the consciousness of the computer as long as the higher level symbols are still given equivalent definitions. Referring again to our square root program, this corresponds to the observation that the process of finding a square root given on level 2 in Figure 2 will remain essentially the same even if the operation of squaring is defined on level 3 in some different but equivalent way.

If we were to adopt a strictly behavioristic criterion for our use of the word "consciousness," then this understanding of computerized consciousness might be satisfactory—granting, of course, that a program with the required higher-order organization could indeed be created. By such a criterion, certain patterns of behavior are designated as conscious and others are not. Generally, a sequence of behavioral events will have to be quite long in order to merit the designation "conscious." For example, a long speech may exhibit certain complex features that identify it as "conscious," but none of the words or short phrases that make it up could be long enough to display such features. Using such a criterion, one might want to designate a certain sequence of computer operations as "conscious" because it possesses certain abstract higher-order properties. Then the overall behavior of the computer might be analyzed as "conscious" in terms of these properties, whereas any single elementary operation would be too short to qualify.

2.3 Subjective Consciousness in Machines and Humans

Yet we are interested not in categorizing conscious behavior, but rather in understanding the actual subjective experience of conscious awareness.

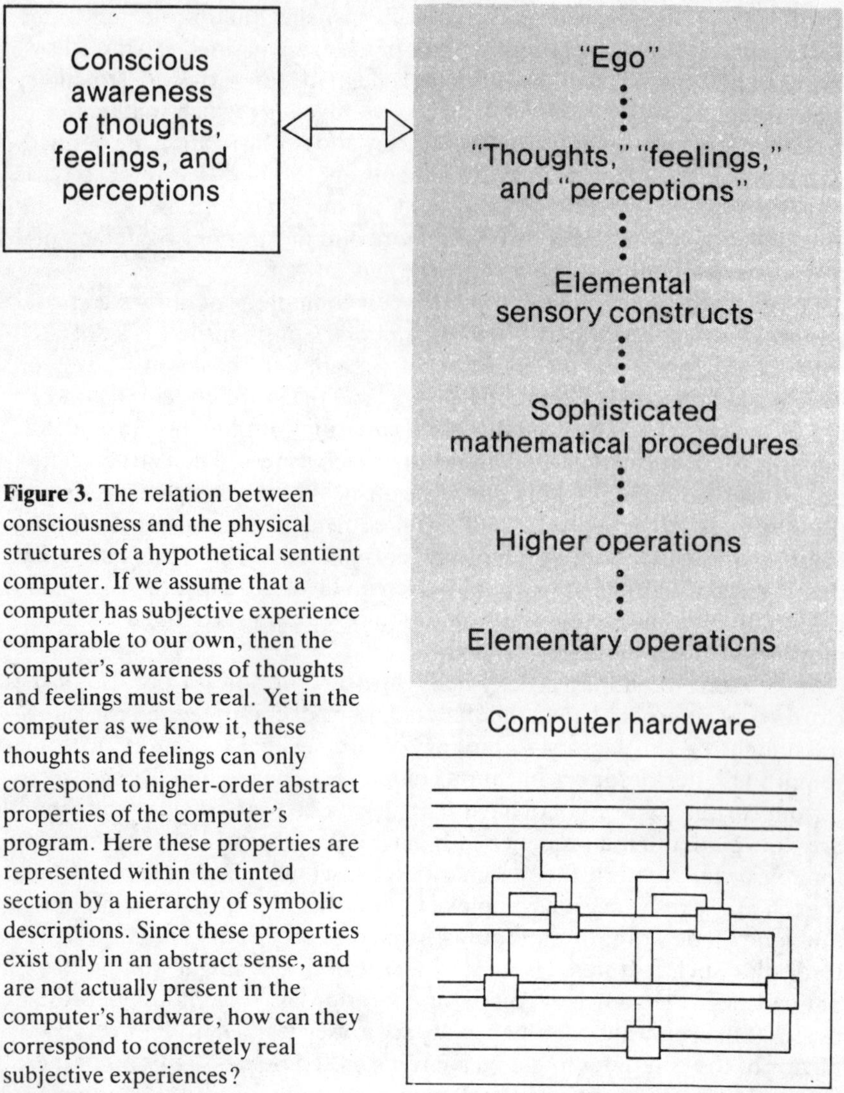

Figure 3. The relation between consciousness and the physical structures of a hypothetical sentient computer. If we assume that a computer has subjective experience comparable to our own, then the computer's awareness of thoughts and feelings must be real. Yet in the computer as we know it, these thoughts and feelings can only correspond to higher-order abstract properties of the computer's program. Here these properties are represented within the tinted section by a hierarchy of symbolic descriptions. Since these properties exist only in an abstract sense, and are not actually present in the computer's hardware, how can they correspond to concretely real subjective experiences?

To clearly distinguish this conception of consciousness from the behavioral one, we will pause here to briefly describe it and establish its status as a subject of serious inquiry. By "consciousness" we are referring to the awareness of thoughts and sensations that we directly perceive and know that we perceive. Since other persons are similar to ourselves, it is natural to suppose that they are similarly conscious. If this is accepted, then it follows that consciousness is an objectively existing feature of reality that tends to be associated with certain material structures, such as the bodies of living human beings.

Now, when a common person hears that a computer can be "conscious," his natural tendency is to interpret this word in the sense that we have just described. Thus, he will imagine that a computer can have subjective, conscious experience similar to his own. Certainly this is the idea behind the fictional stories such as the one with which we began this chapter. One imagines that the computerized "Mr. Jones" is actually feeling astonishment at his strange transformation as he looks about the room through the computer's TV cameras. This implies that his feeling of astonishment really exists.

If this is possible for the computerized Mr. Jones, then we are faced with the situation depicted in Figure 3. On the one hand, the conscious experience of the computer exists—its subjective experience of colors, sounds, thoughts, and feelings is an actual reality. On the other hand, the physical structures of the computer exist. However, we cannot directly correlate consciousness with the concrete physical processes of the computer, nor can we relate it to the execution of individual elementary operations, such as those of Figure 1. According to the artificial intelligence researchers, consciousness should correspond to higher-order abstract properties of the computer's physical states—properties described by symbols such as "thought" and "feeling" that stand at the top of an extensive pyramid of abstract definitions. Indeed, these abstract properties are the only conceivable features of our sentient computer that could have any direct correlation with the contents of consciousness.

Since consciousness is real, however, and these abstract properties are not, we can only conclude that something must exist in nature that can somehow "read" these properties from the physical states of the computer. This entity is represented in Figure 3 by the arrow connecting the real contents of consciousness with higher levels in the hierarchy of abstract symbolic descriptions of the "sentient computer." It must have the following characteristics:

(1) This entity must possess sufficient powers of discrimination to recognize certain highly abstract patterns of organization in arrangements of matter.

(2) It must be capable of establishing a link between consciousness and such arrangements of matter. In particular, it must modify the contents of conscious experience in accord with the changes these

abstract properties undergo as time passes and the arrangements of matter are transformed.

Clearly there is no place for an "entity" of this kind in our current picture of what is going on in a computer. Indeed, we can only conclude that "it" must correspond to some feature of nature that is completely unknown to modern science.

This, then, is the conclusion that we are forced to adopt if we assume that a computer can be conscious. Of course, we can easily avoid this conclusion by supposing that no computer will ever be conscious, and this may indeed be the case. However, what can we say about the relation between consciousness and the physical body in a human being? On the one hand we know that human beings possess consciousness, and on the other we are taught by modern science that the human body is an extremely complex machine constructed from molecular components. Can we arrive at an understanding of human consciousness that does not require the introduction of an entity of the kind described by statements (1) and (2)?

Ironically, if we try to base our understanding on modern scientific theory, then the answer is no. The reason is that all modern scientific attempts to understand human consciousness depend, directly or indirectly, on an analogy between the human brain and a computer. In fact, the scientific model for human consciousness is machine consciousness!

At the present time, most scientists regard the brain as the seat of consciousness. The brain is understood to consist of many different kinds of cells, each of which is regarded as a molecular machine. Of these, the nerve cells are known to exhibit electrochemical activities that are roughly analogous to those of the logical switching elements used in computer circuitry. Even though at present the operation of the brain is understood only in very vague and general terms, scientists generally conjecture that these neurons are organized into an information-processing network that is equivalent to a computer's.

This leads naturally to the picture of the brain illustrated in Figure 4. In this picture thoughts, sensations, and feelings must correspond to higher levels of brain activity that are comparable to the higher organizational levels of a complex computer program. Just as the higher levels of such a program are abstract, these higher levels of brain activity must also be abstract. They can have no actual existence, for all that is actually happening in the brain are certain physical processes such as the pumping of sodium ions through neural cell walls. If we try to account for the existence of human consciousness in the context of this picture of the brain, we can only conclude (by the same reasoning as before) that some entity described

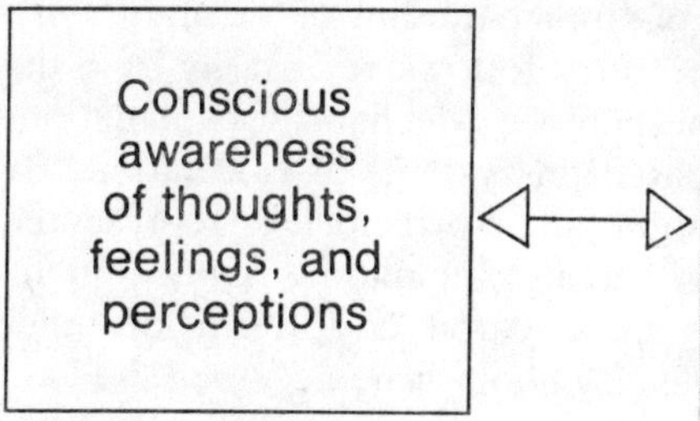

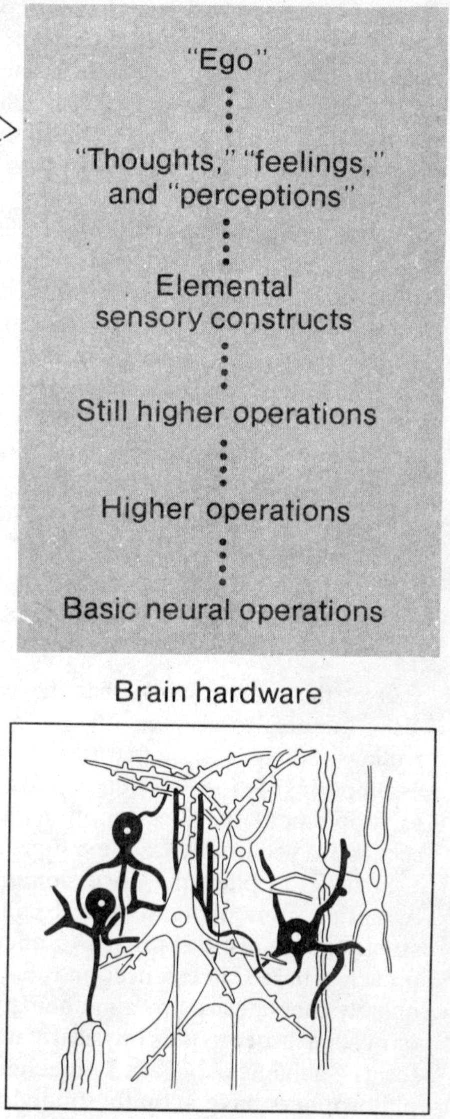

Figure 4. The relation between consciousness and the physical structures of the brain. A person's subjective experiences and the physical phenomena of his brain are both real, but these experiences cannot be correlated with physical brain phenomena in a direct, one-to-one fashion. Rather, the experiences of thoughts and feelings must correspond to higher-order abstract properties of brain states. (As in Figure 3, these properties are represented by the hierarchy of symbolic descriptions within the tinted section.) Since these abstract properties have no concrete existence, and are related only in a very indirect way with the physical structures of the brain, how can they correspond to the person's actual conscious experiences?

by statements (1) and (2) must exist to account for the connection between consciousness and abstract properties of brain states.

Furthermore, if we closely examine the current scientific world view, we can see that the conception of the brain as a computer does not simply depend on some superficial details of our understanding of the brain. On a deeper level we can see that this conception follows necessarily from the fact that the scientific world view is mechanistic. Mechanistic explanations of phenomena are, by definition, based on systems of calculation. By Church's thesis, all systems of calculation can, in principle, be represented in terms of computer operations. In effect, all explanations of phenomena in the current scientific world view can be expressed in terms of either computer operations or some equivalent symbolic scheme.

This implies that all attempts to describe consciousness within the basic framework of modern science must lead to the same problems that we have encountered in our analysis of machine consciousness.[5] Some entity of the kind described in statements (1) and (2) will be required to account for consciousness. Yet in the present theoretical system of science, there is nothing to be found, either in the brain or in a digital computer, that corresponds to such an entity. Indeed, there could not be, for any mechanistic addition to the current picture of, say, the brain would simply constitute another part of that mechanistic system, and the need for entities satisfying (1) and (2) would still arise. Clearly a nonmechanistic approach to consciousness is needed.

2.4 Several Nonmechanistic Theories

Over the years, philosophers have developed a number of nonmechanistic theories to account for our conscious experience of thoughts and feelings. Some of these theories are not compatible with the mechanistic assumptions of modern science, and others have been specifically designed to supplement these assumptions without contradicting them. In this section we will briefly examine some of these theories.

First, let us place the discussion in a formal philosophical perspective, by noting some of the technical philosophical terms associated with the strictly mechanistic approach to understanding sentient beings. This approach is based, in essence, on the idea that a sentient being can be adequately characterized by a mathematical description of its physical states, or of some aspects of its physical states. Although we have used the broad terms "behavioristic" and "mechanistic" to designate this approach, philosophers have actually subdivided it into a number of distinct versions, with names such as radical behaviorism, logical behaviorism, and functionalism.

Of these, functionalism stresses the idea that each sentient being can be characterized by a suitable computer program. Functionalism provides the philosophical framework for research in artificial intelligence, and it can be regarded as the most sophisticated of the various forms of behaviorism.[6] As such, functionalism may seem satisfactory as long as we ignore the existence of consciousness. But since computer coding says nothing about conscious experience, functionalism is completely unable to account for this essential feature of sentient beings. Thus one advocate of functionalism admitted in a recent article, "Many psychologists who are inclined to accept the functionalist framework are nevertheless worried about the failure of functionalism to reveal much about consciousness. Functionalists have made a few ingenious attempts to talk themselves and their colleagues out of this worry, but they have not, in my view, done so with much success."[7]

Let us therefore consider a number of theories in which consciousness *is* granted a real existence. We will begin by examining the identity theory, dual-aspect theories, and the theory of psychophysical parallelism. These theories have many subtle philosophical nuances, but they all share one key feature that is ruled out by the analysis presented in this chapter. We can show this by briefly defining these theories:

(a) *Identity theory.*[8] According to the identity theory, both conscious mental experience and physical phenomena are real. However, mental and neural events are one and the same, and they are basically physical.

(b) *Dual-aspect theories.*[9] Perhaps the most well-known of these theories was devised by Spinoza, who held that there is one underlying substance that has both physical and psychological aspects. Another theory, devised by Alfred N. Whitehead, features one fundamental process that is inherently endowed with "feeling," and that generates both consciousness and physical phenomena.[10] Many of these theories hold that all physical objects are to some extent sentient, a position known as panpsychism.

(c) *Psychophysical parallelism.*[11] This theory holds that consciousness and material phenomena are real, and are correlated with one another in a one-to-one fashion without any causal connection. John von Neumann gave the following interesting definition of psychophysical parallelism: "It is a fundamental requirement of the scientific viewpoint—the so-called principle of the psycho-physical parallelism—that it must be possible so to describe the extra-physical process of the subjective perception as if it were in reality in the physical world—i.e. to assign to its parts equivalent physical processes in the objective environment, in ordinary space."[12]

The common feature of these theories is that they all posit a direct, one-to-one correlation between the contents of consciousness and material phenomena. They maintain that these two things are identical, or that they are aspects of a third thing, or that they somehow run in parallel. Yet we have seen that there can be no one-to-one correlation between the contents of consciousness and the physical phenomena of the brain. Rather, the correlation that must exist between these two real phenomena is highly complex, and possesses the indirect character indicated by statements (1) and (2).

If we posit a one-to-one correlation between the contents of consciousness and certain natural phenomena, then these phenomena must be distinct from the neural interactions of the brain. This conclusion certainly contradicts theories (a) and (c), which are intended to show that consciousness can be comfortably accommodated within the framework of current scientific thinking. This conclusion also contradicts those theories of type (b) which hold that the underlying "substance" is co-extensive with matter. (It is interesting to note that Whitehead's process philosophy does not maintain this, and allows for the existence of extraneural psychic processes that transmit information back and forth between the brain and an extraneural sentient self.[13])

Another theory is idealism,[14] which holds that only conscious minds have actual existence, and that physical objects are nothing but mental perceptions. This implies that the neurons in our brains must also be perceptions, and the question arises, "In what mind are they perceptions?" On the one hand, it is hard to see how the neurons in my brain could be perceptions in my own mind, for I have no direct awareness of them. On the other hand, if these neurons are perceptions in some other mind, then the individual conscious self must be distinct from the brain.

Let us go on to consider two other theories called interactionism and epiphenomenalism. According to these theories, the conscious self is an entity that is distinct from the body, and that can be influenced by physical phenomena occurring in the brain. The difference between these theories is that interactionism allows consciousness to influence the body, whereas epiphenomenalism does not permit this. According to interactionism, the conscious self receives sense impressions from the neural apparatus of the brain, and is able to exert its will on the body by inducing changes in neural activity. In epiphenomenalism the conscious self is simply a passive spectator of events that are conducted entirely by physical processes.

Both interactionism and epiphenomenalism are compatible with the analysis given in this chapter, for we have only considered the transmission of information from the bodily machinery to consciousness. We should note, however, that this process of information transmission, as we have understood it, is quite different from the processes that many proponents of epiphenomenalism seem to envision. Advocates of this theory often convey the impression that consciousness is directly produced by the brain, as we see in the statement that "the brain secretes thought, just as the liver secretes bile."[15] They suggest that matter in appropriate states of complex organization automatically generates conscious awareness reflecting that state of organization.

We have observed, however, that the contents of consciousness cannot correspond directly with the material configurations of either a brain or a hypothetical sentient machine. Rather, as we saw in Figures 3 and 4, the contents of consciousness can only correspond in a one-to-one fashion with higher-order abstract properties of these configurations. Now, why should it happen that certain highly abstract features of complex material systems should come to be represented by real, but nonphysical, conscious perceptions? It is certainly misleading to compare such a process of representation with the secretion of bile by the liver.

As we have pointed out in statements (1) and (2), some entity, process, or law is required that can recognize the appropriate abstract patterns, and modify the contents of consciousness accordingly. This entity or process must be nonphysical or transphysical itself, for otherwise how can it either influence or generate something nonphysical? Furthermore, if it is to be capable of recognizing abstract patterns, this entity or process must be endowed with powers of discrimination of the kind we associate with intelligence.

2.5 The Conscious Self as a Complete Sentient Personality

One natural way of understanding statements (1) and (2) is provided by the model of the conscious self that we introduced in Chapter 1. There we drew upon the *Bhagavad-gītā* to formulate a picture of the conscious self as an independent, irreducible being endowed with its own inherent senses. Here we propose that the entity or process described by statements (1) and (2) corresponds with the innate senses or sensory processes of the conscious self.

We are suggesting that the conscious self, or *jīvātmā,* is a complete sentient personality that is capable of riding in a material body just as a passenger can ride in a vehicle. As such, each *jīvātmā* is conscious and possesses all the attributes of a person, including senses and intelligence. Just as a passenger can obtain information about his vehicle and its surroundings by interpreting certain instruments within the vehicle, so the *jīvātmā* can ascertain the conditions in its body and bodily environment by interpreting the physical states of the body's brain.

We realize, of course, that many other interpretations can be offered for statements (1) and (2). Yet, most of these seem more complicated and obscure than the simple hypothesis we are presenting here. (See Chapter 4 for a discussion of general requirements for a natural law or process that can generate consciousness.) By presenting the body as a vehicle for the *jīvātmā,* this hypothesis enables us to readily understand why nonphysical consciousness should be associated with complex automata. In addition, the hypothesis opens up the possibility that we may be able to enlarge our understanding of the conscious self by direct sensory experience. We shall therefore briefly discuss this hypothesis and consider some objections that might be raised against it.

The position of the *jīvātmā* as the conscious perceiver of the body can be illustrated by the example of a person reading a book. When a person reads, he becomes conscious of various thoughts and ideas corresponding to higher-order abstract properties of the arrangement of ink on the pages. Yet none of these abstract properties actually exist in the book itself, nor would we imagine that the book is conscious of the story it records. As we have indicated in Figure 5, the establishment of a correlation between the book and conscious awareness of its contents requires the existence of a conscious person with intelligence and senses who can read the book. Similarly, we can most readily understand the relation between consciousness and certain abstract properties of brain states by postulating the existence of an intelligent, sentient entity that can read these states.

Now, the objection will be raised that if we try to explain a conscious person by positing the existence of another conscious person within his body, then we have actually explained nothing at all. One can then ask how the consciousness of this person is to be explained, and this leads to an infinite regress.

This objection presupposes that an explanation of consciousness must be mechanistic. But we must simply face the fact that conscious personality cannot be explained mechanistically. An infinite regress of this kind is in fact unavoidable—unless we either give up the effort to understand consciousness or posit the existence of a sentient entity that cannot be reduced to a combination of insentient parts.

The reductionistic approach to explanation will not be fruitful when applied to the conscious self. We will never be able to explain consciousness by breaking it down into combinations of simple insensate components. Nor can it be satisfactory to "explain" consciousness by sticking it

Figure 5. The relation between consciousness and the physical structures of a book. When a person reads a book he becomes aware of higher-order abstract properties of the patterns of ink on paper—properties that are not directly present in these physical structures. This observation suggests an answer to the questions posed in the captions to Figures 3 and 4. We can answer these questions by positing the existence of a nonphysical sentient agency that can read the abstract features of the computer or brain. In the case of the computer there may be no subjective experience, and no need to postulate such an entity. But since the existence of subjective experience in humans is indubitable, we cannot avoid the conclusion that some entity must exist that is capable of reading the physical states of the brain.

awkwardly into a mechanistic world picture as an inexplicable, incompatible element. We *can,* however, seek to discover the true potential of the conscious self, and the nature of its relation with reality as a whole. If the conscious self, or *jīvātmā*, is indeed an independent sentient entity riding in a material vehicle, then the possibility arises that the *jīvātmā* may be able to occupy different kinds of bodies, or function without any material body at all. If the sensory input of the embodied *jīvātmā* is being filtered through a material data processing system, then it is possible that the *jīvātmā* may be able to experience a more direct and vivid mode of sensory perception on a higher level of consciousness. If such possibilities could be realized by direct experience—using practical, reliable methods—then we would indeed be able to feel that we had increased our understanding of consciousness.

In Chapter 9 we will discuss how such a direct investigation of consciousness might actually be carried out. Here we will conclude by making a few observations about the relation between our model of the conscious self and the theories of interactionism and epiphenomenalism. As we have observed, the arguments presented in this chapter do not distinguish between these two theories. However, for the sake of completeness we should point out that our model of the self must be classed under the heading of interactionism. According to the *Bhagavad-gītā,* the *jīvātmā* does influence the functioning of the material body, but this influence is exerted in an extremely subtle way. We will discuss this in some detail in Chapter 7. For now we will briefly mention some of the standard objections to interactionism and show that they do not apply to our model.

In Western philosophy the most famous version of interactionism is that of René Descartes, who proposed that human beings (but not animals) possess a noncorporeal mind that directs the actions of their bodies. According to Descartes, matter has the properties of extension and location in space, but mind does not. Consequently, many people have rejected Descartes' theory on the basis that it is very hard to see how an entity with no spatial properties could possibly interact with something located in a particular position in space.[16]

This objection to interactionism certainly makes sense, but it only applies to Descartes' particular theory. It can easily be answered by noting that a nonphysical entity does not have to be devoid of all physical properties. We have tried to formally define what is meant by "nonphysical" by introducing the idea of numerical indescribability. We say that an entity is numerically indescribable if significant features of the entity cannot be represented by numbers. Yet this does not imply that the entity cannot have any measurable properties at all.

Consciousness provides our archetypal example of numerical indescribability. Yet according to the Vedic literature, the conscious self is localized within the body. For example, the *Muṇḍaka Upaniṣad* states:

eṣo 'ṇurātmā cetasā veditavyo
yasmin prāṇaḥ pañcaḍhā saṁviveśa
prāṇaiś cittaṁ sarvam otam prajānāṁ
yasmin viśuddhe vibhavaty eśa ātmā

"The conscious self is atomic in size and can be perceived by perfect intelligence. This atomic self is floating in the five kinds of air [*prāṇa, apāna, vyāna, samāna,* and *udāna*], is situated within the heart, and spreads its influence all over the body of the embodied living being. When the self is purified from the contamination of the five kinds of air, its spiritual influence is exhibited."[17]

We note that the *jīvātmā* is said to be extremely minute in size, and to be located in the region of the heart (rather than in the brain). However, the *jīvātmā* does not interact directly with the gross physical structures of the body. Rather, it interacts with subtle material elements, and these in turn interact with gross matter in accordance with principles that have yet to be discovered by present-day physicists and chemists.

This brings us to another objection that is commonly raised against the theory of interactionism—the objection that the laws of physics must be violated if a nonphysical conscious entity is able to influence the behavior of matter. We can respond to this objection by pointing out that because of computational difficulties, it is nearly impossible to determine whether or not a complex system really does obey the known laws of physics. Using quantum mechanics, we have great difficulty analyzing a single molecule of benzene, and we cannot even begin to predict what will happen in a brain. Furthermore, developments within the science of physics have led to repeated revisions in the accepted laws of nature, and we may expect to see similar revisions in the future. We can only conclude that we have no justification for rejecting interactionism simply because it contradicts the alleged universality of a given system of physical laws.

As a final point, we note that the physicist Eugene Wigner has invoked the principles of current physical theory to argue in favor of an essentially interactive model of consciousness. Wigner argues that in physics, causation is never a one-way affair. Thus, if consciousness is real, as Wigner believes, then consciousness must exert some influence on matter. Consequently, Wigner concludes that "the present laws of physics are at least incomplete without a translation into terms of mental phenomena. More likely they are inaccurate, the inaccuracy increasing with the increase in the role which life plays in the phenomena considered."[18]

Notes

1. M.I.T. college catalogue, 1979, p. 118.
2. In actual computer applications much more sophisticated methods of calculating square roots would be used. The method presented in Figure 1 is intended to provide a simple example of the nature of computer programs.
3. Kleene, *Introduction to Metamathematics*, pp. 317–322, 377–381.
4. Winston, *Artificial Intelligence*, p. 253.
5. For the sake of clarity, let us briefly indicate why this is so. Suppose that a model of a sentient entity can be described by means of a computer program. Then a certain level of organization of the program will correspond to the elementary constituents of the model. For example, in a quantum mechanical model these constituents might be quantum wave functions. The level of the program corresponding to "thoughts" and "feelings" will be much higher than this level. Hence this "cognitive" level will not in any sense exist in the actual system being modeled. It will correspond only to abstract properties of the states of this system, and thus "something" of the kind described in (1) and (2) will be needed to establish the association between the system and the contents of consciousness.
6. Fodor, "The Mind-Body Problem," pp. 114–123.
7. Fodor, p. 122.
8. Edwards, ed., *The Encyclopedia of Philosophy,* Vol. 5, p. 339.
9. Edwards, p. 340.
10. Whitehead, *Process and Reality*.
11. Edwards, p. 342.
12. von Neumann, *Mathematical Foundations of Quantum Mechanics*, pp. 418–419.
13. In Whitehead, p. 339, we read that the ultimate perception of bodily sensations takes place in a sentient process operating in "empty space amid the interstices of the brain."

14. Edwards, p. 339.

15. Edwards, p. 343.

16. Edwards, p. 341. This point is also raised in Fodor, p. 114.

17. *Muṇḍaka Upaniṣad*, 3.1.9. This verse is cited in A.C. Bhaktivedanta Swami Prabhupāda, *Bhagavad-gītā As It Is*, p. 95.

18. Wigner, "Physics and the Explanation of Life," p. 44.

Chapter 3

Dialogue On Consciousness And The Quantum

A Conversation Between

Dr. Felix Avaroha, Mathematician
Dr. James Yantry, Biologist
Dr. Hans Kutark, Physicist

Who Are Later Joined by Two Physicists,

Dr. Sophus Baum
Dr. Francesco Shunya

The Time: Summer, 1980
The Place: Boston, Massachusetts

This dialogue deals with the question of whether or not modern physics can provide an adequate description of conscious life. The characters are fictitious, but most of the views they express have been expounded by various scientists and philosophers. Sections 3.1, 3.2, and 3.3 are devoted to a discussion of consciousness and the problems of quantum epistemology. In Section 3.4 the concept of the jīvātmā, *or nonphysical conscious self, is introduced, and there is a discussion of how the nonphysical self could be investigated experimentally.*

Avaroha: Over the past three hundred years there has been considerable advancement in many scientific fields, but our understanding of the nature of consciousness has remained in a completely undeveloped state. This imbalance in our scientific world view has resulted in a highly distorted conception of the nature of the conscious self. This conception is rendered particularly unsatisfactory by the widespread tendency to attribute universal validity to scientific hypotheses, and to regard modern science as the only source of true knowledge about the world.

I propose that we need a science of the conscious self, and that such a science requires a source of valid and substantial data directly pertaining to the nature of consciousness. Since such data is lacking in all the fields of modern science, from physics to psychology, I propose that we should turn to ancient and reliable sources of knowledge that we have hitherto neglected in our scientific studies. One such source is the *Bhagavad-gītā,* which presents both a fundamental conceptual framework for the understanding of consciousness, and practical means for directly studying the conscious self.[1]

If the limited and imperfect nature of our current scientific theories is recognized, it will be possible to harmonize the valid insights of modern science with the broader knowledge contained in the *Bhagavad-gītā.* Not only will this provide us with a much-needed advance in our understanding of the nature of conscious life, but also it will yield many stimulating ideas relevant to our existing studies of matter and its interactions.

Yantry: I don't feel that the program you have outlined is at all justified. There are no serious deficiencies in our current scientific world view, especially in my own field of biology. True, there are many mysteries in the science of life, and these are the subject of the most vigorous investigation at the present time. But the basic principles that form the foundation of our scientific research are solidly established. The edifice of scientific progress is firmly founded on the assumption that all phenomena in the universe are due to certain basic physical processes. Therefore, life too must be a result of physical processes only, and the course of life must be determined automatically by the physical and chemical occurrences within living matter.[2]

Although there may be many unsolved problems in high energy physics, these problems all involve extreme conditions that do not arise in living systems. The basis of life is chemistry, and all the phenomena of chemistry are now completely understood in terms of the physics of atomic and molecular interactions.[3] All the elements that make up living systems are known, and the laws governing them are also known. You seem to be advocating the introduction of some kind of nonphysical principles or entities into our scientific picture of life. Since the physical principles underlying life are completely known, there is quite simply no room in our scientific world view for such vitalistic ideas.[4]

Avaroha: It is well known that our experience of conscious perception cannot be described within the mechanistic framework you are advocating as the sole basis for the science of life.[5] As a standard example, consider our conscious perception of the color red. You can specify the wavelength of red light in quantitative terms, and you can also describe how that light induces certain chemical reactions in the retina of the eye. You can go on, at least in principle, to describe a great variety of consequent physical and chemical transformations in the nerve cells of the retina and the brain. But at no time in the course of this description do you say anything at all about the perception of red itself. This perception takes place and is therefore certainly real, but our scientific theories do not enable us to say anything about it.

Yantry: This problem of consciousness has been discussed at great length by many philosophers,[6] but I don't think it has any bearing on our theories of physics and chemistry. The general consensus is that consciousness must be generated by matter when it reaches certain levels of complex organization, as in the brain. Some speak of consciousness as something distinct from matter, and refer to it as an "epiphenomenon." Others speak of it as an aspect of matter. In any event, the important point is that consciousness does not exert any influence on the behavior of matter in living systems.[7] This behavior is entirely determined by the known laws of chemistry and physics.

Avaroha: When consciousness is treated in this way, it occupies a very awkward and artificial position in our theoretical picture. In the science of physics, all other products or aspects of a physical system have some effect on the behavior of the system as a whole. Why should consciousness be an exception?[8]

I suggest that your characterization of consciousness is inadequate, and that a valid account must describe how consciousness interacts with matter. To clear the way for this, I would like to point out that the physical principles underlying the science of chemistry are *not* fully understood. There are serious problems in the theory of quantum mechanics, which describes the behavior of atoms and molecules. These problems have been the subject of great controversy, and they have resulted in a great tangle of speculative interpretations,[9] some of which go to desperate extremes. It is clear that some modification of the theory is necessary. I would suggest that in making such modifications, we should keep in mind the requirements for an adequate theory of consciousness.[10]

Yantry: I am not an expert in the theory of quantum mechanics, but I doubt very much that any of the problems in that field could have any bearing on our established physiochemical understanding of life.[11] Perhaps, Kutark, you could shed some light on this matter.

Kutark: The situation is perhaps more complicated than you seem to think, Yantry. Yet I am convinced that the quantum theory, as it stands, provides a complete and satisfactory account of atomic interactions.[12] In my opinion, Avaroha, the problems you mentioned can be resolved by a proper understanding of the subtle features of quantum epistemology. But if you like we can discuss them, and if your view prevails we can go on to consider your more radical ideas. What do you think, Yantry?

Yantry: I'm surprised you would even consider the idea that our fundamental scientific theories might be in need of significant revision. Well, go ahead. I am sure that your final conclusions, if they are correct, will be consistent with the basic viewpoint on which all our work is based. I simply ask that you try to keep the discussion accessible to persons who are not specialists in the field of physics.

3.1 A Quantum Mechanical Problem

Avaroha: Let us proceed, then, by looking at a simple example. Consider the Wilson cloud chamber. As you know, this device consists of a glass chamber containing a piece of radioactive substance. If the humidity in the chamber is maintained just at the point of saturation, an observer will see thin lines of fog emanating from the radioactive material. Can you explain this?

Yantry: Of course. This is an elementary experiment used in beginning classes to demonstrate the phenomenon of radioactivity. As the radioactive atoms in the chamber decay, they emit subatomic particles that travel at very high velocities. These particles ionize the air along their paths, and water droplets condense around the ions, marking the paths with visible lines of fog.

Avaroha: Presumably, then, the established laws of physics should be able, at least in principle, to give a complete account of a man in a room watching a cloud chamber.

Yantry: Yes. Of course, we should keep in mind that modern physics is not deterministic. An element of chance must enter into the physical description, but this is unavoidable. We now know that chance is part of the nature of things.

Avaroha: Could you give an example of this?

Yantry: You have already mentioned one of the standard examples. The time when a given radioactive atom decays cannot be specified with certainty, even in principle. We can specify at most the probability that the atom will decay within a given interval of time. Likewise, the direction in which the high energy particle is emitted is completely random.

Avaroha: Nonetheless, you do agree, don't you, that a given atom does decay and produce a definite visible track in a particular direction at some particular time?

Yantry: Yes, of course.

Avaroha: Do you also agree that once this happens it will be perceived by the man as a definite event, and that the laws of physics should enable us to give a complete description of the process whereby this perception takes place?

Yantry: This is certainly true.

Avaroha: Very well. For simplicity, let's assume that a single radioactive atom is fixed in the center of the cloud chamber. We expect to find that as

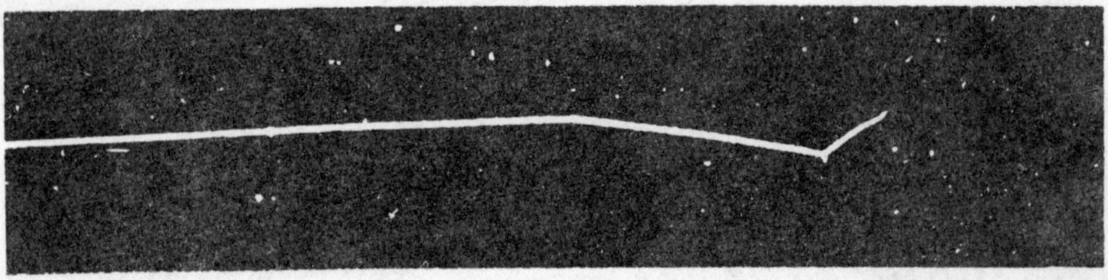

Figure 1. Cloud chamber track produced by the decay of a radioactive atom. The track is believed to have been produced by an alpha particle emitted by an atom of radon situated to the left of the picture. (From C.T.R. Wilson, *Proc. Roy. Soc. London* (A) 87, 277 (1912).)

the man watches, he may see nothing at all for some time. Then, at some particular moment, he will see a single trail of fog extending in a straight line from the center of the chamber. Let us begin by considering what happens within the atom to produce this trail.

Kutark: We can easily explain this in terms of the quantum mechanical "tunneling" effect. We can imagine that the particle is trapped within the nucleus of the atom by a potential barrier so high that the particle lacks sufficient energy to escape. In quantum physics such a particle has a certain chance of passing through the barrier, even though this is impossible from the point of view of classical physics. This phenomenon is called tunneling, and it is the standard explanation for radioactivity.

Avaroha: This kind of verbal account is often given, but quantum mechanical tunneling is not actually described in terms of a localized particle. Rather, it is described in terms of a wave. In this case we can visualize the potential barrier that you mentioned as a partially reflecting glass shell. If some light were trapped within the shell, it would bounce back and forth repeatedly, but with each reflection some light would pass through the shell. Similarly, the process of radioactive decay is described in terms of a wave that is partially trapped within the nucleus, and steadily leaks out, spreading uniformly in all directions.

Kutark: It is true that the word "particle" is used in a metaphorical sense in the quantum theory. Physical descriptions are actually given in terms of waves, or more generally, in terms of "state vectors" in Hilbert space, which can be represented mathematically in various ways.

Yantry: I take it that this talk about waves and particles must be related to

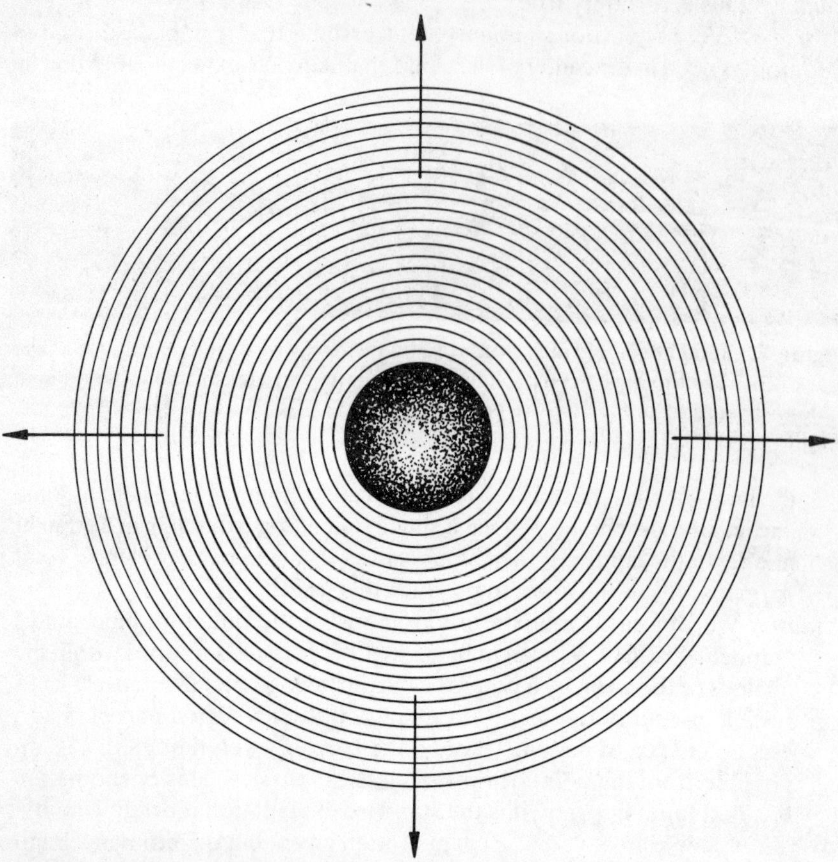

Figure 2. The quantum mechanical wave describing the emission of a particle from the nucleus of a radioactive atom.

the "wave-particle duality" that we often hear about. But your statements seem rather confusing. You say that the quantum theory actually describes radioactive decay in terms of a wave, and that the word "particle" is used metaphorically. Yet I can understand how a particle can produce a definite track, whereas it is hard to see how a wave that spreads uniformly in all directions can do so.

Kutark: The answer is very simple. Thus far, we have considered only the radioactive "particle" itself. To properly describe the cloud chamber tracks, you would have to extend the physical system at least to the point of including the atoms of air within the chamber. You would also have to take into account the interaction between these atoms and the particle. If you do this, you will find that the state vector of the system provides a completely satisfactory account of the origin of the tracks. But in this situation we cannot really call the state vector a wave; it is a much more complicated mathematical construct.

3.2 What Quantum Mechanics is Really Saying

Avaroha: Yes. To really understand the quantum mechanical treatment of our cloud chamber experiment, we will have to deal with much more complicated ideas than we have considered thus far. Let us therefore enlarge our physical system as you have suggested and introduce a general quantum mechanical state vector, $\Psi(t)$, that describes its physical state. In addition, we must introduce the Schrödinger equation,

$$H\Psi(t) = i\hbar\frac{\partial\Psi(t)}{\partial t}$$

which specifies how the state of the system changes with the passage of time. In this equation, the Hamiltonian operator, H, sums up all the physical laws of cause and effect operating within the system.

Yantry: Naturally, I have seen the Schrödinger equation before, but I have not studied it in detail. It involves very complicated calculations that only a specialist can understand. Isn't it possible to make your points about quantum mechanics using simple examples that can be readily visualized?

Avaroha: Superficial verbal accounts of quantum mechanics are generally quite misleading, and may even completely misrepresent the theory. To really appreciate what is going on in the quantum theory, we must obtain some conception of how the theory actually describes nature.

In this case, however, it should be possible to present things in a fairly nontechnical way if we accept one basic mathematical transformation of the Schrödinger equation. We begin by dividing the total system into two parts: the radioactive particle itself, and everything in the system except for this particle. I shall refer to the total system as System I, and I shall refer to the total system minus the radioactive particle as System II.

The state vector $\Psi(t)$ can be expressed as,

$$\Psi(t) = \sum_k F_k(t)\, X_k(t)$$

where the $F_k(t)$'s are state vectors for the radioactive particle itself, and the $X_k(t)$'s are state vectors for the rest of the system. If we choose the $X_k(t)$'s so as to form what is called a "complete orthonormal basis," then we can express any $\Psi(t)$ in this way in terms of some suitable set of $F_k(t)$'s.

Kutark: You are simply describing the standard method of solving differential equations called separation of variables.

Avaroha: That is correct. For our purposes, however, it is sufficient to point out that in the quantum theory the mathematical entities $F_k(t)$ and $X_k(t)$ for $k=1, 2, 3, \ldots$ completely define the state vector of our total physical system at time t.

Yantry: I'm afraid this all seems very abstract. Could you give me some idea of what these "state vectors" really are?

Avaroha: Each $F_k(t)$ refers to the radioactive particle and can be represented as a wave propagating through three-dimensional space. Since $\Psi(t)$ and the $X_k(t)$'s refer to very complicated systems involving vast numbers of particles, they cannot be represented in such a readily visualizable form. We will assume that the $X_k(t)$'s are solutions of the Schrödinger equation for System II, considered by itself. With this assumption you can think of the $X_k(t)$'s as quantum mechanical histories of what will happen in the system in the absence of the radioactive particle. Likewise, you can think of $\Psi(t)$ as a history depicting what will happen if the particle is present.

Yantry: Could you explain this in more specific terms?

Avaroha: Yes. Consider this example: Suppose that System II consists of n molecules of gas located at fixed positions in the cloud chamber.[13] You can think of these molecules as potential targets for the radioactive particle. The following drawing shows how you might visualize this situation in terms of classical physical concepts. [See Figure 3.] Here the particle is depicted as a small sphere that has emerged from the

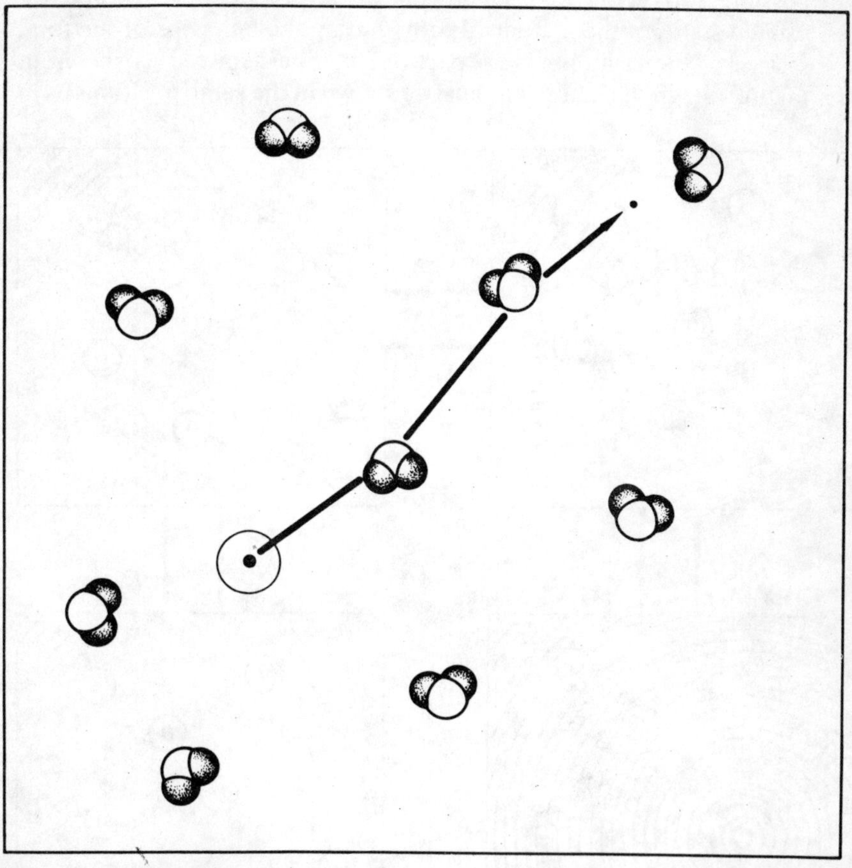

Figure 3. The process of radioactive decay as it might be visualized from the viewpoint of classical physics.

radioactive nucleus at a high velocity and is in the process of colliding with three of the target molecules.

Unfortunately, although this diagram is readily understandable, it completely misrepresents the process of radioactive decay as described in the quantum theory. To present the quantum mechanical description, I will assume, for simplicity, that System II consists of *n* idealized target atoms, each of which can be either excited (*e*) or unexcited (*u*). Since these atoms interact only with the radioactive "particle" and not with one another, System II remains unchanged with the passage of time. Thus each history, $X_k(t)$, of System II is static, and there are 2^n

possible $X_k(t)$'s, one for each possible arrangement of excited and unexcited states of the n atoms. In this setting the behavior of the total system of target atoms plus "particle" can be depicted as shown in Figure 4. Here nine target atoms are shown in the same positions as in

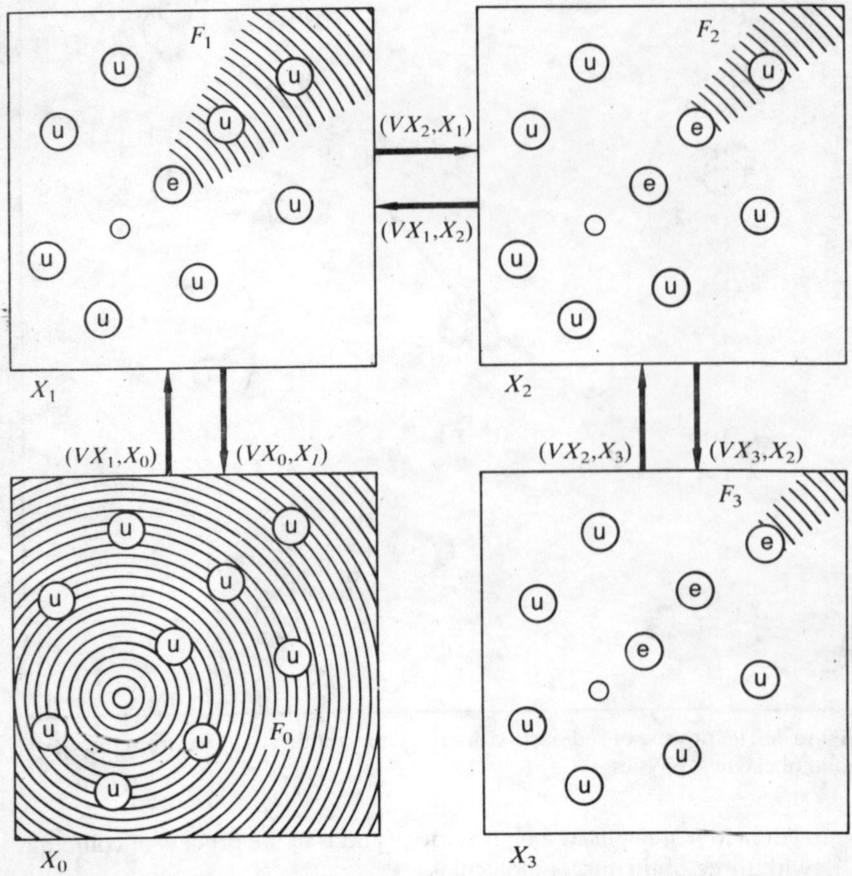

Figure 4. Part of the state vector for a system of nine target atoms and a radioactive nucleus. Each target atom can be in an excited state (e) or an unexcited state (u). The state vector is represented by waves F_0, F_1, F_2, . . . ,F_{511}, corresponding to the 512 possible combinations of excited and unexcited states of the nine atoms. Each box depicts a combination of excited and unexcited states, and the corresponding wave. These waves can "flow" from one box to another if the two boxes differ in the state of excitation of one atom, and the waves and atoms are lined up properly. (For mathematical details see Note 24.)

Figure 3. The circles marked with *e* or *u* represent the nine atoms, and four of the $2^9=512$ possible patterns of excitation are shown.

Corresponding to each $X_k(t)$, or pattern of excitation, there is an $F_k(t)$ which is depicted as a wave flowing through space. The wave $F_0(t)$ flows radially out of the radioactive nucleus, and is similar to the wave shown in Figure 2. This wave generates respective waves $F_1(t)$, $F_2(t)$, and $F_3(t)$, which are associated with X_1, X_2, and X_3, as shown in the figure. The general principle is that F_i can generate a wave F_j if the corresponding X_i differs from X_j in the state of excitation of a single atom, and this atom lies in the path of F_i. The figure shows how the *F*-waves, by propagating in this way, can start from $X_0(t)$, where there are no excited atoms, and eventually reach $X_3(t)$, where there is a line of three excited atoms extending out from the radioactive nucleus.

Kutark: This shows in a pictorial way how a trail of excited atoms is formed. If X_i corresponds to a chain of *m* excited atoms extending in a straight line from the nucleus, and X_j corresponds to the same chain with one additional excited atom at the end, then the *F*-waves can pass from X_i to X_j if this atom is lined up with the chain. Otherwise they cannot do this, for the waves tend to propagate in a straight line.

We can also see why a particle of lower energy will tend to produce a crooked track: At lower energies the *F*-waves will have longer wavelengths, and they will tend to spread out more. Thus the *F*-waves will be able to reach X_k's corresponding to curved tracks of various shapes.

Yantry: This seems very obscure. Why, if we are dealing with one radioactive particle, are you considering many different *F*-waves propagating through three-dimensional space? Do your successive waves F_0, F_1, F_2, and F_3 correspond to successive stages in time in the formation of the chain of excited atoms? Also, out of all possible straight chains of atoms extending from the nucleus, how is it determined which one will be traversed by these waves?

Avaroha: It is actually incorrect to think of the *F*-waves as real phenomena occurring in three-dimensional space. Rather, each F_k is an abstract mathematical function associated with a possible arrangement of excited and unexcited atoms in the cloud chamber. Rather than flowing through three-dimensional space, the *F*-waves are flowing through an abstract realm of possibilities. In principle, any of the 2^n different patterns of atomic excitation are possible, but due to the way the *F*-waves propagate, only those patterns representing straight tracks are associated with a non-zero F_k. Nothing has been said, however, about choosing a particular direction of propagation. Tracks in all possible directions are equally and simultaneously represented in the total state vector, $\Psi(t)$, that we are trying to describe.

I should also point out that the figure is referring to one moment in time. The successive X_k's and F_k's do not refer to successive steps in the propagation of the "particle." In fact, the $F_k(t)$'s remain practically unchanged during the period of perhaps an hour or so, in which the observer is watching the cloud chamber. This is because the intensity of the F_0 wave emanating from the radioactive nucleus is diminished by one half during a period of time equal to the "half-life" of that radioactive element. If this is substantially longer than the period of observation, we can assume that $\Psi(t)$ remains nearly static during this time.

Yantry: That means that this complicated $\Psi(t)$ specifies neither the time of formation of the cloud chamber track, nor its direction. Doesn't this mean that $\Psi(t)$ must refer to a set of alternative events from which the real event is chosen by some stochastic process? What do you mean, then, by saying that $\Psi(t)$ refers to the physical state of the system at a particular moment in time?

Avaroha: That is an interesting question. As far as the quantum theory is concerned, the state vector for a physical system provides a *complete* description of the state of that system, in the sense that the system actually possesses no physically relevant properties or characteristics not specified by the state vector. Isn't this so?

Kutark: That is true. We would be contradicting the quantum theory if we were to attribute to a physical system any property not specified by its state vector.[14]

3.3 Threading the Labyrinth of Quantum Epistemology

Avaroha: So, we seem to have a situation in which the state of our physical system is not characterized by any particular time of appearance of the track, or any particular direction of propagation. How do we reconcile this with the fact that, at a particular time, our observer witnesses the appearance of one particular track?

Kutark: The answer to this question involves an analysis of the quantum mechanical process of measurement. The state vector $\Psi(t)$ refers to phenomena that are atomic, and not directly observable. To be observed, they must produce effects that are amplified to a macroscopic level by some suitable apparatus, in this case the cloud chamber. Normally, certain features of the state vector will correspond with certain gross features of the measuring apparatus—features that can be directly observed and then described in the language of classical physics. In this case the different X_k's representing straight tracks correspond to different visible trails of fog within the chamber. Here, amplification of the quantum phenomena is due to the process of condensation, whereby droplets of water coalesce about the ionized atoms.

At the time of the measurement, we say that the apparatus will be in the macroscopic state corresponding to X_k, with a probability of (F_k,F_k). Here (F_k,F_k) represents what we could call the *total weight* of F_k, and it is interpreted as a probability. If X_k represents either a straight track or no track at all, then, as we have seen, F_k will have some positive weight. Thus these X_k's correspond to possible observable alternatives. In contrast, if X_k represents some highly irregular arrangement of excited atoms, then F_k will be zero, and we will not expect to observe a track corresponding to this X_k. Is this satisfactory?

Avaroha: Are you trying to say that the cloud chamber must be described in terms of classical physics?

Kutark: Yes. Niels Bohr pointed out that the quantum theory is meaningless unless it can be translated into the language of classical physics, which we use to describe our observations of the world.[15] Therefore, in the quantum mechanical process of measurement, we must change from the quantum mechanical to the classical mode of description at some point. In this case it is natural to do this at the point where the ion trails, which we describe quantum mechanically, give rise to visible vapor trails within the cloud chamber.

Avaroha: Is classical physics capable of giving an adequate account of the structure of matter?

Kutark: No. As you well know, the quantum theory was developed because classical physics could not successfully describe the atomic constituents of matter.

Avaroha: Are you saying, then, that it is not possible for us to give an adequate description of the cloud chamber?[16]

Kutark: Not necessarily. We could describe the cloud chamber by means of quantum mechanics and revert to classical physics at another point in the process of observation. For example, we could do this at the point where light reflecting from the cloud chamber was focused on the retina of the observer's eye. John von Neumann pointed out that the boundary between the observer and the observed system can be arbitrarily shifted, with everything on the observed side being completely describable by quantum mechanics.[17]

Avaroha: This procedure leaves the conscious observer on the side of the boundary where phenomena are to be described in terms of inadequate classical concepts. If you are truly forced to divide the world into two parts in this way, then it would seem that the quantum theory is incapable of adequately describing the observer. Furthermore, since your boundary singles out one potential observer for unique treatment, you seem to be introducing an element of solipsism into your theory. If the quantum theory simply describes one individual's subjective impressions of the part of the world external to him,[18] then it can provide neither a complete description of reality nor an adequate account of consciousness.

Kutark: Actually, the observer is irrelevant. Once the observer is brought into the picture the impression is created that a subjective element has been introduced into physics. This simply entangles us in muddled thinking! To maintain scientific objectivity we should exclude all conscious observers from the physical system and define the measuring process in terms of some automatic recording device describable in terms of familiar, classical physical concepts.[19]

Avaroha: What do we do if we want to give a theoretical account of the actual human observer of our cloud chamber? Are you saying this can't be done?

Kutark: Of course it can be done. You can use one comprehensive state vector to describe the cloud chamber, the human observer, and as much of his environment as you may wish to include. We should simply keep in mind that the state vector must be interpreted as an objective description of physical reality.

Avaroha: Very well, then, let's try to do this. Why don't we adopt our previous notation to this enlarged system? We can refer to the enlarged system as System I, and let $\Psi(t)$ designate its state vector. Similarly, we can define System II as the enlarged system minus the radioactive particle. The $F_k(t)$'s and $X_k(t)$'s can then be defined as before.

If we adopt these conventions, we can view the $X_k(t)$'s as possible histories of the total system minus the radioactive particle. Most of these histories will presumably represent matter in various chaotic states. But if quantum mechanics can actually describe System II adequately, then some of these histories must represent the formation of a vapor trail in the cloud chamber, followed by the perception of this trail by the observer.

Kutark: Yes. For each possible track in the cloud chamber there will be an X_k that represents the formation of that track through condensation, and its subsequent perception by the observer.

Avaroha: Can you use the Schrödinger equation to demonstrate rigorously that these X_k's really will adequately describe the physiological processes going on in the body of the observer?

Kutark: Of course not. That would plainly be asking too much. We simply assume this because if it were not so, then our theory would be wrong.

Avaroha: All right. Let's make this assumption for the sake of argument. If we do this we will find, as before, that the total state vector $\Psi(t)$ corresponds to a superposition of $X_k(t)$'s representing either particle tracks in various directions, or no track at all. Now, however, the $X_k(t)$'s also represent physical states of the observer corresponding to his perception of these conflicting alternatives. In other words, at a given time t, the state vector $\Psi(t)$ represents the observer as being simultaneously in a large number of different physiological states corresponding to mutually contradictory perceptions. If $\Psi(t)$ is indeed a complete description of the physical state of the system, then how do you account for this?

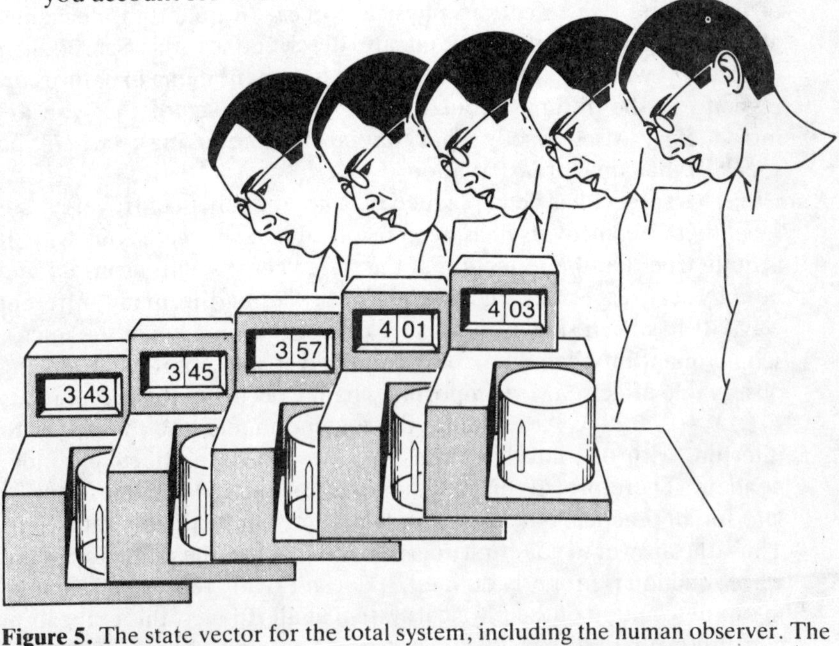

Figure 5. The state vector for the total system, including the human observer. The five images correspond to five situations of the observer, involving distinct experiences and perceptions. The state vector gives nearly equal representation to many such situations.

Kutark: We deal with this situation by employing what is known as the "reduction of the wave function." Essentially, I have already described this procedure. At the time of observation the state vector $\Psi(t)$ is replaced by one of its unambiguous components, $F_k(t)X_k(t)$, with a probability of $(F_k(t),F_k(t))$. We can also express this by saying that at the time of observation, $\Psi(t)$ is replaced by the statistical mixture of states,

$$M(t) = \sum_k (F_k(t),F_k(t))\, P_{X_k}(t)$$

Here we represent the statistical mixture by what is known as a von Neumann density matrix.[20]

Avaroha: Since $\Psi(t)$ is intended to represent the physical state of the system, naturally we would suppose that changes in $\Psi(t)$ must correspond to changes occurring in nature in the physical system itself. In the science of physics we normally suppose that natural transformations of matter are due to certain physical forces. In quantum mechanics all transformations of this kind are described by the Schrödinger equation. I would therefore like to ask what phenomena in nature correspond to the abrupt "reduction" of the state vector that you are introducing. Also, exactly what time are you referring to when you speak of the "time of observation"?

Kutark: This subject has been plagued by a great deal of controversy, but recently this controversy has been resolved in a very satisfying way. It is quite true that the reduction of the state vector seems arbitrary and nonphysical, especially because it can be defined in many different ways. It has been shown, however, that at the time when the microscopic quantum phenomena are amplified to the point of producing observable effects, a very important change occurs in the components $F_k(t)X_k(t)$ of $\Psi(t)$. At this time these components lose the power to interfere with one another, and thus they become effectively independent. Therefore, at this time our expression $M(t)$ becomes equivalent for all practical purposes with $\Psi(t)$, and can justifiably replace it. Thus, the answer to your first question is that when the reduction of the wave function is properly defined, it doesn't really represent a change in our description of the physical system at all. In fact, this realization constitutes the indispensible completion and natural crowning of the magnificent edifice of quantum mechanics![21]

Avaroha: There seems to be some ambiguity in your statements. $M(t)$ may resemble $\Psi(t)$ in certain respects. But it is formally different from $\Psi(t)$ and does not, for example, satisfy the Schrödinger equation. The most striking *similarity* between $M(t)$ and $\Psi(t)$, however, is that both of these mathematical entities fail to specify the specific alternative state $F_k(t)X_k(t)$ corresponding to the unique conscious experience of the observer. Therefore, the original problem we encountered with $\Psi(t)$ is not solved if we simply replace $\Psi(t)$ by $M(t)$.

Moreover, you also said earlier that $M(t)$ means that the system is in a *specific* state $F_k(t)X_k(t)$, and that this came about abruptly with a probability of $(F_k(t),F_k(t))$. Thus you are using $M(t)$ in two ways: to describe the state of the system at time t, and to describe a process whereby the system reached a completely different state by a random jump. Which of these two conflicting usages would you like to choose? You certainly cannot use both consistently.

Kutark: Many physicists have concluded that quantum mechanical statements must always refer to statistical ensembles. All we can say is that out of N identically prepared systems, $N(F_k(t),F_k(t))$ will be in the state $F_k(t)X_k(t)$ at the time of observation. $M(t)$ in fact expresses this property of a large ensemble of systems.[22]

Avaroha: Do you mean to say that in quantum mechanics we cannot refer to the specific situation that is actually experienced by the observer at a particular time? If this is so, doesn't it follow that quantum mechanics is indeed drastically incomplete?

Kutark: Certainly not, for I have already said that you can refer to the specific state of the observer by using a particular $X_k(t)$.

Avaroha: You are saying then that the state of the system changes abruptly from $\Psi(t)$ to some particular $F_k(t)X_k(t)$ at the time of observation?

Kutark: That is certainly one standard interpretation of quantum mechanics.[23]

Avaroha: I would like to refer once again to my question about the "time of observation." You said that the time of observation is, approximately, the time when the quantum phenomena are amplified from the microscopic to the macroscopic level. But in our system, this process is occurring continuously during the entire period of, say, an hour in which the cloud chamber is being observed.

Kutark: Oh? I would think that the amplification must occur directly after the chamber is triggered and the process of condensation can begin.

Avaroha: It is true that some cloud chambers are triggered at specific times. But let's consider what happens if our cloud chamber is of the type that operates continuously. In that case we will find that the state vector $\Psi(t)$ for our total system does not single out any particular time of occurrence for the event of radioactive decay. Rather, $\Psi(t)$ is a superposition of $F_k(t)X_k(t)$'s, representing all possible times of observation for the track.

The structure of $\Psi(t)$ in this situation is rather interesting. As we know, each $X_k(t)$ can be thought of as a possible history of events in System II. In $\Psi(t)$ each $X_k(t)$ is present to a degree determined by the magnitude of its coefficient, $F_k(t)$. If $F_k(t)$ is zero, then we can assume that $X_k(t)$ is not represented in $\Psi(t)$.

I can show by a diagram how a history representing the observation of a track becomes represented in $\Psi(t)$. [See Figure 6.] Here the history X_0 represents what happens in System II when there is no ion trail

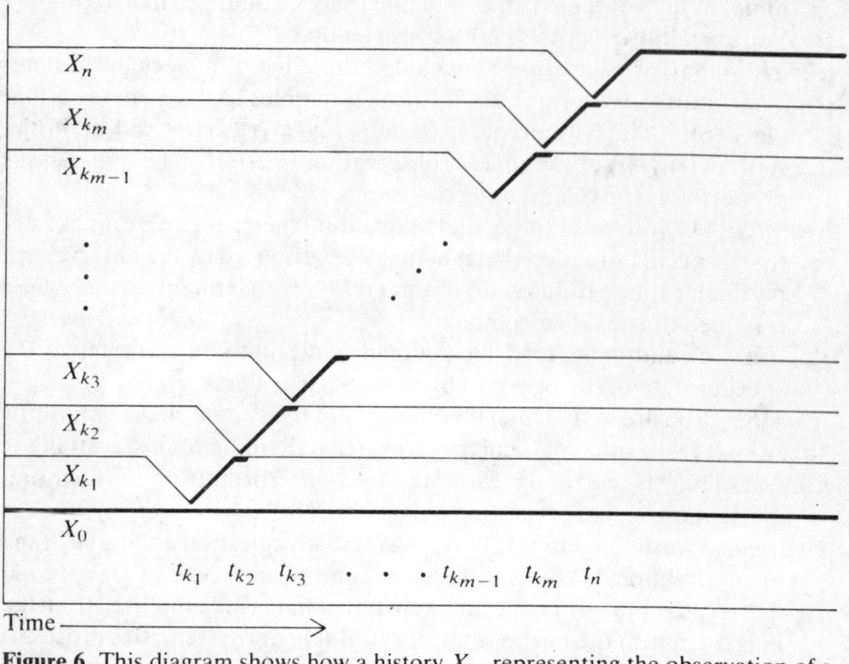

Figure 6. This diagram shows how a history X_n, representing the observation of a particular track, is added to the total state vector. This is a process involving a number of intermediate histories, $X_{k_1}, X_{k_2}, \ldots, X_{k_m}$, that represent the observation of partial tracks of greater and greater length. Here each history is indicated by a line, and the line is made thicker during the period when that history is represented in the total wave function. Vertical distance between histories designates similarity, and we can see that a history can be added to the total state vector only at a time when it is very similar to another history that is already represented there.

in the chamber. I shall assume that X_0 represents a situation in which the observer sits for one hour and sees nothing. You should note that since System II omits the radioactive particle, none of the X_k's can depict the formation of a track due to the event of radioactive decay.

Kutark: Certainly, though, some of the X_k's will represent tracks, for otherwise $\Psi(t)$ could not represent the observation of any track at all.

Avaroha: That is true. Roughly speaking, for each possible track and each possible time, there will be an X_k that represents the observation of that track at that time. But in a history X_k representing the observation of a track at time t_0, the appearance of the track will be due to some events other than radioactive decay that take place in System II before time t_0.

Kutark: What do you mean? What happens in $X_k(t)$ before t_0?

Avaroha: We may not be able to say exactly. Due to the time reversibility of the Schrödinger equation, we know that X_k must have some history before time t_0, and since System II omits the radioactive particle, this history must depict the formation of the track by some spurious process.

Referring again to Figure 6, we see that X_n represents a history in which a complete track appears in the chamber, beginning at time t_n. Each X_{k_i} in the figure represents a history in which a partial track appears at time t_{k_i}. Starting with X_{k_1}, which represents a very short track, histories representing successive prolongations of the track at successive times are briefly represented in the total state vector, one after another. Finally, at time t_n the history representing the complete track becomes represented in $\Psi(t)$.

Kutark: What causes a particular X_k to join the total state vector at a particular time?

Avaroha: If X_i is already represented in the state vector, and X_j is very similar to X_i at time t, then at this time it is possible for X_j to acquire a non-zero F_j and thereby join the total state vector. According to the mathematics of the Schrödinger equation,[24] when X_i and X_j are sufficiently similar, the wave F_i can induce the development of a non-zero F_j. The situation was similar in the simpler case we discussed earlier, in which the X_k's represented combinations of excited and unexcited states of target atoms. There we saw that F_i could influence F_j only if X_i and X_j differed in the state of excitation of a single target atom.

Kutark: So all the X_k's simply exist as unrealized alternative histories, and when they happen to exhibit certain relationships of similarity to one another, they can join or leave the total state vector.

Avaroha: That is what the mathematics of the theory indicates. Each of the histories, $X_{k_1}, X_{k_2}, \ldots, X_{k_m}$, involves many events that occur before and after its brief period of "existence" in $\Psi(t)$. These histories serve only as stepping stones for the establishment of X_n, which represents a complete track. For every possible time and every possible track direction, there will be a similar system of histories. Thus the total state vector will have a structure we can depict graphically in the following way. [See Figure 7.] Here each line segment refers to a possible history during its time of representation in $\Psi(t)$. All possible observations of tracks at all possible times are represented. I should point out that the pattern of branching here is fairly simple because we are dealing with only one radioactive atom. In a realistic case with many atoms, each branch would also have many sub-branches and sub-sub-branches.

Kutark: You are right. The mathematical structure of $\Psi(t)$ is indeed fascinating! In the total state vector there are not only "realized" histories depicting different possible experiences of the observer, but there are also histories that largely involve impossible or highly improbable experiences. For example, a history entailing a partial track is represented only for the short time required for it to serve as a stepping stone. It is not part of the total state vector once it depicts the observation of a track that has abruptly stopped!

Avaroha: We might ask, however, just what this mathematical structure has to do with reality, and how we can correlate its components with the conscious experiences of the observer.

If we are to avoid contradicting the uniqueness of the observer's conscious perceptions, we cannot restrict ourselves to performing the operation of reduction of the state vector at some one particular time. As I pointed out, in a case where there are many radioactive atoms, each branch will repeatedly subdivide, and each time we reduce the state vector we will have to reduce it again almost immediately.

We are faced with a situation of almost continuously having to make abrupt, nonphysical modifications in our description of the physical state of the system, simply to prevent this description from contradicting some of the most obvious aspects of our ordinary experience. We have no basis for deciding at what frequency these modifications are to be made. We know only that they are necessary if we are to avoid an absurdity.

Kutark: I can give you an example from ordinary, classical physics in which such repeated reduction is necessary. Consider a rotating wheel. The angular position *a* of the wheel is given by the simple formula

$a=vt$, where v is the wheel's angular velocity, and we assume that $a=0$ when the time t is zero.

Now, in physics we cannot define v with perfect accuracy, and due to the influence of the environment, v will always fluctuate slightly. As time passes, however, this uncertainty in the definition of v will result in a large cumulative uncertainty in a. Therefore, it will be necessary to repeatedly redefine a. Isn't this situation very similar to the one you are describing?[25]

Avaroha: It is different in a very significant way. In your wheel example, the repeated reduction or redefinition is necessary because our information about the physical system is incomplete. In the quantum mechanical situation, this information is supposed to be completely specified by the state vector, $\Psi(t)$. The very point I've been trying to make, of course, is that the state vector does not, in fact, provide a complete description of the system.

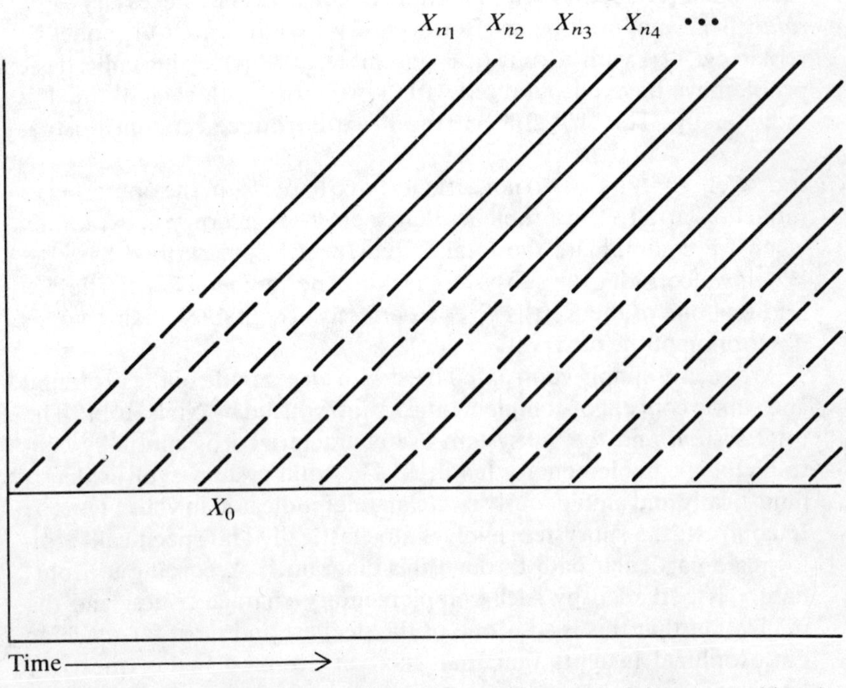

Figure 7. The total state vector. Within any small interval of time, many histories ($X_{n1}, X_{n2}, X_{n3}, \ldots$) representing different experiences of the observer are added to $\Psi(t)$.

I should note that some physicists have tried to make quantum mechanics complete by introducing what are known as "hidden variables." Their idea is that the state vector corresponds to a statistical distribution over the hidden variables. This means that the state vector is an incomplete description of the system, and must therefore be periodically "reduced" for the same essential reason that your wheel's position has to be periodically redefined. As you know, of course, the hidden variable theories are all very controversial, and none has met with widespread acceptance.[26] They simply constitute another symptom of the unsatisfactory character of the quantum theory.

Kutark: In practice, however, we can never describe large physical systems with single state vectors such as $\Psi(t)$. We must always use statistical distributions, as is done, for example, in statistical mechanics. Also, we must always consider the effects of minute fluctuations arising from the influence of the external environment. Thus, in a realistic model the kind of reduction I have mentioned will always be necessary.

Avaroha: That may well be so. But even if we complicate our model by replacing $\Psi(t)$ with a statistical ensemble of $\Psi_j(t)$'s, the same basic problem we have encountered with Ψ will arise with each of the Ψ_j's individually. This will still be true if we introduce random fluctuations.[27]

Kutark: Well, for $\Psi(t)$ we do not actually have to perform the operation of reduction at all. The problems that seem to concern you arise only when we contemplate the total system, which is described by $\Psi(t)$. When we consider the subsystem lacking the radioactive particle, we find that one of the $X_k(t)$'s gives a perfectly acceptable, unambiguous description of the observer.

Are we not simply confronted here with an example of the profound and subtle concept of complementarity introduced by Niels Bohr? The total system and the subsystem are characterized by mutually contradictory, complementary features. The total system evolves deterministically and ambiguously in the manner indicated in your Figure 7. In contrast, the subsystem evolves stochastically and specifically, following a particular path through this diagram.[28] According to Bohr, nature is pervaded by such complementary characteristics, and the realization that this is so is one of the deepest and most far-reaching philosophical insights that man has yet attained in his quest for knowledge.

Avaroha: If the total system is ambiguous in certain of its gross features, then how can a subsystem, which is part of it, be unambiguous in these very same features?

Kutark: According to the principle of complementarity, when we refer to a system we cannot attribute any real existence to its subsystems. This, in fact, is Bohr's solution to the problem of wave-particle duality. If we try to attribute real existence to an electron in certain experimental settings, then we seem to encounter a contradiction, for it sometimes exhibits the properties of a wave, and sometimes the properties of a particle. The contradiction evaporates, however, if we simply refer to the experimental apparatus plus electron as an indivisible total system, and do not try to break it down into parts.

Avaroha: Does this mean that when we refer to the total system, we cannot refer at the same time to the observer, or to his state of consciousness?

Kutark: Yes, that is correct.

Avaroha: But when we speak of System II, we can refer to the observer as having specific conscious experiences. Is that right?

Kutark: Yes. You find this confusing only because you do not grasp the principles of quantum logic. Just as the general theory of relativity has forced us to accept new axioms of geometry for our descriptions of space and time, so the quantum theory has forced us to adopt new rules of logic.[29] It just takes some time to get used to this.

Avaroha: Let me ask you this. Do the magnitudes of the F_k's in $\Psi(t)$ have any bearing on your application of the principle of complementarity to $\Psi(t)$? Let's imagine that by increasing the half-life of the radioactive atom, we increase the relative magnitude of F_0 with respect to all the other F_k's. Is there some point at which you would drop your stricture of not attributing reality to System II when speaking of System I?

Kutark: As long as the other F_k's are not all zero, I can think of no reason to do this.

Avaroha: In that case, consider what happens when we isolate a single electron from System II, and designate the remainder of System II as System III. If we carry out an analysis similar to the one that we have done for Systems I and II, we will find that the state vector of System II is a macroscopically ambiguous combination of state vectors for System III. Do you agree that this is so?

Kutark: It is certainly possible that some unlikely quantum transitions of the electron could result in gross variations in the behavior of the system. Therefore it is reasonable to suppose that the state vector for System II is macroscopically ambiguous.

Avaroha: Would we also expect to find that the state vectors for System III are macroscopically ambiguous combinations of state vectors for a System IV, obtained by removing a particle from System III?

Kutark: Yes, although the relative magnitude of the grossly contradictory terms in the state vector may be very small. The same thing can be said of the sequence of subsystems you will no doubt want to construct by isolating successive particles one at a time. The state vector of any subsystem may exhibit macroscopic ambiguities.

Avaroha: Doesn't this mean that we cannot associate the unique conscious experiences of the observer with any subsystem of the total system, including the man's brain or any part of it? Unless we do perform the operation of reduction, we are likely to meet ambiguities in any subsystem that contradict the specificity of conscious experience. It does not help us very much to simply maintain that whenever we speak of one of these subsystems, we cannot attribute reality to any of its sub-subsystems.

Kutark: All I can really say here is that we have simply become mired in useless hair splitting. Since science has to be practical, the best thing to do is revert to a classical or semi-classical description of the system at some point.[30]

Yantry: I'm relieved to hear you say that Kutark! This entire discussion of quantum physics seems very bizarre and unreal to me. In biology and chemistry we have solid, three-dimensional molecular models that are as real as your bedroom furniture! We also have practical, comprehensible mathematical schemes, such as systems of reaction-diffusion equations, that describe the behavior of these models. Certainly this represents the soundest approach to the study of living systems.

Kutark: Yet these mathematical systems can be only approximations at best. I'm afraid the point will be made that our scientific picture of life is incomplete if we are forced to resort to such approximations.

3.4 A Discussion of Contrasting World Views

(*Dr. Sophus Baum and Dr. Francesco Shunya have been listening for some time, and at this point they join the conversation.*)

Baum: I would like to point out that in the midst of all these complicated deliberations, you have overlooked what is at the same time the simplest and grandest interpretation of quantum mechanics. In this interpretation we completely reject all *ad hoc* schemes that attempt to adjust the state vector in a nonphysical way so as to bring it into line with our narrow, preconceived views of what reality should be. Rather, we accept the state vector as a complete description of reality as it is, with all the staggering implications this entails. Reality consists of an infinite system of bifurcating, noncommunicating universal realms in which all the manifold possibilities described in the quantum mechanical state vector are factually realized.[31] In this interpretation all transformations of the physical system take place completely in accordance with the laws of physical causation, as described by the Schrödinger equation. Chance is completely eliminated in the sense that a factual universe exists for every alternative state of affairs described by the quantum theory.

Avaroha: You seem to be referring here to a state vector for the entire universe.

Baum: Yes, that is correct. Our scientific world view can be complete and satisfying only if it is universal. Since the world is quantum mechanical, we must postulate a universal state vector, and the simplest interpretation of such a state vector is that it describes multiple universes. In fact, this is the only interpretation of the state vector suitable for the grand synthesis of general relativity and quantum mechanics that shall provide the final, unified description of universal reality.[32]

Avaroha: Has a mathematically consistent synthesis of quantum mechanics and general relativity yet been worked out?

Baum: No, but we are working on it.

Avaroha: Could you explain what happens to the consciousness of the observer when your universes bifurcate?

Baum: That is very easy to explain. Just as the universe splits into multiple universes, so the observer splits into multiple observers, one for each universe. In each universe the corresponding observer is conscious of the particular course of events that occurs there. In many of these universes our observer will not even exist. In others, someone similar to him will exist, and in still others he will exist but will have different experiences. Actually, each one of us has innumerable near-duplicates of ourselves living separate lives in different universes.

Avaroha: Is it possible for us to communicate with these parallel universes?

Baum: No. Once a universe bifurcates into two copies, there can be no communication between them.

Avaroha: Then it is not possible for us to obtain any empirical evidence for the existence of these universes?

Baum: No. However, this interpretation of the state vector is justified, because it allows us to retain the absolute statistical laws of quantum mechanics, which have been verified again and again by experiment.

Avaroha: If every possible quantum mechanical alternative is represented by a real universe, then there must be universes in which very improbable sequences of events are the rule.

Baum: I know what you are going to say. The only possible answer is that we just happen to be in the universe that we are in. Of course, the universes that obey certain statistical laws are the most prominently represented, and this is what we *mean* when we say that these statistical laws are valid. We just happen to be in a typical universe that obeys the universal laws, but some of our near-duplicates are now experiencing life in a universe in which all of these laws have just begun to be completely violated. That's just the way things are.

Shunya: The absurd conclusions you are now contemplating are clearly due to a serious misunderstanding of the true nature of *all* scientific theories. All your attempts to associate some concept of reality with the algorithms of scientific theories are based on hopelessly muddled thinking. When making scientific statements, we must speak only about patterns of correlation in sense data. A theory is of value insofar as it accurately describes such patterns, and all attempts to associate a theory with "reality" are simply an irrelevant and meaningless misuse of words.[33] This is the real import of the quantum theory.

Avaroha: Do your strictures on admissible types of statements apply just to scientific statements? Could there be true and meaningful statements of some other kind that *do* refer to reality?

Shunya: No. Only statements that refer to patterns of correlation in sense data should be made.

Avaroha: The very statement that you have just made is not of this type. Your limited system of discourse seems to depend on the existence of a higher reality for its very definition—a reality to which it cannot refer. Also, is it possible to live by the system of philosophy that you have outlined? Do you regard other persons simply as patterns of correlation in sense data, and do you think that it constitutes hopelessly muddled thinking to suppose that they really exist?

Shunya: The path of scientific truth is a difficult and lonely one. We must come to the stark realization that most of our desires for meaning, purpose, and understanding can never be satisfied, or even meaningfully discussed. This applies even to the desire to understand the real basis of our own existence as scientific investigators. At most we can obtain some consolation by admiring the beauty of a symmetrical system of equations, or the elegance of a concise deductive argument. In this way we can spend the brief interval of time that we somehow pointlessly occupy between two infinite, meaningless voids.

Kutark: This is becoming very exhausting. I must admit that there seems to be some inadequacy in our scientific understanding that is preventing us from coming to a satisfactory conclusion. Possibly this inadequacy does have something to do with consciousness. It is true that the subject of consciousness seems to arise naturally in our discussion, in various direct and indirect ways. For example, the multiple universe idea really amounts to a proposal for associating multiple conscious awarenesses with the state vector. It is also true that we have no idea of how to deal with consciousness scientifically.

Let me ask you this, Avaroha. No doubt you are aware that some prominent physicists have proposed that consciousness is directly responsible for the reduction of the state vector.[34] Some of them maintain, as you do, that consciousness is something fundamental.[35] They argue that the state vector is somehow reduced at the moment it begins to display ambiguities that can be perceived by the observer. For example, the moment the observer of your cloud chamber begins to develop an ambiguous brain state representing the perception of two different particle tracks, the state vector is reduced, and the new state vector involves just one of these tracks. This is supposedly done by "consciousness," but how it is done is not at all clear. Some other physicists have even speculated that consciousness can cause systematic reductions of the wave function that violate the statistical rules of quantum mechanics.[36] They use this idea to explain various phenomena such as the "psychokinesis" of the parapsychologists. Are you perhaps in favor of some of these ideas?

Avaroha: The basic approach that underlies these ideas is to repair the defects of quantum mechanics by grafting something new onto it. Of course, it is understandable that a person steeped in the concepts of modern physics would try to begin in this way. But I would suggest that this is not the right approach. Someone once pointed out that Newton's theory of gravitation could not be amended by making some small alterations, since these would simply clash with the existing structure of the theory. Rather, Newton's theory could be supplanted only by something fundamentally different, such as the general theory of relativity, which provided a completely new perspective. I would propose that if we are to obtain an adequate understanding of consciousness and its relationship with the physical world, we will similarly have to approach the subject from a radically different point of view.

Kutark: What do you have in mind?

Avaroha: I will begin by outlining the fundamental understanding of the nature of consciousness presented in the *Bhagavad-gītā.* As you have said, even though consciousness is a fundamental aspect of reality, it has not proven possible to adequately explain or even describe consciousness within the framework of modern science. The problem, in fact, is not that we presently have an inadequate theory of consciousness. Rather, we find that our scientific statements do not even refer to consciousness. This is a fundamental limitation of the mechanistic point of view, in which we try to reduce all explanations to mathematical calculations involving measurable quantities.

The *Bhagavad-gītā* states that each individual living organism consists of an irreducible conscious entity riding in a physical body composed of gross material elements. The body is insentient, and it is described in the *Bhagavad-gītā* as a complicated machine.[37] In contrast, the conscious entity, or *jīvātmā,* is the actual sentient self of the living being, and it cannot be explained in mechanistic terms.[38] Each *jīvātmā* possesses all of the attributes of a person, including consciousness, intelligence, and innate sensory faculties. These attributes cannot be reduced to the interplay of some underlying impersonal entities that we might hope to describe by a mechanistic theory. In a sense, we can compare the *jīvātmās* with the hypothetical fundamental particles sought by physicists. Just as these particles are envisioned as having certain irreducible material properties, so the *jīvātmās* can be thought of as fundamental units of conscious personality endowed with certain irreducible personal traits.

Kutark: So, you are proposing a theory that features a transcendental soul as a primitive element. *A priori,* I suppose there's no reason why we can't propose such a thing. But are there any experiments proving the existence of the soul?

Avaroha: To answer this question, let's consider how physical experiments are conducted. In physics we can show that an entity exists only by an experiment that takes advantage of that entity's mode of interaction with other matter. For example, we have been discussing the cloud chamber tracks made by charged particles such as electrons. These tracks result from the ionization of atoms near the path of the particle, and this ionization comes about as a result of the electromagnetic interaction between the particle and the electrons in the atoms. Neutral particles do not interact in this way and thus leave no tracks. The neutrino, for example, is famous for interacting with matter in a very weak fashion—by what is known as the weak force, in fact—and thus it is very hard to detect experimentally.

Kutark: So to detect the soul in an experiment we would have to take advantage of the soul's particular mode of interaction. That is reasonable. But what is that mode of interaction? At present, physicists know of four basic types of force: strong, weak, electromagnetic, and gravitational. You are suggesting, I gather, that the soul does not interact in any of these modes?

Avaroha: That is correct, and consequently we couldn't hope to directly detect the presence of the *jīvātmā* with any of our customary physical instruments. The *jīvātmā does* interact with matter, but in a very indirect and subtle way. As a result of the *jīvātmā's* primary interaction, secondary interactions are induced in the body, and these affect the nervous system in particular.[39] These electromagnetic effects are detectable in principle, but they are very complex. Therefore, it would be very difficult to unambiguously single out the influence of the *jīvātmā* on the body by analyzing physical measurements. [The precise nature of the interaction between the *jīvātmā* and matter is discussed in Chapter 7.]

Shunya: This makes it seem very implausible that you could ever verify the existence of this hypothetical *jīvātmā.* But I would like to make another, more fundamental point. Suppose you could demonstrate from experimental data that some new fundamental law of nature was needed to explain the functioning of the brain. A theory incorporating this law would still be mechanistic. All our scientific statements—and, in fact, all valid statements of *any* kind—refer to patterns in measured data, and they are therefore necessarily mechanistic, even though we may not always try to express them in formal mathematical language. Since you are describing consciousness and personality as nonmechanistic, you are in effect saying nothing at all. It is meaningless to even talk about verifying such statements by experiments.

Avaroha: You are partly right. It is indeed true that we cannot study consciousness *per se* by examining its influence on the motion of matter. Of course, we can make indirect inferences about consciousness by such methods. But to make a real study of consciousness we have to take advantage of the higher cognitive potencies of the *jīvātmā* itself.

As I have pointed out before, many of your own statements cannot be translated into strictly mechanistic terms. When you spoke of desires and hopes that cannot even be meaningfully discussed, you were in fact referring to aspects of reality that transcend the domain of mechanistic description. To understand these things and deal with them in a practical way, we need to enter a domain of discourse and experience that goes beyond the mechanistic world view. If we were simply machines, then this would not be possible. However, according to the *Bhagavad-gītā* our own existence transcends the mechanistic realm.

When the *jīvātmā* is embodied, its innate senses are linked up with the information processing system of the physical body, and thus the normal sensory perceptions of the *jīvātmā* refer almost exclusively to the physical states of machines, including the machine of the brain.[40] In this condition, only the *jīvātmā's* direct perception of its own internal sensory and cognitive activities involves something that cannot be described in terms of mechanical configurations. For this reason, there is a strong tendency for the *jīvātmā* to overlook its own nature and view the world in an entirely mechanistic way.

But the inherent senses of the *jīvātmā* are not limited to observing the states of the physical body. The *jīvātmā* is capable of a relation of direct reciprocation both with other *jīvātmās* and with the *paramātmā*, or the Superconsciousness. This mode of interaction directly involves the use of all personal attributes and qualities, and thus it cannot be described in mechanistic terms. It can be understood and meaningfully discussed only by persons who have attained to this level of experience by direct realization.

Shunya: Such "realization" is purely subjective! Anyone can claim to have all kinds of remarkable realizations and mystical visions, and in fact there are many thousands of such people, and thousands of conflicting sects composed of their gullible followers! But science is limited to knowledge that can be verified objectively. For an observation to be considered objective it must be possible for several different people to make the observation independently, and then compare their results.

Avaroha: Two persons able to function on a higher level of consciousness will certainly be able to recognize each other as realized souls, and they can also meaningfully discuss their realizations with other similarly endowed persons. We can partially illustrate this by the example of two seeing persons discussing the sunset in the presence of a congenitally blind person. The blind person would not be able to appreciate their statements, and he might take the skeptical viewpoint that talk about sunsets is simply meaningless. Nonetheless, the seeing persons can discuss the sunset, and each can feel confident that the other is sharing his experience and understanding what he is talking about.

Another point is that realized persons are able to perceive themselves and others directly with their innate transcendental senses. They are not restricted to observations of external behavior. Thus, confirmation of higher states of consciousness is not limited simply to the subjective perception of each separate person.

You are certainly correct in pointing out that there are many people who delude themselves and others by claiming to have attained various kinds of mystical realizations. But the existence of such cheating does not imply that a genuine science of higher consciousness is not possible. Such a science must indeed be based on verification of crucial observations by more than one person, but such verification is possible by realized persons.

The *Bhagavad-gītā* outlines a practical system for the attainment of higher realization. In this system the seeker of knowledge must take instruction from a realized soul.[41] By following these instructions, the person's higher cognitive faculties are awakened by the grace of the Supreme.[42] His realizations, however, can be readily evaluated by his teacher, who is fully capable of detecting mistakes and illusions. Furthermore, one can check the conduct of both teacher and disciple by consulting other self-realized souls, and by referring to a standard body of authoritative literature. This system can be compared with that of modern science, in which the findings of individuals are scrutinized by their peers, and evaluated in the context of standardized knowledge.

Kutark: You have referred to the Supreme and to Superconsciousness. What do you mean by these terms? Also, just what is realized in this process of higher realization? Can this be conveyed to a person whose experience is limited to the ordinary functioning of the five senses?

Avaroha: The *Bhagavad-gītā* explains that consciousness exists in two aspects, the infinite and the infinitesimal. The infinite consciousness is the very basis of reality and the ultimate source of all phenomena. This absolute consciousness is understood to be a Supreme Person, who is fully endowed with all personal attributes—such as senses, will, and intelligence—and who is known in the Vedic literature by many names, such as Kṛṣṇa and Govinda. This is, of course, the same Supreme Being known as God in the Judeo-Christian tradition, or as Allah in Islam.

The infinitesimal aspect of consciousness consists of the innumerable atomic selves called *jīvātmās*. We can illustrate the relation between atomic and infinite consciousness by a simple analogy. In classical physics we can fully characterize an electron as a minute charged particle that interacts in a certain way with an electromagnetic field. Similarly, we can understand the true character of the *jīvātmā* in terms of its natural interaction with the Supreme Person. Just as we can think of the electron as being defined by its interaction with an electromagnetic field, we can understand the *jīvātmā* as being defined by its personal interaction with the Supreme Conscious Being.

Thus, the ultimate goal of self-realization is to attain to this state of natural reciprocation with the Supreme. This mode of interaction is entirely personal, being based on the exchange of loving service. We get some hint of the quality of this exchange from the following characterization of the Supreme Person in the *Brahma-saṁhitā:*

premāñjana-cchurita-bhakti-vilocanena
santaḥ sadaiva hṛdayeṣu vilokayanti
yaṁ śyāma-sundaram acintya-guṅa-svarūpam
govindam adi-puruṣaṁ tam ahaṁ bhajāmi

"I worship Govinda, the primeval Lord, Who is Śyāmasundara, Kṛṣṇa Himself with inconceivable innumerable attributes, Whom the pure devotees see in their heart of hearts with the eye of devotion tinged with the salve of love."[43] Of course, we can attain full understanding of what this description entails only by direct experience, just as we can understand the taste of a fruit only by actually eating it.

Baum: It seems that you are simply expounding a religious doctrine here. How can you seriously introduce such ideas into a scientific discussion? From the viewpoint of science, such ideas are simply fantastic and unverifiable. You can hold them only by taking a blind leap of faith. To proselytize these doctrines in the guise of science is reprehensible!

Avaroha: It is ironic that you should say this after advocating the multiple splitting universe theory, which is indeed unverifiable. In contrast, direct verifiability is the whole point of the approach to higher consciousness that I have been outlining. It is certainly true that you cannot prove the existence of God on the basis of reasoning and a few pieces of empirical data—at least, you cannot prove anything very interesting about God in this way. But if God is real and the conscious self is endowed with suitable innate capacities, then we should be able to know God directly.

Unfortunately, some scientists have unnecessarily ruled out the very possibility of doing this by propounding universal theories that leave no room for the conscious self, what to speak of anything higher. By extrapolating empirical findings beyond all justifiable bounds, they arrive at world views that are truly fantastic and unverifiable. Contemplating such views, they come to the inevitable conclusion that "the more the universe seems comprehensible, the more it also seems pointless."[44] To widely disseminate such pointless theories among the people in general is indeed proselytization of a reprehensible kind, for these theories provide no tangible benefit, and they block the path of spiritual progress by filling people's minds with misconceptions.

Yantry: This all seems very far removed from the subject matter of physics, chemistry, and biology. Why is it necessary for you to introduce such an elaborate scheme, which involves so many concepts foreign to our current scientific way of thinking? Of course, we don't fully understand consciousness, and we may have much to learn about the fundamental principles underlying physical reality. We should certainly be cautious about the temptation to over-extrapolate and prematurely generalize. Indeed, it seems to me that as scientists, we should take a very conservative approach.[45] We should simply try to proceed step-by-step with our research, building gradually on the platform of existing scientific knowledge.

Avaroha: The trouble with this idea is that modern science doesn't possess a sufficient body of data about consciousness. A scientific theory is no better than the data on which it is based, and so progress in understanding the relation between consciousness and matter is bound to be very slow and uncertain. This is why the various attempts to introduce consciousness into the quantum theory are premature. For example, one physicist may know nothing about consciousness beyond the fact that persons are normally conscious of definite macroscopic arrangements of matter. Since he knows that this fact makes the reduction of the state vector necessary in quantum mechanics, he proposes a theory in which consciousness causes this reduction. Yet this theory may fail to take many aspects of consciousness into account.

The advantage of the *Bhagavad-gītā* is that it provides extensive information about consciousness, and it also provides scientific procedures whereby a person may make practical use of this knowledge. Since "conservative" means to retain what we already have, a truly conservative approach to science should not disregard this body of knowledge.

Kutark: You seem to be trying to build a bridge between a religious approach to reality and the methodology and world view of modern science. But aren't these two things completely incompatible? For example, you are proposing that nature must ultimately be understood in nonmechanistic terms. If this is true, doesn't it mean that our scientific approach to understanding nature is futile?

Avaroha: If we adopt a nonmechanistic view of nature, then we must regard any mechanistic theory as approximate at best. But this will not put scientists out of business. In principle, the measurable phenomena generated by nonmechanistic entities can be at least partially described by an open-ended hierarchy of mechanistic theories of ever-increasing complexity.[46] Thus there is no lack of available subject matter for mechanistic theorization. For example, there is no doubt much to be said in mechanistic terms about the interaction between the *jīvātmā* and the physical body, and there is extensive information on this subject in the Vedic literature. In contrast, if it were true that a complete mechanistic theory could be devised, then once it was worked out in detail, no further discoveries would remain to be made, and science would be a closed subject.

Of course, the real interest of the world view presented in the *Bhagavad-gītā* lies in the direct study of the *jīvātmā* and its relation with the Supreme Person, Śrī Kṛṣṇa. Since this study is based on reliable and systematic procedures for obtaining knowledge, it should certainly appeal to the genuine scientist, even though it completely transcends the domain of mechanistic theory. This study is of great significance because it provides a truly satisfying understanding of the nature and meaning of the conscious self—an understanding that can be realized through practical experience.

Notes

1. A.C. Bhaktivedanta Swami Prabhupāda, *Bhagavad-gītā As It Is.*
2. Weisz, *Elements of Biology,* p. 8.
3. Watson, *Molecular Biology of the Gene,* pp. 54, 87.
4. Sherman and Sherman, *Biology: A Human Approach,* p. 6.
5. See, for example, Huxley, *Essays upon Some Controverted Questions,* pp. 220–221, and Wigner, "Two Kinds of Reality," pp. 248–263.
6. Edwards, ed., *The Encyclopedia of Philosophy,* Vol. 5, pp. 336–345.
7. Rensch, *Evolution Above the Species Level,* p. 356.
8. Wigner, "Remarks on the Mind-Body Question," p. 294.
9. Jammer, *The Philosophy of Quantum Mechanics.*
10. Wigner, "Physics and the Explanation of Life," p. 44.

11. Eigen, "Selforganization of Matter and the Evolution of Biological Macromolecules," p. 467.
12. Slater, *Quantum Theory of Molecules and Solids,* Vol. 1, pp. *vii–viii.*
13. Mott, "The Wave Mechanics of α-Ray Tracks," pp. 79–84.
14. Wigner, "Remarks on the Mind-Body Question," p. 286.
15. Jammer, pp. 100–101.
16. Wigner, "Epistemological Perspective on Quantum Theory," pp. 379–380.
17. von Neumann, *Mathematical Foundations of Quantum Mechanics,* pp. 419–421.
18. Heisenberg, "The Representation of Nature in Contemporary Physics," pp. 99–100.
19. Rosenfeld, "The Measuring Process in Quantum Mechanics," p. 224.
20. von Neumann, chap. V.
21. Daneri, Loinger, and Prosperi, "Quantum Theory of Measurement and Ergodicity Conditions," pp. 297–319, and "Further Remarks on the Relations Between Statistical Mechanics and Quantum Theory of Measurement," p. 127.
22. Freundlich, "Mind, Matter, and Physicists," pp. 129–147.
23. Dewitt, "Quantum Mechanics and Reality," pp. 32.
24. Here is a more precise mathematical analysis of the state vector. Write the state vector as

$$\Psi(t) = \sum_k F_k(x,y,z,t)\, X_k(t)$$

where the X_k's represent histories of the behavior of the apparatus and observer. Take $\{X_k\}$ to be a complete orthonormal set and suppose, in accordance with our assumptions, that each X_k satisfies the Schrödinger equation for the system of observer plus apparatus (omitting the radioactive particle). Let $F_k\ (x,y,z,t)$ be the wave functions for this particle for $k \geqslant 0$. Start at $t=0$ with $\Psi_0 = F_0\ X_0$, representing unexcited target atoms and no observation of a track. The Schrödinger equation becomes

$$\left[i\hbar \frac{\partial}{\partial t} + \frac{\hbar^2 \nabla^2}{2M} \right] F_k(t) = \sum_n F_n(t)\ (V\ X_k, X_n)$$

where V is the potential of interaction between the particle and the target atoms.

In this equation the operator in brackets on the left represents the free propagation of the F_k's as waves in three-dimensional space. In addition to this free propagation, these waves also directly influence one another due to the terms (VX_k,X_n), and thereby transfer weight from X_0 to histories X_k with $k \neq 0$. The wave F_i can influence the wave F_j only at a time t_* when $X_i(t_*)$ is nearly identical with $X_j(t_*)$, for only at such a time is it possible for $(VX_i(t_*),X_j(t_*))$ to be different from zero. For any given pair of histories this could happen at most for a brief moment, and the histories would be expected to diverge from one another at earlier and later times. Thus weight within the total state vector will be transferred from one history to another at times depending on the structure of the histories themselves. This would result in the development of a total state vector of the form shown in Figures 4, 6, and 7.

25. Jauch, *Are Quanta Real?* pp. 40–47.

26. Here is a selection of articles on the theory of hidden variables: Bell, "On the Problem of Hidden Variables in Quantum Mechanics," pp. 447–452; Bohm and Bub, "A Proposed Solution of the Measurement Problem in Quantum Mechanics by a Hidden Variable Theory," pp. 453–468; Wigner, "Epistemological Perspective on Quantum Theory," pp. 377–378; and Wigner, "On Hidden Variables and Quantum Mechanical Probabilities," pp. 1005–1009.

27. Freundlich, pp. 132–133.

28. Jauch, p. 89.

29. Jammer, chap. 8.

30. Hans Bethe (personal communication) has pointed out that due to the problems involved with the reduction of the wave function, it does not make sense to try to devise a quantum mechanical description of living organisms. He recommends an empirical, semiclassical approach.

31. Dewitt, pp. 30–35.

32. Dewitt, "Quantum Gravity: the New Synthesis," p. 744.

33. Nagel, *The Structure of Science,* chap. 6.

34. von Neumann, chap. VI.

35. Wigner, "Two Kinds of Reality."
36. Mattuck and Walker, "The Action of Consciousness on Matter: A Quantum Mechanical Theory of Psychokinesis," pp. 112–159.
37. A.C. Bhaktivedanta Swami Prabhupāda, *Bhagavad-gītā As It Is,* p. 830.
38. Ibid., chap. 2.
39. A.C. Bhaktivedanta Swami Prabhupāda, *Śrīmad-Bhāgavatam,* 3rd Canto, Part 4, p. 112.
40. A.C. Bhaktivedanta Swami Prabhupāda, *Bhagavad-gītā As It Is,* pp. 702–704.
41. Ibid., pp. 259–260.
42. Ibid., pp. 506–509.
43. Bhakti Siddhanta Saraswati Thakur, *Shri Brahma-Samhita,* p. 124.
44. Weinberg, *The First Three Minutes,* p. 144.
45. Heisenberg, *Physics and Beyond,* p. 112.
46. Bohm, *Causality and Chance in Modern Physics,* p. 133.

Chapter 4

Karl Popper On the Mind-Body Problem

—A Review—

In *The Self and Its Brain,* the well-known philosopher Karl Popper and the eminent neurophysiologist John Eccles have collaborated to develop a theory of mind-brain interaction. Their book contains three sections. In the first section Karl Popper does two things: he presents a philosophical analysis of the mind-body problem, and he outlines a basic conceptual framework for an understanding of the mind as an entity that is distinct from the brain but that interacts with it. In the second section John Eccles surveys our current knowledge of the anatomy and function of the brain and introduces a specific model for the process of mind-brain interaction. The third section consists of a series of dialogues between the two authors, in which they explore some of the strengths and shortcomings of their ideas.

In this review we discuss Popper's analysis of the mind-body problem. In his portion of *The Self and Its Brain,* Popper discusses two basic subject matters: the nature of mind, and the mind's temporal origin. His aim is to establish that the fundamental features of personality, such as consciousness, thought, emotion, and purposeful action, are not simply patterns of chemical interaction (as much current scientific and philosophical thinking would have it) but rather aspects of a real yet nonphysical entity called the mind. In Popper's view, the mind should be considered neither an aspect nor a byproduct of physical processes. Instead, it should be regarded as an independent entity that influences the physical processes of the brain and that is influenced by them in turn.

While propounding this bold thesis, Popper simultaneously tries very hard to show how mind can be understood to have originated in a world of matter governed solely by physical laws. He does this by elaborating a theory of *emergent evolution,* which holds that entirely new and unpredictable qualities, processes, and laws can "emerge" spontaneously in nature and thereby completely transform the character of reality. Although the idea of emergent evolution is not new, Popper has developed it in great detail and has made it the cornerstone of his philosophy of mind.

Popper maintains that at one time the universe consisted solely of matter interacting with itself according to laws similar to or identical with those studied by the physicists. At this time nothing resembling mind or consciousness existed. Then, as matter gradually coalesced into various combinations by purely physical processes, totally new entities appeared and began to interact with matter in novel yet lawful ways. Thus life emerged, then dimly conscious animal minds, and finally fully self-conscious human minds.

Popper holds that the mind is an emergent entity "utterly different from anything which, to our knowledge, has previously existed in the world" (page 553). He has indeed presented a good case for the view that the mind is real, that it is independent of the brain, and that its properties are completely different from those of matter (as understood by the chemists and physicists). However, in his attempt to reconcile this view with the theory of evolution, he has shown only that evolutionary theory is unable to account for the origin of the mind. Although Popper has distorted the standard neo-Darwinian theory of evolution almost beyond recognition, his system of emergent evolution contributes nothing to our understanding. In fact, it raises more questions than it answers.

In the end Popper admits his failure: "Now I want to emphasize how little is said by saying that the mind is an emergent product of the brain. It has practically no explanatory value, and it hardly amounts to more than putting a question mark at a certain place in human evolution" (page 554). After giving a short account of Popper's arguments for the nonmaterial nature of mind, we will show that emergent evolution is, in fact, logically untenable. Then, salvaging some of the good points of Popper's presentation, we will consider an alternative approach to understanding the nature of the mind.

One of Popper's most basic arguments for the nonphysical nature of the mind is that, contrary to the opinions of the behaviorists, conscious subjective experience is both real and completely unexplained by our concepts of matter. The existence of conscious awareness is directly experienced by the conscious self, and this by itself refutes *radical materialism,* the view that matter (as understood by modern physics and chemistry) is all that exists.

Popper also points out that living beings, and especially human beings, exhibit behavior that cannot be reasonably explained in material terms, but that can be understood very clearly in terms of the actions of mind. For example, it certainly seems very remarkable that a lump of matter in the form of a human being should detach itself from its substrate and, say, climb up the side of Mount Everest. Although one could dabble with explanations for this phenomenon in terms of cybernetic brain mechanisms, it is very hard to see in purely physical terms how or why such mechanisms should ever have come to be. In general, it is hard to explain long-term and elaborately purposeful action—from the building of nests, to the construction of skyscrapers, to the formulation of philosophical theories—in terms of intermolecular forces. Yet we *can* systematically explain these things in terms of a mind endowed with purpose and desire.

Popper argues that morality and concepts of good and evil cannot be understood in purely physical terms. We cannot adequately explain these manifestations by totally denying the existence of consciousness. We also cannot explain them by any theory that grants the existence of consciousness, but maintains that it cannot influence matter and that matter behaves entirely in accordance with known physical laws. (There is a wide range of such theories, including parallelism, the panpsychism of Spinoza, epiphenomenalism, and the identity theory.) Popper holds that the existence of standards of moral behavior requires a nonphysical mind that can influence matter.

The same nonphysical mind is necessary to explain our standards of aesthetics. In Popper's words, "To assume that Michelangelo's works are simply the result of molecular movements and nothing else seems to me very much more absurd than the assumption of some slight . . . violation of the first law of thermodynamics" (page 544). He also argues that it is only in terms of the actions of the mind that we can understand—or even talk about—truth, falsehood, and validity in language. In purely physical terms these concepts refer to arbitrary patterns of symbol manipulation, and they play no essential or meaningful role. They can be meaningfully discussed only in the context of a reality higher than that of material interactions.

Popper further points out that the mind and its attributes play an explanatory role in psychology analogous to the explanatory role electrons play in physics (although there is, of course, no corresponding mathematical development in psychology). Thus it is as reasonable to attribute reality to the mind as it is to attribute it to electrons. We may add in this connection that behavioral psychology has provided us with remarkably little insight into the nature of human behavior, its avowed subject. We might suggest that psychology will make significant progress only by developing an adequate understanding of the mind as a real entity.

In refuting the theories based on the idea that consciousness exists but does not influence the behavior of matter, Popper points out that these theories conflict with the Darwinian theory of evolution, for they do not provide a means whereby natural selection can act to bring about the evolution of consciousness. Thus the strict Darwinist must either deny the reality of consciousness or attribute full consciousness to inanimate matter. Otherwise he must explain why consciousness should develop progressively without the aid of natural selection. This argument should be of interest to the orthodox adherents of neo-Darwinian evolutionary theory. As we shall see, Popper himself proposes a very different theory of evolution.

Popper also confronts the challenge that since the known laws of physics cannot be violated, a nonphysical mind must be ruled out. His main point here is that the program of reductionism in physics and chemistry is drastically incomplete. Because of difficulties in computation, we simply do not know what the quantum theory says about most chemical processes. Also, there have been many revolutionary developments in physics in this century, and we may confidently expect more.

Adding a final point, Popper warns of the danger of cutting off healthy inquiry by prematurely imposing a rigid view based on known physical principles. In philosophy, this warning applies to the indiscriminate application of Occam's razor as a means of ruling out hypotheses. Popper also condemns what he calls "promissory materialism," or the argument that materialistic claims should be accepted because proof for them will surely be found some time in the future.

Thus Popper gives many arguments indicating that mind must involve a higher reality—a reality that cannot be reduced to matter as it is understood by modern science. However, when he tries to account for the *origin* of this higher reality by means of his theory of emergent evolution, he sticks essentially to the reductionistic approach, and he is unable to avoid its shortcomings. We will now briefly outline the theory of emergent evolution and indicate why this is so.

First we shall consider Popper's concept of "downward causation." According to this idea, when many parts combine to make a whole, the whole is an entity in and of itself, and it is capable of acting on each of its parts individually. The formation of heavy nuclei in the center of a star by the action of intense heat and pressure is regarded as an example of downward causation, in which the whole star acts on its individual constituent particles.

This concept amounts to a deceptive way of introducing higher entities into the material picture without really introducing them. A physicist would immediately reply that the behavior of the star can be fully explained (in principle) in terms of the material interaction of its component parts, without any reference at all to the star as a whole. Thus the concept of downward causation is simply a disguised form of reductionism.

In fact, Popper *does* believe that new entities can appear in the world, and that these entities amount to more than simply names for collections of existing entities. In particular, he believes entirely new laws or modes of operation of the universe can come into being, and thus "the first emergence of a novelty such as life may change the possibilities or propensities in the universe" (page 30). Popper maintains that the inherent indeterminacy of quantum mechanics makes it possible for new laws to appear without violating the old ones. Thus he believes that "all physical and chemical laws are binding for living things" (page 36), even though living things involve the "emergence of new lawlike properties" (page 25).

Popper does not like the idea of substance or essence, and thus he tends to refer to his emergent entities in terms of their behavior. However, in addition to exhibiting novel patterns of lawful behavior, emergent entities like life and mind possess, according to Popper, entirely new qualities and properties—such as consciousness. Thus they add to nature something concretely new, and very much like a substance or essence.

Although Popper believes the appearance of these entities to be completely unpredictable, even in principle, he still claims that their appearance is lawful. Accordingly, Popper repeatedly stresses natural selection as a basic principle underlying the development of mind, although mind is a totally novel, emergent entity that cannot be reduced to a combination of material elements. At the same time, Popper agrees with Jacques Monod when he says that the chance that life would appear on earth was virtually zero, and he cites this as an example of how emergent entities are completely unpredictable in terms of the universe as it exists before the time of their emergence.

Generally, Popper gives the impression that emergent entities appear gradually in a step-by-step fashion over the course of evolutionary development. According to this view, mind as a fundamental entity in its own right must have emerged at a certain stage of evolution, thereby altering the basic character of nature from then on. However, in their dialogues Popper and Eccles also seem to agree that mind emerges anew from matter in the brain of each newborn child—a position that Eccles supports by saying that a girl who had been brought up for 13½ years without learning how to speak did not have a mind during that time (page 564). This appears to be contradictory, but in any event Popper seems to require that the emergence of mind must be lawful.

We can raise many objections to this theory of emergent evolution, and it is clear that Popper has not formulated it consistently. However, we will restrict ourselves to making two basic points. The first is that the theory of emergent evolution is very different from the standard neo-Darwinian theory of evolution, and thus it should be understood that Popper is actually rejecting the standard evolutionary theory. The second point is that for new entities to emerge in a lawful fashion, as Popper certainly requires, there must be a preexisting higher law that regulates their emergence. This higher law must already incorporate, in potential form, the qualities and features of the emergent entities.

As a concrete example, suppose that the state of a physical system is changing according to a Markovian probability law, L.[1] The state X of such a system makes random jumps at successive discrete times, $t=1, 2, 3, \ldots$, and these jumps are governed by the law L. The behavior of the system is summed up by the rule that at each time t,

$$X \longrightarrow X' \text{ with probability } L(X,X')$$

For example, suppose that X represents the position of a drunkard who is staggering back and forth at random on a steep hillside. Then the formulas, $L(X,X-1)=2/3$ and $L(X,X+1)=1/3$, would mean that the drunk always takes a step of one unit, but is twice as likely to step downhill as uphill.

Now let us imagine that the system can develop an emergent property characterized by a new law, L', and let us suppose that in the state X, this emergence can take place with a probability of $p(X)$. If we try to formulate this, we can see that it entails a metasystem in which both L and X are varying. The behavior of this enlarged system, if it can be described at all, must be given by a more complex meta-law. For example, we might stipulate that at each time t,

$$(X,L) \longrightarrow (X',L') \text{ with probability } L(X,X')\,\mathbf{L}(X,L,L')$$

This meta-law necessarily entails a function $\mathbf{L}(X,L,L')$ giving the probability that the law L' will emerge when the system is in the state X and is operating under the law L.[2] In our example, all of the possible emergent laws L' can be expressed by formulas, and thus $\mathbf{L}$ can also be represented mathematically. But what can we say about the meta-law $\mathbf{L}$ in Popper's system, where mental properties may emerge that are qualitatively different from anything contemplated in present-day physics? Certainly this meta-law would also have to be qualitatively different from any of the laws known to physical science. Indeed, if anything, it would have to possess qualities even more remarkable than those of the various possible entities that may emerge under its regulation.

Now, if the meta-law $\mathbf{L}$ is not itself an emergent entity, it must represent a permanent state of affairs, and its qualities must correspond to absolute features of reality. If **L** is an emergent entity, we can inquire about the law governing its emergence, the law governing the emergence of this law, and so on. Unless we propose an infinite regress of laws, we must posit some ultimate, absolute law that can be discussed only in terms of nonphysical entities and qualities.

Thus Popper's theory of emergent evolution requires the existence of laws that already embody qualities equal or superior to all the supposedly novel qualities and properties that may "emerge." Such laws must be invoked to account for lawlike regularities in the emergence of new qualities, and to explain, for example, why we should expect mind to emerge from a highly organized brain and not from a clod of earth.

This conclusion certainly contradicts the basic purpose of Popper's system of emergent evolution. We would like to suggest that this system should, in fact, be discarded, for it is an attempt to carry out the impossible task of accepting reductionism and rejecting it at the same time. A more satisfactory development of Popper's ideas about mind can be obtained if we boldly reject reductionism altogether and simply accept that principles and entities higher than those known to modern science are, and always have been, a permanent part of the world.

Two aspects of our world that are particularly significant are the presence of conscious selves, and the presence of standards of meaning and value. These are certainly of central importance, for it is ultimately the self that understands and seeks to find explanations, and in so doing the self is always referring to standards of meaning. It is therefore interesting to note that Popper comes close to attributing real, irreducible existence to the self and to absolute standards of meaning.

Thus Popper describes something he calls "World 3," the realm of abstract concepts, mathematical truths, and moral and ethical principles. "World 3 is a kind of Platonic world of ideas, a world which exists nowhere but which does have an existence and which does interact, especially with human minds" (page 450). Popper stresses the role of World 3 as a final standard of reference for questions of truth, validity, and meaning (page 77).

If there is no fundamental basis for meaning, then it is hard to see how we can ultimately justify any philosophy of life, on either a theoretical or practical level. However, if we grant the existence of a factual, absolute source of standards for truth and meaning, then a possibility opens up—we may be able to gain access to this source and thereby obtain a genuine understanding of the world. And if we at least tentatively accept the self as a real entity, then we can entertain the possibility that the self may have a meaningful place in the larger order of reality as a whole. A direct investigation of the role of the self in the context of a higher, meaningful reality could lead to practical realization of our true potentialities as conscious beings—potentialities that presently lie dormant and unexplored.

Popper tends to speak of the self in rather vague reductionistic terms as some kind of pattern of interaction between the mind and the body. Yet he also sometimes refers to the self as a real entity. In one passage he says that "the talk about a substantial self is not a bad metaphor" (page 146), and he proposes that "selves are the only active agents in the universe: the only agents to whom the term activity can be applied" (page 538). This is really Popper's best bet, and one wishes he had the boldness to follow his idea where it leads and straightforwardly consider the self as a fundamental entity in its own right.

On the basis of such a hypothesis, a direct investigation of the self as such is at least a formal possibility. We suggest that only an investigation of this kind can yield satisfying answers to the basic questions that gave rise to *The Self and Its Brain* in the first place. As Eccles points out in one of the dialogues, "Man has lost his way these days . . . . He needs some new message whereby he may live with hope and meaning. I think that science has gone too far in breaking down man's belief in his spiritual greatness and in giving him the idea that he is merely an insignificant material being in the frigid cosmic immensity" (page 558). If we can candidly consider that the self may be a real, conscious entity in a world with inherent meaning and purpose, we may hope to come to a practical and coherent world view that does violence neither to reason nor to our natural spiritual aspirations.

Notes

1. A simple Markov chain is used in this example, but the same argument could be framed using the more sophisticated laws studied in physics.

2. There are many different ways of formulating such a meta-law. The basic point is that the meta-law must govern the emergence of certain "novel" properties, and thus it must be able to deal with these properties. A law defined in the customary language of physics could not govern the emergence of consciousness, since consciousness belongs to a category lying outside the scope of this language. If we suppose that there are laws of nature governing the emergence of consciousness, then we must conclude that nature has inherent features falling outside the realm of discourse of physics. The simplest hypothesis about such features is, of course, that consciousness itself is an inherent feature of reality, and not an emergent property.

PART II

FORM

Chapter 5

Information Theory And the Self-organization Of Matter

In this chapter we use information theory to show that the laws of nature, as understood by modern science, are insufficient to account for the origin of life. The basic argument is the following: The laws of nature and the corresponding mathematical models of physical reality can all be described by a few simple equations and other mathematical expressions. This means that they possess a low information content. In contrast, there is good reason to suppose that the intricate and variegated forms of living organisms possess a high information content. It can be shown that configurations of high information content cannot arise with substantial probabilities in models defined by mathematical expressions of low information content. It follows that life could not arise by the action of natural laws of the kind considered in modern science.

This argument bypasses the proposition made by many evolutionary theorists that even though the steps leading to life are improbable, they are nonetheless likely to happen, given the immense spans of geological time available. We show that no period of time, from zero to billions of billions of years, will suffice to render probable the evolution of life from matter by known physical processes. Indeed, we show that over periods many times the estimated 4.5-billion-year age of the earth, the probability of the evolution of higher life forms remains bounded by upper limits of $10^{-150,000}$, an almost infinitesimal number. This implies that the entire history of the earth would have to be repeated over and over again at least $10^{150,000}$ times for there to be a substantial chance that higher living entities would evolve even once.

At the basis of these figures lies an intuitive reason for the impossibility of organic evolution. We show that the process of natural selection—the alleged mechanism of evolution—must have specific direction if it is to bring about the development of complex living organisms. Without such direction, this process is unable to discriminate among random events (mutations) in such a way as to bring complex order out of chaos. For this reason, the standard argument that evolution will occur, given long enough time spans, is false. Natural selection will lack direction if the causal principles underlying this selection, namely the laws of nature, do not have sufficient information content to specify such direction.

Our fundamental argument is that in a physical system governed by simple laws, any information present in the system after transformations corresponding to the passage of time must have been built into the system in the first place. Random events cannot give rise to definite information, even when processed over long periods of time according to simple laws. It follows that mathematical models based on simple laws cannot account for the origin of such highly variegated and complex entities as living organisms. Using such models, we can only explain the existence of complex order here and now by postulating that equivalent complex order was present at an earlier time, or was transported into the system from the outside. These postulates do not account for the origin of such order, but simply confront us with either an infinite regress or an eternal source of order containing the information necessary to specify all life forms.

These arguments suggest that the scientific program of describing the world by mathematical models is severely limited, and can serve only to impede our understanding of nature. This program is based on the conviction that the simple regularities observed by physicists and chemists in experiments with inanimate matter will suffice to account for every phenomenon in the world. But since we show here that this program cannot succeed in accounting for the origin of life, we suggest that a different approach should be explored. The direct implication of the information theoretic analysis is that nature is inherently complex, and encodes the designs of living organisms—both lower and higher—in some form. Although this in itself does not tell us very much, we suggest that it may be fruitful to consider the possibility that life is built into nature as a fundamental principle, and represents more than simply a temporary collocation of material elements.

The program of science during the last two or three hundred years has been to reduce life to matter and to deny the existence of any higher life-principle transcendental to matter. In this program, the idea that matter is both simple and conceivable has been essential. But if, as shown here, we must attribute all the characteristic features of life to matter in order to explain the origin of life from matter, then we can conclude that this program has failed.

One way of responding to this failure is to consider the universe as a whole to be an incomprehensible welter of arbitrary complexities. A more promising response is to consider that if the natural causes underlying life must entail all the detailed features of life, then perhaps life—and intelligent life in particular—is the fundamental cause underlying the phenomena of the universe. This possibility opens up many new avenues of empirical investigation, but it also implies that traditional empirical methods can take us only so far in our effort to understand nature. Yet, if the ultimate cause of the universe is not merely "life," but is an irreducible intelligent being, then the possibility arises that we may be able to transcend the process of experimental dissection and hypothesis, and obtain knowledge by direct communication with this absolute source.

In this chapter we touch on these points only briefly and concentrate on the analysis of natural processes using information theory. We develop the basic arguments in Sections 5.1, 5.2, and 5.3, and outline their broader implications in Section 5.4. A more detailed mathematical treatment of some of the arguments is presented in Appendices 1 and 2.

5.1 The Theme of Simplicity in the Theories of Physics

One of the fundamental principles of modern physics has been that the laws of nature can be described by very simple and general mathematical relationships. Perhaps the most famous advocate of this principle was Albert Einstein, who strove during the major portion of his life to find a "unified field theory," which would derive all the forces and laws of interaction of the physics of his day from a single, unifying mathematical rule. In more recent times, the search for a unified physical theory has been avidly pursued by many physicists, such as Steven Weinberg, Abdus Salam, and Sheldon Glashow, who in 1979 shared the Nobel Prize in physics for their contributions in this field.

Weinberg and his colleagues have not yet been able to formulate the "grand unified theory" with which they hope to pin down, once and for all, the ultimate reality underlying the phenomenal world.[1] Such a theory would account for the observed behavior of subatomic particles at high energies and would provide a complete theoretical description of the origin of the universe from a primordial cosmic explosion, or "big bang." Although many researchers have tried to construct such a theory, serious mathematical difficulties have thus far impeded their efforts. For example, the quantum field theory is plagued by a tendency for important calculations to diverge to infinity when they should yield finite answers. Also, no one has yet been able to devise a consistent mathematical system that joins together quantum mechanics and general relativity, the two most fundamental theories of modern physics.[2]

As a result of these difficulties, it is not possible at the present time to formulate a complete mathematical model of the universe. But scientists widely believe that a complete physical theory has been established for phenomena involving moderate masses, energies, and velocities. In particular, scientists generally believe that the nonrelativistic theory of quantum mechanics is sufficient to account for all the phenomena of chemistry, and that all the phenomena of life can be reduced to chemistry. (Nonetheless, some long-standing controversies about the validity of quantum mechanics remain unresolved. These were discussed in Chapter 3.)

According to the physicist John Slater, "The success of exact calculations for the helium atom and the hydrogen molecule convinced physicists that wave mechanics provided a framework which was at least in principle capable of giving theoretical explanations of any desired accuracy for the phenomena of atoms, molecules and solids."[3] The idea that life, in turn, is a molecular phenomenon is summed up by the molecular biologist James Watson: "We see not only that the laws of chemistry are sufficient for understanding protein structure, but also that they are consistent with all known hereditary phenomena. Complete certainty now exists among essentially all biochemists that the other characteristics of living organisms (for example, . . . the hearing and memory processes) will all be completely understood in terms of the coordinative interactions of small and large molecules."[4] Taken together, these statements of Slater and Watson imply the widely accepted conclusion that life is a quantum mechanical phenomenon.

The laws of quantum mechanics must be very remarkable if all the characteristics of living beings do indeed depend on them. We will therefore briefly outline the mathematical structure of the quantum mechanical laws. Our objective is twofold: first, to clearly define what we mean by simplicity in a system of natural laws; and second, to clarify the nature of the hypothetical relationship between the quantum mechanical laws and the phenomena of life.

First, let us consider the laws of nature in classical physics. These can be summed up by the following equations:

$$\frac{dq_j}{dt} = \frac{\partial H}{\partial p_j}(p_1, \ldots, p_n; q_1, \ldots, q_n) \qquad (1)$$

$$\frac{dp_j}{dt} = -\frac{\partial H}{\partial q_j}(p_1, \ldots, p_n; q_1, \ldots, q_n) \qquad (2)$$

In classical physics the state of a physical system at any given time is completely described by the position coordinates, q_j, and momentum coordinates, p_j. These coordinates comprise $6N$ numbers for a system of N material particles, and equations (1) and (2) describe how these numbers change with the passage of time. In classical physics the function H, which is called the Hamiltonian, is generally given by a simple formula:

$$H = \sum_{j=1}^{n} p_j^2 / (2m_j) + V(q_1, \ldots, q_n) \tag{3}$$

where

$$V = \sum_{i<j} A_{ij} / |\mathbf{r}_i - \mathbf{r}_j| \tag{4}$$

and

$$|\mathbf{r}_i - \mathbf{r}_j| = \sqrt{(q_{3i} - q_{3j})^2 + (q_{3i+1} - q_{3j+1})^2 + (q_{3i+2} - q_{3j+2})^2} \tag{5}$$

We have written these formulas out in full to show how very simple the laws of classical physics are. This is quite literally the full extent of the laws of nature as understood in classical physics up to the time of Maxwell. According to those scientists who adhered to the philosophy that nature could be completely described by mathematical laws, all the phenomena of nature could be calculated using equations (1) through (5) and initial values of the q_j's and p_j's at some arbitrary starting time, t=0.

This philosophy received its initial impetus in the eighteenth century from Isaac Newton. He summed it up as follows: "I . . . suspect that [the phenomena of nature] may all depend upon certain forces by which the particles of bodies . . . are either mutually impelled towards one another and cohere in regular figures, or are repelled and recede from one another."[5] Equation (4) specifies these forces, which attract if A_{ij} is positive and repel if it is negative. In the nineteenth century the physicist Hermann Von Helmoltz expressed the same view: "The task of physical science is to reduce all phenomena of nature to forces of attraction and repulsion, the intensity of which is dependent only upon the mutual distance of material bodies. Only if this problem is solved are we sure that nature is conceivable."[6] Needless to say, Von Helmoltz included life as a "phenomenon of nature."

With the advent of Maxwell's electromagnetic theory, Einstein's theory of relativity, and the theory of quantum mechanics, the simple view of nature summed up by equations (1) through (5) underwent a considerable change. But the basic concept—that natural phenomena are reducible to the interplay of elementary material forces—has been retained. In the present dominant theory of quantum mechanics, arrangements of numbers still describe physical systems, although the particle coordinates of classical physics have given way to Hilbert space vectors. The laws of transformation of these numbers are still given by simple equations that may be written down in a few lines.

In quantum mechanics, the basic equation of motion for a physical system is the Schrödinger equation:

$$\frac{i\hbar\partial\Psi}{\partial t} = H\Psi \qquad (6)$$

Here the state, or exact physical description, of the physical system is given by the Hilbert space vector, Ψ, which can be represented in various ways as a mathematical function or as a sequence of numbers. The Hamiltonian function, H, has been adopted from classical physics and now appears as an operator capable of acting on Ψ to produce a new vector. In analogy with equation (3), H could be given by:

$$H = \sum_{k=1}^{n} \frac{-\hbar^2}{2m_k} \frac{\partial^2}{\partial q_k^2} + V(q_1, \ldots, q_n) \qquad (7)$$

where V is the same as in equation (4).

Equations (6) and (7), along with (4) and (5) and an initial value for Ψ at the time t=0, completely specify the quantum mechanical picture of a physical system of n/3 particles moving according to the attractive and repulsive forces given by V.

In further developments of the theory of quantum mechanics, things become somewhat more complicated. In addition to equation (4), various other terms are added to V to represent different kinds of forces believed to be acting in physical systems. These include terms for "spin" and electromagnetic interactions. Also, the basic form of H in equation (7) is sometimes modified in various ways. It remains true, however, that very brief formulas can express the Hamiltonian for any system that is supposed to represent the fundamental laws of nature. When the abbreviated notations in these formulas are written out in full (as we did for the classical case) the resulting equations occupy a few lines at most.

This is true in particular of the physical model of chemical interactions that Watson and his colleagues believe to be sufficient for a complete understanding of life. The Hamiltonian for this model should include terms for electric forces, spin interactions, and electromagnetic interactions (plus gravity). This Hamiltonian is illustrated in Figure 1.[7]

If the laws of physics can account fully for the moment-to-moment flow of life processes, one might suppose that they also can account for the origin of living organisms over the course of time. In the development of modern science, Charles Darwin was one of the first persons to seriously work out the consequences of this idea. Darwin based his theory of evolution on hypothetical processes of random variation and natural selection that he regarded as natural byproducts of underlying physical processes. Since Darwin's time, biologists have ascribed his random variations to the processes of genetic mutation and recombination. They have also carried his ideas to their logical conclusion by introducing the theory of molecular evolution. This theory attributes the origin of the first living organisms to purely physical processes of "self-organization" acting in a primordial soup of disorganized chemical compounds.

It is our thesis that equations as brief and simple in form as those of Figure 1 cannot contain sufficient discriminatory power to summon forth from a chaos of randomly distributed atomic particles the complex and variegated world of life we see about us. Both the Darwinian and the molecular

$$(a)\ H\Psi = i\hbar \frac{\partial \Psi}{\partial t}$$

$$(b)\ H =$$

$$\sum_n \frac{1}{2}\left[-\hbar^2 c^2 \frac{\partial^2}{\partial q_n^2} + \eta_n^2 q_n^2\right] + \sum_k \frac{-\hbar^2 \nabla_k^2}{2m_k}$$

$$+ \sum_k \frac{i\hbar e_k}{m_k c} \mathbf{A}(\mathbf{Q}_k)\cdot\nabla_k + \sum_k \frac{e_k^2}{m_k c^2} |\mathbf{A}(\mathbf{Q}_k)|^2$$

$$- \sum_k \frac{e_k}{2m_k c} \bar{\sigma}_k \cdot \nabla_k \times \mathbf{A}(\mathbf{Q}_k) + \sum_{i>j} \frac{e_i e_j - G m_i m_j}{|\mathbf{Q}_i - \mathbf{Q}_j|}$$

$$\mathbf{A} = \sum_n q_n \mathbf{A}_n$$

Figure 1. The laws of nature underlying chemistry.

theories of evolution are based on the processes of random variation and natural selection. These theories hold that "chance" will provide various combinations of molecules which may or may not be useful to living organisms, and that "natural selection" will pick out those which are useful and eliminate those which are not. Geneticists such as Ronald Fisher have argued statistically that even if natural selection only slightly favors one form over another, in a sufficient length of time the favored form will nonetheless be found to predominate over the unfavored one.[8]

Yet natural selection must have some direction if it is consistently to choose certain material configurations out of the myriads of configurations possible. The local selective advantages within particular populations must add together (as in a vector sum of vectors added tail to head) to produce a general trend from primordial soup to higher organisms. Ultimately, the fundamental laws of nature must provide this direction. At least, this must be true if nature is indeed to run in accordance with such laws.

It is very hard to see, however, why "forces of attraction and repulsion . . . dependent only upon the mutual distance of material bodies" should select trees, amoebas, bumblebees, or human beings in favor of other possible material configurations, such as inert globs or blotches. Enhancing the theoretical picture with spin interactions following the Pauli matrices, or electromagnetic fields composed of harmonic oscillators, does not seem to add more plausibility to the idea that natural selection could do this. We will argue that, in current physical theories, the very brevity of the laws of nature makes them incapable of selecting the complex forms of living organisms from an initial state of molecular chaos, no matter how much time is allowed for the process. Basically, we shall show that for natural laws to select a complex form out of a random distribution of matter, the laws must themselves possess a corresponding level of complexity. This implies that the Hamiltonian for a quantum mechanical system will require many pages of symbols (as many as thirty at the very least) if that system is to be capable of selecting configurations with the complexity of living organisms. In other words, the known laws of physics are insufficient to account for the origin of life, and for a system of physical laws to do so, its sheer size and complexity would make it impossible for the human mind to handle.

In neither the classical nor the quantum mechanical theories of physics have mathematicians ever been able to exactly solve the equations of motion for systems containing more than two particles. Since systems capable of representing living organisms must contain enormous numbers of particles (on the order of 10^{23}), we can see that it is not practical to study the nature of such organisms by explicitly solving the equations of motion. But such solutions must exist for the theory to be valid at all. Generally scientists have argued on the basis of abstract reasoning that solutions to the equations of motion can be calculated in principle. They have then attempted to apply and verify the theory by making logical deductions about the properties of the solutions without actually seeing them. We shall proceed on the assumption that the required solutions always do exist and could be calculated.

We shall formally define the information content of a theory to be the length of the shortest computer program that can numerically solve the equations of motion for the theory to within any desired degree of accuracy. For consistency, we shall stipulate that all programs used in the estimation of information content must be written in a fixed programming language. The Schrödinger equation (Equation 6) can be solved in principle by a simple numerical algorithm. Consequently, the information content of a theory having this equation as its basic equation of motion is nearly proportional to the number of symbols needed to write out the Hamiltonian for that theory in the programming language. We can also estimate the information content of a configuration of matter, such as the body of a living organism, to be the length of the shortest program needed to generate a complete numerical description of that configuration. We shall use this measure of information content to provide a clear-cut quantitative demonstration that the known laws of physics, or any similar system of laws, must fail, even in principle, to account for the origin of life.

In a mathematical model of a physical system, two other ingredients are needed along with the laws of motion. These are the initial conditions and the boundary conditions of the system. Normally, a physical system is confined within a certain fixed volume of space. To calculate the events occurring within this volume, we must know the physical conditions along the boundary of the volume during the time the system is being studied. In most physical models the behavior of the system is studied during a finite time interval, $0 \leq t \leq t_1$. It is therefore also necessary to specify the physical state of the system at the beginning of this time period, or $t=0$.

In a theory of the origin of life, the initial conditions typically represent a "primordial" situation possessing a very low degree of organization, if any. For example, most theories of the chemical origin of life postulate that life arose from a "primordial soup" consisting of a mixture of water and simple compounds such as CO_2, CH_4, N_2, NH_3, and H_2S, and a reducing atmosphere composed mainly of CH_4 and NH_3.[9] This mixture of chemicals is presumed to receive radiation from the sun, to receive supplies of gases from the earth (volcanic venting), and to radiate heat and light into outer space. This sums up the initial and boundary conditions for this model.

As another model, one could start with the supposed origin of the solar system from a cloud of gas. The initial conditions would then consist of a description of the initial gas cloud, and the boundary would correspond to an unlimited vacuum surrounding this cloud (if we ignore the influence of distant stars). In this model the laws of nature would first generate the solar system, complete with primordial soup, and then generate life in the soup. Or one might consider a model of the universe as a whole, such as that proposed by the "big bang" theory. Most versions of this theory feature a superhot soup of subatomic particles as the initial condition of the universe. (Of course, there are no boundary conditions in a universal model.)

We should observe that the quantum mechanical laws of Figure 1 are not adequate for the last two of these three models. Since the second model includes the sun, it must deal with nuclear reactions, and these are not described by nonrelativistic quantum mechanics. This model would require some form of quantum field theory. Likewise, the third model calls for a theory combining quantum mechanics and general relativity. It will not be possible to precisely define these models until substantial advances are made in theoretical physics. Yet it is interesting to note that the existing equations of quantum field theory are much more streamlined and elegant than the nonrelativistic equations of Figure 1. Since the general program of physics is to explain nature in terms of the simplest possible principles, we can anticipate that physicists will exert every effort to devise universal equations of motion that are even simpler in form than the quantum field equations.

We should also observe that the initial and boundary conditions of the three models are quite simple to describe and that they become progressively simpler as we go from model to model. The basic idea behind current scientific theories of the origin of life from matter is that one need propose only a very simple set of conditions to hold in the beginning. After all, the purpose of such theories is to "explain" all the features of life, and the more intricate the specifications required for the initial conditions, the less complete the explanation becomes. Many scientists would feel a need to explain complex initial conditions in terms of some earlier and less complex state of affairs.

In this regard it is interesting to consider in greater detail the initial conditions that scientists have proposed for the big bang theory. One of the basic requirements of this theory is that it should account for the distribution of matter in the universe into galaxies and clusters of galaxies. Yet scientists have noted that an initial superhot plasma will tend not to give rise to such a distribution. At high temperatures, diffusion will tend to smooth out all irregularities in a gas, and the later development of a highly irregular distribution of matter can be assured only by building very large irregularities into the initial plasma. Some theoreticians, including the astrophysicist David Layzer, have felt dissatisfied with this idea. They have introduced an alternative theory in which the universe begins in a perfectly homogenous state of global thermodynamic equilibrium at zero temperature.[10] In their theory, the irregularities in mass distribution are produced by the fracturing of the solid universal substance as the universe expands. Their initial conditions are thus as simple as possible, and they require that all diversity in the universe must arise from the action of processes governed by the natural laws.

A typical initial condition for a model of the origin of life will consist of an ensemble of possible initial states, such as one of the thermodynamic ensembles of statistical mechanics or some simple combination of these. This certainly holds true for the models referred to above. Such an ensemble can be specified by a simple equation or a brief set of equations. For example, in the theory of quantum mechanics one of the standard thermodynamic ensembles, known as the canonical ensemble, is given by the equation

$$\rho_0 = K^{-1} \exp(-H/kT) \qquad (8)$$

where H is a Hamiltonian operator.[11]

In this equation, ρ_0 is called a density matrix. It corresponds to a collection, or ensemble, of quantum mechanical states, each of which has a statistical weight giving the probability that the physical system will be found in that particular state. This means that the initial state of the system is left ambiguous to a very large extent. In fact, one of the basic principles of statistical mechanics is the assignment of equal probabilities to all initial states satisfying certain simple restrictions, such as a certain particle density or a certain range of energies. In such statistical formulations of initial conditions, many of the alternative initial states of the system will have a very high information content. However, the statistical ensemble as a whole can be described by a few simple criteria, and therefore it possesses a low information content.

The boundary conditions for the physical system should also be definable in simple terms. At most, one would expect radiant energy or simple material particles to pass back and forth across the boundary. In some models the boundary might consist of reflecting or noninteractive walls, or a limitless vacuum, or there may be no need for explicit boundary conditions at all. Any interaction between the system and matter or energy beyond its boundary should be describable in simple statistical terms, as can be done, for example, for cosmic rays or the influx of solar radiation. Boundary conditions, like initial conditions, must be relatively simple: if intricate specifications were required for the boundary conditions, then one would need to explain their origin also.

Once the initial and boundary conditions are defined, the state of the physical system at each time t between 0 and t_1 can be calculated using the natural laws of the system. The basic situation is summed up in Figure 2. A theory of the origin of life from matter should predict that after some period of time, perhaps in the range of four billion years or so, the system will have a reasonably high probability of exhibiting the molecular configurations characteristic of living organisms.

Let us consider how we can mathematically represent the presence of these configurations in the physical system. We will do this in particular for the theory of quantum mechanics. In this theory, any state of affairs one might want to observe in the system is represented by a mathematical operator called an "observable." We can denote the situation to be observed by **B**, and we can denote the mathematical operator to which it corresponds by B. Then the probability of finding the system in the situation **B** is given by

$$\text{Prob}(\mathbf{B}) = \text{Trace}(\rho B) \tag{9}$$

where ρ is the density matrix defining the state of the system. This formula can be evaluated in principle by a brief set of computer instructions.

We are interested in the case where **B** represents the presence of a particular molecule or collection of molecules in the system. For example, **B** might represent the presence of a DNA molecule expressing the genetic specifications of an organism. One way of describing such a molecule is by means of a numerical code indicating which atoms are to be found in close proximity to which other atoms—that is, indicating the pattern of chemical bonds that characterizes the molecule. If X represents such a molecular code, then the operator $B(X)$ corresponding to it can be expressed by a simple formula. (This is described in greater detail in Appendix 2.)

The boundary conditions, initial conditions, and laws of nature determine the density matrix ρ describing the physical state of affairs at time t_1. From ρ we can (at least in principle) calculate the probability, $M(X)$, that any particular molecule described by a code, X, can be found somewhere in the system at time t_1:

$$M(X) = \text{Trace}(\rho B(X)) \tag{10}$$

The probability function $M(X)$ determines what molecular configurations can be expected to have evolved in the system by the time t_1. If $M(X)$ is fairly large, X can be expected to have evolved, but if it is very small the evolution of X is unlikely.

According to our formal definition of information content, the information content, $L(M)$, of the function M is equal to the length of the shortest computer program that will calculate this function. This length is no greater than the total length of the programming for all the various calculations we have just described, and it should correspond to about three or four pages of tightly packed programming instructions for a model based on an initial primordial soup evolving in the presence of solar radiation by the laws given in Figure 1. (We can envision this program as being written in a programming language that provides for handling numbers with an arbitrary number of significant digits. This language and the estimation of $L(M)$ are discussed in Appendix 2.)

We shall see in Section 5.3 that $M(X)$ must be exceedingly small if $L(X)$, the information content of X, is very much greater than the information content of M. The difference between the information in X and that supplied by the system (represented by $L(M)$) must be made up by pure chance, and therefore the probability of X goes down exponentially with this difference. Thus the evolution of life forms in such a system is extremely unlikely, for it can be argued that the length of the shortest program needed to calculate the essential molecular structures of even a "primitive" living organism should be a great deal longer than three or four pages. This argument is discussed in detail in the next section.

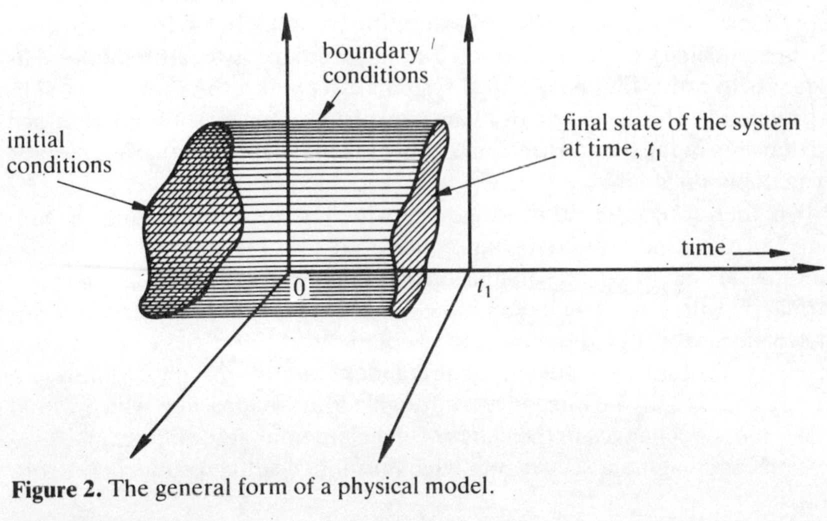

Figure 2. The general form of a physical model.

We should note the ways in which "chance" enters into the function $M(X)$ for the probability of finding X in the system. There is an element of randomness in the thermodynamic ensembles defining the initial conditions and the boundary conditions. This is one source of randomness for the "random" mutations of the theory of evolution, which are supposed to be due to chance molecular collisions and bombardment by cosmic rays. Also, randomness is built into the basic structure of quantum mechanics, since the quantum mechanical states are essentially statistical in nature.

Thus the random mutations of the theory of evolution are automatically built into our physical models. As we have pointed out before, natural selection is also implicit in these models, for it is not an independent principle, but must simply be a consequence of the underlying natural laws.

As a final point, we would like to mention another class of models that exhibit the processes of mutation and natural selection involved in the theory of evolution. These are the cellular automaton models pioneered by John von Neumann.[12] In these models an elemental finite-state automaton is placed on each square of a large two-dimensional lattice. The state of the system is given by specifying the states of all the automatons in the lattice. The system changes in the following way with the passage of time: Let t be a small, fixed time interval. At the end of each successive interval t, each automaton changes to a new state in a way which depends only on the states of the automatons occupying the immediately adjacent squares.

By properly adjusting the states of the automatons in a region of the lattice, one can create an "organism" that functions through the interaction of the automatons in its constituent cells. Von Neumann has shown that a self-reproducing organism capable of exhibiting complex behavior (a universal Turing machine) can be constructed in his cellular automaton model. His idea was to prove that mechanical systems can exhibit the property of self-reproduction characteristic of living organisms. This was intended as one further step in the demonstration that life is a mechanical process governed by mathematical laws.

It is therefore interesting to inquire whether self-reproducing "organisms" of the kind von Neumann considered could evolve in his cellular automaton system in a reasonable length of time. The system's law of transformation with time should determine the natural selection of various forms of organisms through the same sort of competitive processes envisioned in ordinary evolutionary theory. The random mutations of evolutionary theory could easily be introduced through a Markov process, which would make random changes in the states of the elemental automatons.

One can imagine a scenario in which primitive self-reproducing organisms could gradually arise through processes of self-organization in an initial "soup" consisting of automatons with randomly chosen states. These organisms might then evolve sensory systems and arrangements for defense and offense. Finally, intelligent beings might arise who would build the equivalent of cities and empires, and create art, technology, and even cybernetics.

But one could not expect such evolution to occur. Owing to the great simplicity of von Neumann's system, the function corresponding to $M(X)$ for the system can be defined by a very brief list of equations. In contrast, von Neumann's self-reproducing machines are very complicated, and he required several hundred pages to describe them in his book. It therefore seems reasonable to suppose that their information content greatly exceeds that of M. As we shall see in Section 5.3, this rules out the evolution of such configurations within the system.

5.2 The Great Complexity of Biological Form

In this section we shall discuss four aspects of the bodily structures of living organisms: the molecular structures of cells, the genetic coding (genotype), the visible bodily form (phenotype), and the behavioral patterns of organisms. Under the last heading we shall be particularly concerned with human behavior and its byproducts, including language, literature, technology, and scientific theories.

First, let us consider the molecular structures of cells. One of the most thoroughly studied organisms is the bacterium *Escherichia coli,* a unicellular organism about 500 times smaller than the average cells of higher plants and animals.[13] This is one of the smallest and simplest of all living organisms. Yet it is estimated that a single *E. coli* cell contains between 3,000 and 6,000 different types of molecules. Among these are some 2,000 to 3,000 different kinds of proteins, with an average molecular weight of 40,000. James Watson, one of the foremost authorities on molecular biology, admits that most of these large biological molecules do not obey any simple structural rule:

> Most of these macromolecules are not being actively studied, since their overwhelming complexity has forced chemists to concentrate on relatively few of them. Thus we must immediately admit that the structure of a cell will never be understood in the same way as that of water or glucose molecules. Not only will the exact structures of most macromolecules remain unsolved, but their relative locations within cells can be only vaguely known.[14]

Biochemists describe proteins as chains built up from twenty different varieties of amino acid molecules. A typical protein molecule in an *E. coli* cell will contain some 300 of these amino acid subunits. Since each subunit may be any one of twenty different amino acids, this means that the number of possible protein molecules of typical size is about 20^{300}. In general, a binary number of $\log_2 N$ digits can be used to identify a particular member of an N-element list. It follows that no more than $\log_2 N$ bits of information are required to specify the member, given that the structure of the list is known. (A bit is a binary digit of 0 or 1.) This comes to about $300 \log_2 20 \approx 1{,}297$ bits for a typical protein molecule in an *E. coli* cell. Since there are approximately 2,000 to 3,000 different proteins of this kind in a cell, the total information content for cellular protein is bounded by an upper limit of between 2,594,000 and 3,891,000 bits.

Each *E. coli* cell contains at least one chromosome, which consists of a circular molecule of DNA with a molecular weight of about 2.5×10^9. This DNA molecule is believed to contain coded instructions that determine the structures of all the other molecules in the cell. DNA molecules can be visualized as helical chains composed of successive pairs of DNA bases. There are four different kinds of bases—adenine (A), thymine (T), guanine (G), and cytosine (C)—and these are limited to forming four different kinds of base pairs: A-T, T-A, C-G, and G-C. Biochemists have worked out a genetic code, whereby sequences of DNA base pairs represent sequences of amino acid molecules. In this code, each group of three base pairs along the DNA chain specifies a particular amino acid in a corresponding protein molecule, or it codes for the termination of a protein chain.

Each DNA base pair has a molecular weight of about 660, and so a group of three pairs has a molecular weight of about 1,980. Since the molecular weight of haploid *E. coli* DNA is about 2.5×10^9, this means that the genetic coding for this organism will consist of some 1.3×10^6 triplets of bases. Since each triplet can discriminate between 21 alternatives (20 amino acid types and a stop code), this gives us an upper bound of about 1.3×10^6 times $\log_2 21$, or some 5.5×10^6 bits, for the genetic information content of an *E. coli* cell. (In this section we carry out all calculations to several decimal places, and then round off all numbers cited in the text to a few significant figures.)

Yet the *E. coli* bacterium is a very simple organism. In the cells of higher plants and animals, much larger amounts of DNA are found than in *E. coli*. It is estimated that mammalian cells contain some 800 times as much DNA, yielding an upper limit of about 4.4×10^9 bits for the genetic information content of these cells.[15] Some idea of the size of these numbers can be obtained by considering the number of pages of print required to write down such large amounts of genetic coding in full. In a typical book there are some 70 characters per line and 40 lines per page. This gives us about 1.7×10^4 bits per page if we use an alphabet of 64 characters. (Since $\log_2 64=6$, we can use 6 bits to encode each character.) At this rate it would take about 330 pages to write down the coding for *E. coli,* and about 264,000 pages to write down the coding for a mammalian cell.

One of the dogmas of molecular biology (called the central dogma, in fact) is that all the information needed to specify a cell is contained in the cell's DNA coding, and that this coded information is not changed except by random mutations. Of course, DNA cannot generate a functional cell out of disorganized components by itself, and cells may therefore contain structural information that is not coded in DNA. Also, the recent discovery of reverse transcription shows that information can be transferred to the DNA molecules from other molecules in the cell.[16]

Nonetheless, the amount of DNA in cells should give us some idea of the amount of information needed to adequately describe them. According to the central dogma, the figures we have derived thus far should provide upper limits for the essential information content of cells. We would now like to estimate reasonable lower limits. To do this we shall need to consider the variety and complexity of the structures cells are found to contain. Since some genes in the chromosomes of higher animals apparently exist in multiple copies, it would seem that the total genetic information content for these organisms must be lower than the figures suggested by their total DNA content. This conclusion is also indicated if, as some biologists have argued, the chromosomes of higher organisms contain many stretches of random, nonfunctional coding.[17]

Yet based on the great complexity of structure visible under the microscope in vertebrate cells, Watson estimates that such cells must be "at least 20 to 50 times more complex genetically than *E. coli*."[18] By this he means that such cells should contain coding for at least 20 to 50 times as many kinds of protein molecules as *E. coli.* We would need between 6,600 and 16,500 pages to write down this amount of coding, based on our 330-page estimate for *E. coli.* This corresponds to between 1.1 and 2.8×10^8 bits of information, and between 84,000 and 210,000 proteins, with an average of 300 amino acid subunits apiece.

To determine a lower limit for the genetic information content of cells, let us consider how information may be distributed among the protein molecules of a typical mammalian cell. From the figures we have cited, the lowest estimate for the number of distinct proteins in such a cell is $2{,}000 \times 20 = 40{,}000$. A protein of 300 amino acids can be specified by a string of 1,297 bits, or binary 1's and 0's. Since the size of proteins can vary, let us assign a string of 10,000 bits for each protein. We shall label these strings $Y_1, \ldots, Y_N$, where $N=40{,}000$, and the strings are listed in numerical order. We can join $Y_1, \ldots, Y_N$ together to form a large string, X, of 4×10^8 bits, and for each integer $n=1, \ldots, N$ we can form a string X_n of intermediate length by joining together $Y_1, \ldots, Y_n$.

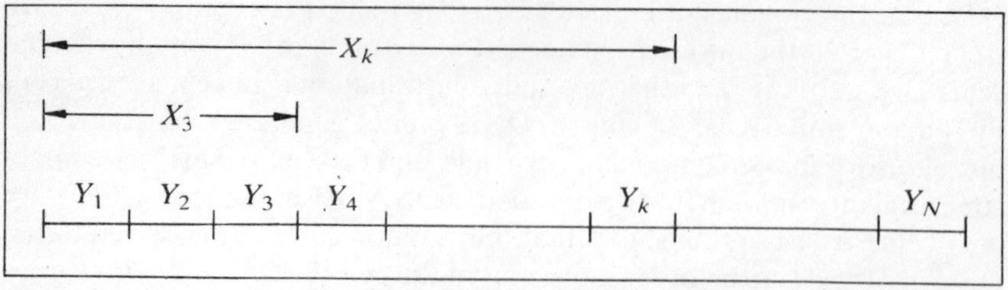

Figure 3. The structure of the bit string, X, representing the amino acid sequences for the proteins of a typical mammalian cell.

The information content of X can be approximated by adding together the amounts of information contributed by each of the blocks, Y_n, into which X is divided. This idea can be formally expressed in the following way. There is a special mathematical function, F, called the *generating function*. This function can be used to calculate $Y_1, \ldots, Y_N$ by means of the formula,

$$Y_n = F(w_n, X_{n-1}) \tag{11}$$

where n runs from 1 to N, and $w_1, \ldots, w_N$ are suitably chosen bit strings. (Here we define $X_0=1$, so that the formula can be applied when $n=1$. The mathematical terms and formulas we shall use are discussed in Appendix 1, and we present only a brief introduction here.)

The idea of this formula is that Y_1 can be calculated from w_1. Then Y_2 can be calculated from w_2 and $Y_1=X_1$. In general, each Y_n can be generated from w_n and the Y_k's that have been already calculated. Each bit string w_n represents the information that has to be introduced to specify Y_n, given that $Y_1, \ldots, Y_{n-1}$ are known.

The w_n's are related to $L(X)$, the total information content of X, by the following inequality:

$$L(X) \geqslant \sum_{n=1}^{N} (l(w_n) - 1) \tag{12}$$

Here $l(w_n)$ represents the number of bits in the bit string w_n. This inequality says, in essence, that the information content of X is at least as great as the sum of the amounts of information introduced step-by-step as X is assembled from $Y_1, \ldots, Y_N$.

Suppose for the sake of argument that $L(X) \leq 6\times10^5$ bits. Inequality (12) can be rephrased as

$$1+\frac{L(X)}{N} \geq \underset{n=1,\ldots,N}{\text{Average of }} l(w_n) \qquad (13)$$

If we substitute 6×10^5 for $L(X)$ and 4×10^4 for N, we find that the average value of $l(w_n)$ is no greater than 16 bits. This means that a typical block Y_n can be calculated exactly from X_{n-1} using no more than 16 bits of information.

Now, Y_n represents a protein molecule built from an average of 300 amino acids, and to directly spell out the amino acid sequence of such a protein requires some 1,297 bits. It is possible, of course, to specify some sequences of 300 amino acids with much less information. For example, if a protein consists of a pattern of 10 amino acids repeated 30 times, then the protein can be specified by about 43 bits of information. The amino acid sequences of actual proteins do not seem to follow any simple rule, however, and it is therefore hard to believe that they could be consistently generated using such small amounts of information.

We can obtain an intuitive idea about the structural requirements of proteins by considering the roles they play in the metabolism of cells. The exact way these proteins function is far from being known at the present time. But it is known that they are able to behave like small computers. Here is an example taken almost at random from Watson:[19] In *E. coli* there occurs a sequence of chemical reactions that convert the compound threonine into isoleucine in five steps, each of which is catalyzed by a particular enzyme, or protein macromolecule. The first step in this sequence can occur only with the aid of the enzyme threonine deaminase. When the final product, isoleucine, has reached sufficiently high concentrations, it interacts with the threonine deaminase molecules in such a way that they no longer catalyze the first reaction of the series. This prevents the manufacture of more of the product than the cell needs. We may note that each enzyme is so structured that it catalyzes only a few specific reactions. While not affecting the rates of other chemical reactions at all, such biological enzymes are known for their ability to cause certain chemical reactions to occur millions of times faster than they will occur under laboratory conditions in which the enzyme is not present. We may also note that threonine deaminase is inhibited specifically by isoleucine at the proper level of concentration, and not by any other chemical that would normally be present in the cell (for otherwise this control system wouldn't work).

Molecular biologists hypothesize that many of the amino acids in an enzyme are organized into "recognition sites" that respond to specific molecules in the cell in the same way that a lock responds to a particular key. The enzyme is so structured that its properties change in a systematic way when it interacts with these molecules, and this enables it to act as a logical unit in the overall functioning of the cell. According to this conception, an enzyme may be compared with a subroutine in a complex computer program, and its constituent amino acids may be compared with elementary programming operations that are combined to form a logical network.

If we consider that 16 bits are not sufficient even to define an arbitrary sequence of four amino acids, we can only conclude that most enzymes cannot be independently specified by such small amounts of information. Now, if one enzyme were very similar to another, it might be possible to define its structure by specifying small modifications in the structure of the other enzyme. This would make it possible to calculate the Y_n for this enzyme using the $Y_{n'}$ for the other enzyme plus a small amount of additional information. Yet if we examine the structure and function of cells, we find that they contain many diverse and complex enzymes. There is no reason to suppose that these enzymes can be systematically transformed from one into another using on the average only 16 bits of new information per transformation.

Also, there is no reason to suppose that the generating function, F, has unique properties that enable it to produce the amino acid sequences of proteins. After all, F is determined by a simple mathematical definition that has nothing to do with living organisms. (F is defined in Appendix 1.)

We conclude that we must be incorrect in assuming that the information content, $L(X)$, of mammalian proteins is less than 6×10^5 bits. We therefore propose that this figure can be taken as a reasonable lower bound for $L(X)$.

$$\text{Lower bound of } L(X) > 6\times10^5 \text{ bits} \tag{14}$$

This conclusion is given further support if we perform the calculation in formula (13) using a value of N=210,000 corresponding to our upper estimate for the number of distinct proteins in mammalian cells. Using this N, we find that $l(w_n)\leq 4$ bits on the average if we assume that $L(X)\leq 6\times10^5$ bits.

We can even go further and let X designate a string of 4.4×10^9 bits representing the complete genetic coding of a higher plant or animal. As we have already mentioned, this X corresponds to 264,000 pages of coding at 1.7×10^4 bits per page. If we let N=264,000 and let $Y_1, \ldots, Y_N$ represent these pages, then we can again perform our calculations.[20] We find that if $L(X) \leq 6 \times 10^5$, then the average $l(w_n)$ must be less than 4 bits. This implies that, on the average, each successive page of the mammalian genetic coding introduces no more than 4 bits of new information. In other words, the typical page Y_n is given by $F(w, X_{n-1})$, where w is an integer between 1 and 15, and X_{n-1} represents the preceding pages. This strongly suggests that $L(X) > 6 \times 10^5$ for this X.

At this point the objection might be raised that while X must indeed have a high information content, most of this information may well consist of insignificant nonsense. One reason for supposing this is that molecular biologists have discovered in the cells of higher organisms sections of DNA coding that serve no obvious purpose. These sections of coding can presumably change freely under the influence of mutations, and thus they may be expected to consist largely of random noise.

This objection can be answered by pointing out that while such random noise may be present, the structural and functional requirements of living organisms clearly call for large amounts of meaningful information. This was the basis for our argument that the information content of mammalian proteins must be at least 6×10^5 bits. In addition, biologists generally find that structures in living organisms have some important function, even though it may not be immediately obvious what this function is. This suggests that most of the DNA coding in the cells of higher organisms should contain some significant information.

We can conclude that our estimates of minimal information content reflect the presence of significant information, but that the strings, X, to which these estimates refer may also contain some irrelevant noise. We shall therefore introduce the idea of a *symbolic description* that represents essential biological information, while omitting irrelevant details. Our string of protein sequences is an example of such a description, although it may have the shortcoming of including some insignificant features of proteins. In general, a symbolic description is a bit string that encodes biological information, but which does not necessarily correspond directly to the genetic coding of an organism. Such a description can omit random noise that may be present in the genome, while at the same time including an account of important features of the organism.

At the present stage of biological knowledge, it is not possible to define in detail an adequate symbolic description of a cell. Yet if a symbolic description could be formulated that extracted only 24 bits of significant information from each (17,000 bit) page of the mammalian genome, then the information content of this description would be at least 6×10^6 bits.

To give a further indication of the complexity of living organisms, let us now describe a number of different categories of organic structure. The structures in each of these categories could, in principle, be formally represented by symbolic descriptions that capture their essential features. Since these structures tend to be highly complex and variegated, we suggest that their corresponding formal descriptions must have a large information content.

We shall consider the following hierarchy of structure and function in living organisms.

(a) *The chemical reactions involved in cellular metabolism.* These involve respiration, the synthesis of various chemicals needed in the cell from food molecules, photosynthesis in plants, and the processes involved in the orderly breakdown of different molecules. It would appear that most of the genetic coding of *E. coli* must be devoted to metabolism, since these bacterial cells do very little but grow and divide in half. Even though *E. coli* is one of the simplest of organisms, its metabolic interactions are so intricate that "the exact way in which all these transformations . . . occur is enormously complex, and most biochemists concern themselves with studying (or even knowing about!) only a small fraction of the total interactions."[21] That these interactions must be governed by a complex system of logic rivaling the most sophisticated programs of modern electronic computers is certainly indicated by the descriptions in Watson's book.

(b) *The morphology of cells.* The *E. coli* cell appears to possess a relatively simple gross structure, but many cells, even among the algae and protozoa, have a very complex morphology. For example, the cilia of protozoa such as the paramecium have been shown to possess an intricate structure. The cilia function cooperatively under the direction of versatile cellular control mechanisms to produce a synchronized rowing machine.[22] They are assembled within the cell according to a regulated program, and the process of construction must also require complex molecular machinery.

In the cells of higher organisms, we find many examples of complex morphology. For example, biologists have discovered several kinds of structures that join cells together and enable them to communicate.[23] These junctions display an elaborate architecture of sheets, tubes, and filaments, and some of them are designed to open and close systematically in response to cellular conditions. It seems very doubtful that precise plans for this cellular machinery could be specified by a small amount of information. It also seems doubtful that these plans could be generated by adding a few bits of information to, say, the plans for the enzymes regulating the Krebs cycle of cellular respiration.

(c) *The varieties of cells making up the tissues of higher organisms.* We can easily write down a long list of types of cells appearing in diverse bodily organs. These include muscle cells, nerve cells, bone cells, different kinds of blood cells, glandular cells, liver cells, epithelial cells, and so forth. The study of a particular kind of cell can be a whole academic subject in itself, and doctoral dissertations are frequently devoted to the study of a detail of a detail of the structure and function of such cells. The complete instructions for constructing all these cells must be contained in the genetic coding of any higher organism, at least according to the understanding of modern biology. There must also be instructions controlling the development of these cells during the growth of the embryo.

(d) *The structure and function of the organs in higher plants and animals.* The various organs of the body perform a vast array of complicated functions, most of which are poorly understood. Examples include the disease-fighting system of the blood, the image-producing eye and its retina, the brain, the endocrine gland system, and the heart and circulatory system.

The functions of a typical organ are carried out through the cooperative interaction of many complex subsystems. For example, the subsystems of the eye include the lens, the muscles supporting it, the iris, the cornea, the retina, the nerve connections, and the muscle system that moves the eyeball. Many of these subsystems are very intricate. For example, the iris contains a muscle system for opening and closing the pupil; the lens must be transparent and shaped so as to focus a sharp image on the retina; the retina contains systems of cells and nerves designed to detect elementary visual patterns such as lines and edges; the light-sensitive cells contain complex chemical systems designed to respond to different colors of light; and so forth. It would not be surprising if significant amounts of information were required to represent each of these subsystems as combinations of their underlying cellular components. In general, we would expect the basic plans of organs to have a high information content.

(e) *The behavior of animals other than man.* Many patterns of complex behavior are exhibited by lower animals. We may note, for example, the social systems of bees and ants, the spinning of spider webs, and the trans-continental migrations of birds. Biologists generally think that these instinctive behavioral patterns are built into the genetic material of the organisms. This suggests that they must be represented biochemically as a series of logical "if–then" instructions similar to the program of a computer.

It might be an interesting challenge for a student of animal behavior to try to write computer programs that would duplicate the behavior of a particular animal. As an indication of the difficulty this would involve, consider the problem of pattern recognition. Many birds are highly discriminating in their response to the coloring and physical shape of other birds. This means that they are able to make fine distinctions between complex patterns of color and form. Yet computer programs that can discriminate between simple geometric shapes have proven very difficult to write, and have involved many elaborate programming procedures. (For example, one such program, called the "MIT robot," requires some 3.6×10^6 bits of programming instructions.[24]) We can conclude that the coded instructions specifying animal behavior may be expected to entail a great deal of information.

(f) *Human personality*. This is perhaps the most complex topic of all, and it is presently beyond the reach of the reductionistic methods of modern science. There are substantial reasons for believing that the conscious self cannot be understood in physical terms, and this suggests that the behavior of conscious beings also cannot be fully explained in terms of physical processes. Nonetheless, scientists who accept the mechanistic world view are committed as a matter of consistency to suppose that all aspects of personality can be described in terms of interacting molecules.

For the sake of argument, let us consider the hypothesis that personality can be adequately defined in this way. Our question is: How much information would be required to write down a symbolic description capturing the essential features of human personality?

Such a symbolic description would have to define human intelligence, and it would have to explain the faculty of speech and the abilities involved in artistic and musical creativity. In addition, this description would have to represent the basic qualities that characterize interpersonal behavior. The following list of personal attributes may give some idea of what this entails:

> Anger, anxiety, apprehension, arrogance, bashfulness, conceit, compassion, courage, determination, doubt, dread, envy, faithfulness, forbearance, forgiveness, gratitude, gravity, greed, guilt, haughtiness, humility, impudence, lamentation, mercy, patience, peacefulness, perseverance, pride, renunciation, respectfulness, tactfulness.

We may obtain some idea of the amount of information needed to define these attributes by considering the great diversity and complexity of human artistic and literary productions. Of course, it is not possible at the present time to distill a precise characterization of personality from this source of raw data. Yet we wonder whether the information content of a full symbolic description of human personality could be as low as our minimum estimate of the information content of a higher cell. We recall that this was 6×10^5 bits, or about 36 pages.

5.3 Information-theoretic Limitations on the Evolution of Complex Form

In Section 5.1, we discussed the mathematical models of natural phenomena used in modern physics, and pointed out that the fundamental program of the physicists is to make these models as simple and general as possible. The basic format for a physical model is as follows: We have a system, S, in which events take place in accordance with a set of natural laws, F. Generally, F will be defined by a set of differential equations. The system S will have initial conditions, S_0, and boundary conditions, B. These will be described by probability distributions which may consist of combinations of thermodynamic ensembles such as the Gibbsian canonical ensemble. The probability distribution, P_t, for the state of the system at time t can be calculated, at least in principle, from the equations for the initial conditions, boundary conditions, and natural laws.

We have argued that simplicity in a mathematical model can be measured by the amount of coding needed to express the model in a fixed programming language. The mathematical models of physics tend to be simple in the sense that they can be specified by relatively small amounts of coding. For example, the Schrödinger equation of Figure 1 can be solved numerically by a program occupying less than one solid page of programming instructions. (This is discussed in greater detail in Appendix 2.) If we allow four additional pages for initial and boundary conditions, we find that we can express in less than five pages a model of a primordial planet evolving in accordance with the laws of chemistry and electromagnetism. The information content of P_t for this model is no more than 14,000 characters (at 2,800 characters per page), or

$$L(P_t) \leqslant 6 \times 14{,}000 = 84{,}000 \text{ bits} \tag{15}$$

(Recall that each character in our 64-character alphabet requires six bits.)

From the probability distribution P_t we can calculate the probability, $M(X)$, that a particular molecular configuration described by a code, X, will be found somewhere within the system at time t. $M(X)$ can be interpreted as the probability that the configuration X will have "evolved" within the system by the time t. To calculate $M(X)$ given X and P_t, we need a function that can analyze the state of the system at time t and report whether or not the configuration represented by X is present. One can define an adequate function of this kind in less than one page of condensed programming instructions. (Again, see Appendix 2.) This gives us an upper bound for $L(M)$ of less than six pages, or

$$\text{Upper bound of } L(M) \leq 100{,}800 \text{ bits} \tag{16}$$

In contrast, in Section 5.2 we estimated a lower bound for the information content of a configuration X representing the genetic coding for a cell of a higher organism. This estimate was:

$$\text{Lower bound of } L(X) > 600{,}000 \text{ bits} \tag{17}$$

The following inequality reveals the implications of these bounds for the theory of evolution:

$$M(X) \leq 2^{c + \log_2 T + L(M) - L(X)} \tag{18}$$

where c is a constant of 326 bits, and

T = The maximum number of distinct configurations, X, that can coexist within any one state of the physical system. (19)

The molecular configurations should be defined in such a way that no two distinct configurations share atoms in common. (For example, a part of a configuration should not count as a distinct configuration.) Then T is no greater than the total number of atoms in the system. For a system the size of the earth, this should be no more than $T = 10^{51}$. Some physicists have estimated that the total number of subatomic particles in the universe is less than 10^{80}. Using this speculative figure,[25] we can estimate $\log_2 T \leq 266$ in a universal model.

Putting these values together, we find that

$$M(X) \leq 2^{326 + 266 + 100{,}800 - 600{,}000} \leq 10^{-150{,}000} \tag{20}$$

According to inequality (20), the probability that the configuration X will be found anywhere within the system at time t can be no greater than one out of $10^{150{,}000}$. Suppose that t is 4.5 billion years—the estimated age of the earth according to present geological theories. Multiplying $M(X)$ in inequality (20) by $365 \times 4.5 \times 10^9$, we see that the probability of finding X in the system at the end of any day in a 4.5-billion-year period is also much less than $10^{-150{,}000}$. We can conclude that the entire course of events in S over a 4.5-billion-year period would have to be repeated over and over again at least $10^{150{,}000}$ times for there to be a reasonable expectation that the configuration X would be seen in S even once. (This is in accordance with what is known as the frequency interpretation of probabilities. See Chapter 6 for a discussion of probability and its interpretation.) Since

$10^{150,000}$ is an enormous number, to say the least, it is reasonable to suppose that X will not evolve within the system in 4.5 billion years.

Now, X could represent the genetic coding for a higher animal, and S could be a mathematical model of an earth-sized physical system in which the evolution of life might be expected to occur. Our conclusion is that higher life as we know it will not evolve in such a system in any realistic span of time. For the time t we could have chosen any time period for which $L(t)$ is small, for the only property of t that affects our considerations is the number of characters needed to express t in the program for calculating P_t. This means that our t could be anything from one year to billions of billions of years, and the conclusion expressed in inequality (20) would still hold.

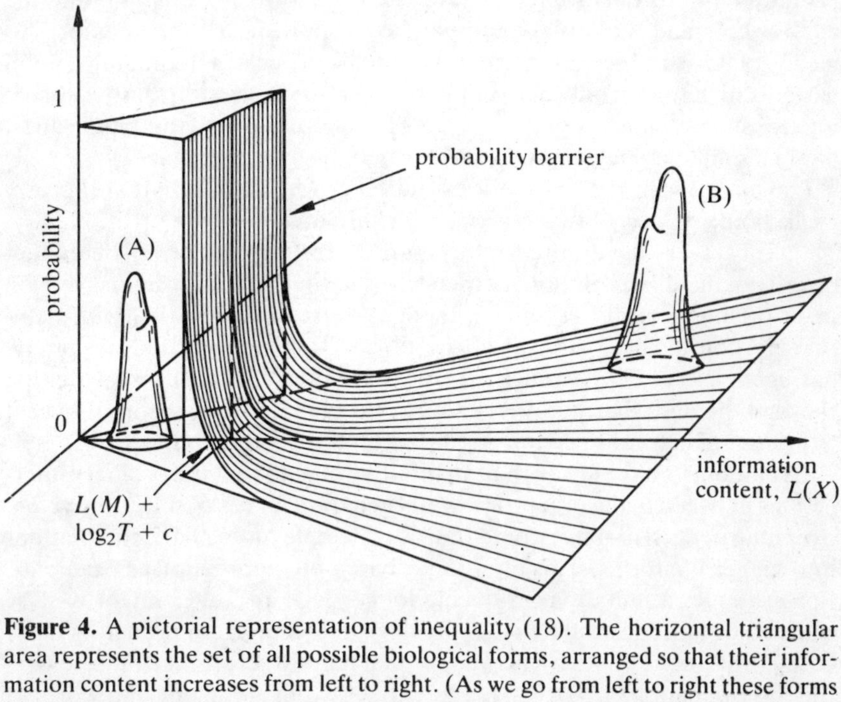

Figure 4. A pictorial representation of inequality (18). The horizontal triangular area represents the set of all possible biological forms, arranged so that their information content increases from left to right. (As we go from left to right these forms become more densely packed since the number of possible forms of information content $L(X)$ increases exponentially with $L(X)$.)

The vertical axis represents probability. Peaks (A) and (B) represent probability distributions for the forms generated by a physical process with information content $L(M)$. The curved surface represents the restriction on probabilities imposed by inequality (18). The distribution (B) of complex forms violates this restriction and is therefore ruled out. In contrast, inequality (18) does not rule out the distribution (A) of simple forms.

It is often said that while it is highly unlikely that any given complicated structural part of a living organism will arise by chance, still, given the immense span of geological time, such organisms are bound to evolve eventually. Self-reproducing systems of molecules will automatically arise through the effects of random combination and processes of chemical self-organization. These systems will be modified by random mutations, and they will gradually evolve through the culling action of natural selection.

Yet, although this evolutionary picture may seem superficially plausible, the analysis presented here rules it out in a system characterized by simple natural laws and simple initial and boundary conditions. The reason for this is easy to understand. Natural selection is supposed to direct the process of evolution, but its only source of guidance is the information built into the natural laws and the initial and boundary conditions of the system. This means that natural selection can constrain the processes of random combination and mutation only in a simple way. Natural selection may be able to impose simple patterns on the welter of randomly distributed molecules, but in a simple model, complex order can only arise by chance.

For this reason, the theory of evolution can be seen to fail at the very weak point that has been criticized by so many students of the theory. Many observers have noted that natural selection has never been adequately defined in evolutionary theory, either in Darwin's original version or in the more recent "synthetic theory."[26] According to Darwin, natural selection means "survival of the fittest," but no one, unfortunately, has been able to define which creatures are fittest, except by saying that they are the ones that survive. A similar problem plagues the more recent definition of natural selection as "differential reproduction."

Evolutionists have always had an intuitive feeling that the ordinary interactions between living organisms would generate forces of selection which, over long periods of time, would transform simple molecular combinations into higher life forms. This intuition is based on commonplace examples. For example, a mutation producing longer legs in a deer might well be selected because it would enable the deer to escape from predators more easily. Yet, this is no reason to believe that natural selection would possess the discriminating power needed to guide the development of a world of plants and animals from an inanimate primeval slime. What we have shown here is that in a system governed by simple natural laws, no process is sufficient to do this, whether it be natural selection or any other imagined process of evolutionary development.

At this point, let us consider one possible objection that could be raised to our interpretation of inequality (18). We have discussed the question of whether or not a configuration represented by X could evolve within the system S. But do the X's we have considered represent objects of real interest? Suppose, for example, that X represents the exact DNA coding of a particular cell. Many mutations are believed to have a neutral effect on cellular development, and many others might affect the cell in a relatively insignificant way. By combining, say, 10,000 mutations of this type in various ways, one could conceivably produce $2^{10,000}$ different cells, all nearly identical in form and function. One might argue that while the evolution of any one of these cells is highly improbable, it might nonetheless be probable for at least one out of the total collection to evolve. If p is the probability for the evolution of each individual genotype, then the probability for the evolution of at least one of the genotypes might be in the order of $2^{10,000}p$. This probability could be fairly large, even if p were very small.

Perhaps the most comprehensive way to answer this objection is to make use of the concept of symbolic descriptions that we introduced in Section 5.2.[27] Recall that a symbolic description of an organism is a sequence of coding that specifies significant features of the organism, while omitting unimportant details. We argued in Section 5.2 that an adequate symbolic description of a higher organism should possess a high information content, and we argued that the same could be said of the symbolic descriptions defining many important general features of living organisms.

The following diagram sums up the relationship between a symbolic description and the many individual instances to which it refers.

$$\left.\begin{array}{c} X_1 \\ X_2 \\ \cdot \\ \cdot \\ \cdot \\ X_n \end{array}\right\} \xrightarrow{\mathrm{G}} Y \qquad (21)$$

Here $X_1, \ldots, X_n$ represent distinct configurations of matter, and Y represents a symbolic description of these configurations. G designates an "observation function," or a process of analysis that can be applied to any of the X_j's to yield Y.

Computer programs for pattern analysis provide many examples of observation functions. For example, consider a program for the analysis of handwriting. If $X_1, \ldots, X_n$ were different handwritten copies of a particular text, this G could produce a printed version of the text by analyzing any one of the copies. The printed text Y would contain the essential information in $X_1, \ldots, X_n$, while omitting all reference to the individual styles of handwriting they might display. We can think of Y as a symbolic description that applies equally well to each of the handwritten copies, even though these copies may differ greatly from one another in detail.

In the field of biology there are many applications for the concepts of symbolic descriptions and observation functions. For example, consider a particular species of animal, such as the horse. Horses vary greatly in individual detail. But if there is any meaning to the term "horse," there must be certain specific information that is common to all normal horses and that fully defines this category of organic form. It should be possible to ascertain this information by observing any horse that is not defective in some way, for otherwise it could not be said that the information truly characterizes horses. This suggests that there should exist a symbolic description characterizing horses, and an observation function G that can analyze any given horse and generate this symbolic description.

In general, an observation function can be constructed from any systematic process of observation that abstracts certain features from observed objects and ignores others. One of the principles of reductionistic science is that all such processes can be defined mathematically as algorithms. Of course, no one has yet devised algorithms for the kind of sophisticated observational processes that we are considering here. In this chapter, however, we will assume for the sake of argument that this is possible, and we will treat observation functions as computer programs. (A technical discussion of observation functions is given in Thompson, (1980).)

If Y is a symbolic description produced by an observation function G, we can measure the information content of Y by $L(Y|G)$. The symbol $L(Y|G)$ designates the amount of information required to specify Y, given that G is known. The idea is that we only want to measure information in Y that is obtained from $X_1, \ldots, X_n$. We do not want to consider any information in Y that is contributed by the observation function itself.

We can clarify this idea by referring once again to the example of handwriting analysis. In this example, Y might consist of the original text printed in a particular typeface. In that case the information defining this typeface could be ascertained by inspecting Y. Yet this information has nothing to do with the original handwritten texts, $X_1, \ldots, X_n$, and is simply a byproduct of the observation function, G. The quantity $L(Y|G)$ represents the amount of information in Y that is not derived from G, and thus $L(Y|G)$ represents information that is coming solely from $X_1, \ldots, X_n$.

Using the concept of observation functions, we can generalize inequality (18) in the following way:

$$M(X_1) + M(X_2) + \ldots + M(X_n) \leq 2^{c' + \log_2 T + L(M) - L(Y|G)} \quad (22)$$

Here c'=446 bits, and T is the same as before. Y represents a symbolic description of organic form, and G represents an observation function. $X_1, \ldots, X_n$ represent all the individual configurations of matter to which G assigns the description Y. For example, Y might be a symbolic description of a horse, and $X_1, \ldots, X_n$ might represent all the possible individual horses satisfying this description.

We have argued in Section 5.2 that an adequate symbolic description of, say, a horse must have an information content of 6×10^5 bits at the very least. (Recall that such a description must define from scratch all significant structural features of the horse—from cellular organelles to gross anatomy.) Since this information should be independent of the function G used to observe it, we would expect to find $L(Y|G) \geq 6 \times 10^5$ bits. We can thus recast inequality (20) in the form.

$$M(X_1) + M(X_2) + \ldots + M(X_n) << 10^{-150.000} \qquad (23)$$

Here the summation, $M(X_1) + \ldots + M(X_n)$, is an upper bound on the probability that some one of the forms $X_1, \ldots, X_n$ will evolve within the system S. Our conclusion is that since $10^{-150,000}$ is an exceedingly small number, it is nearly certain that none of these forms will ever evolve in S. In the particular case we are considering, this means that no instance of a horse will ever be found in S. In general, it means that no form with a symbolic description of high information content can be expected to evolve in a system characterized by natural laws, initial conditions, and boundary conditions of low information content.

Let us examine inequality (22) more closely to understand the basic principle behind it. First of all, note that the upper bound this inequality places on $M(X_1) + \ldots + M(X_n)$ will become reasonably large only if we increase the complexity of our model to the point where $L(M)$ is nearly equal to $600{,}000 - 266 - 446$ bits, or nearly 36 solid pages of coding. There are three ways of increasing $L(M)$. One way is to increase the complexity of the laws of the system. We note, however, that scientists have not yet reached the point of even considering natural laws requiring 36 pages of coding, and it is unlikely that such considerations could ever be practical, given the limitations of the human mind. At any rate, the laws of present-day physics are based on the Schrödinger equation and a few potentials, and the fundamental program of physics has been to simplify these as much as possible.

$L(M)$ might also be increased by increasing the complexity of the initial conditions or the boundary conditions of the system. As we shall see, this would amount to building data for the symbolic description, Y, into the initial or boundary conditions. If specifications for Y were built into the boundary conditions, then as time passed we would find information for Y

coming into the system from across the boundary. If such specifications were built into the initial conditions, it would appear that information for Y had existed in the system from its very beginning. In either case, the mathematical model provides us with no satisfactory explanation of the original source of the information for Y. Certainly neither alternative is acceptable from the point of view of current evolutionary theory.

We can clarify these points by considering the following stronger version of inequality (22):

$$M(X_1) + \ . \ . \ . + M(X_n) \leqslant 2^{c' + \log_2 T - L(Y|G,M)} \qquad (24)$$

Here $L(Y|G,M)$ designates the amount of information needed to specify Y, given that both G and M are known. This is formally defined as the length of the shortest program that can calculate Y, using the functions G and M as built-in subroutines.

If $L(Y|G,M)$ is small, most of the information for Y can be obtained from G and M. We have already postulated that $L(Y|G) \geqslant 6 \times 10^5$ bits. In order for $L(Y|G,M)$ to be much smaller than this, it is necessary to adjust M very carefully and, in effect, build specifications for Y into M. Inequality (24) shows that there can be a reasonable probability of finding an X_j in the system at time t only if $L(Y|G,M)$ is not very much greater than $c' + \log_2 T$. This constant is no more than 712 bits, or about 119 characters. This means that nearly all the information needed to specify Y must be built into M in the form of natural laws, boundary conditions, or initial conditions.

This is an appropriate time to consider one objection that might be made to our arguments. One might point out that the information content of ordinary matter is certainly very high. For example, the information needed to specify the positions of the billions of molecules in a gas must be enormous. How, then, are we justified in saying that $L(M)$ for a physical model should be small? The answer to this question is that we have described the initial state of our physical system by means of thermodynamic ensembles that specify only broad statistical properties of matter. However, we could also consider a model in which the initial conditions stipulated a particular arrangement of subatomic particles in a primordial gas.

In such a model, $L(M)$ would be extremely large, and inequality (22) would not tell us very much. But what should we expect of $L(Y|G,M)$ in this situation? There are essentially two alternatives. If the arrangement of our primordial gas were chosen at random, then we would expect the information specifying this arrangement to be irrelevant to the construction of Y, and thus we would expect $L(Y|G,M)$ to be large. According to (24), this would mean that $M(X_1) + \ . \ . \ . + M(X_n)$ would be very small. (This line of reasoning is automatically incorporated in the derivation of (22) and

(24) if we use statistical ensembles in the definition of M.) Conversely, if $L(Y|G,M)$ were small, specific information for Y would have to be built into the initial distribution of particles in the primordial gas. One would then be led to ask how this information came to be encoded in such a strange form in the beginning of the history of the physical system.

The same considerations apply to boundary conditions. For example, if cosmic rays entered the system from outside, and their energies and directions of motion were given by a simple statistical distribution, then the system could not be expected to extract a large amount of specific information from them in the form of an organism with a symbolic description, Y. In order for this information to be obtainable from the cosmic rays, their statistical distribution function, D, would have to be highly complex. Furthermore, it could not be just any complex function, but would have to be chosen so that $L(Y|G,D)$ was small. In other words, a large amount of specific information for Y would have to be coded into the cosmic ray stream.

This brings to mind the panspermia hypothesis of Svante Arrhenius. According to this theory, life never had an origin, and it has been disseminated throughout the universe in the form of spores that travel in outer space from one favorable planet to another. Arrhenius thought these spores would be primitive and would independently evolve into higher forms on various planets. We can see, however, that "primitive" spores would not do—the spores would have to contain instructions for all of the organisms that later evolved.

The theory of Arrhenius holds that life is eternally existent as a material phenomenon. This theory suffers from the drawback that natural processes tend to obliterate information, thereby making it very unlikely that a large store of information could be maintained eternally in a material system. Also, the theory is no more satisfying as an explanation of origins than a modified "big bang" theory, with instructions for life forms encoded in the initial state of the universe.

Yet in a system having a low value of $K=L(M) + \log_2 T + c'$, the probability is practically zero that life as we know it will arise. This K can be regarded as a universal constant of the physical system that constrains its evolutionary potential. If any category of form can be characterized by a simple description having information content less than K, then it is possible for representatives of that category to arise in the system. But if the members of the category satisfy a description of higher information content than K, then they are highly unlikely to evolve.

This applies to categories such as species, classes, and phyla of plants and animals. It also applies to more abstract categories such as intelligence or personality. We can conclude, for example, that personality will not evolve in a system of low K value unless we define personality so broadly that it becomes practically devoid of meaning. This can be appreciated if we contemplate the list of features of personality given in Section 5.2. Unless these features can be adequately defined by a description of low information content, we cannot expect to see entities that display them arising in a system of low information content. (Here, of course, we are speaking of personality as a purely physical phenomenon, in accordance with the reductionistic philosophy of modern science.)

At this point we would like to briefly discuss some recent theories of the self-organization of matter. These theories are based on nonequilibrium thermodynamics and the theory of chemical kinetics, and they have been developed by researchers such as Ilya Prigogine[28] and Manfred Eigen. In these theories, systems of chemicals are modeled with differential equations of a kind known as reaction-diffusion equations. By studying such equations, the theoreticians hope to show how disorganized molecules in a primordial soup could combine together chemically to produce the first self-reproducing cell.

Perhaps the most well-known example of this work is Eigen's theory of self-reproducing hypercycles.[29] In this theory, Eigen proposes that systems of polypeptides and self-replicating RNA molecules will arise spontaneously in a suitable chemical soup. A collection of RNA molecules, $R_1, \ldots, R_n$, will be able to perpetuate itself in the soup if each R_j generates polypeptides that catalyze the reproduction of R_{j+1}, and R_n similarly catalyzes the production of R_1. Eigen calls such systems of molecules "hypercycles," and he proposes that they might have filled the evolutionary gap between disorganized chemical compounds and living cells.

Here we will not attempt to discuss Eigen's theory in detail. We will simply point out that Eigen has not even begun to explain the origin of the self-reproducing machinery of living cells. In existing cells, the DNA molecules carrying genetic information are reproduced with the aid of highly complex and specific enzymes, such as "DNA polymerase" and "DNA gyrase." These enzymes all perform functions which are apparently necessary for cellular reproduction, and which frequently involve remarkable feats of molecular manipulation. For example, recent work suggests that DNA gyrase is able systematically to break a DNA strand, pass a nearby strand of DNA through the break, and then rejoin the broken strand.[30] Since long DNA chains automatically become tangled during replication, this capacity to tie and untie knots in DNA appears essential for cellular reproduction.

All these enzymes are manufactured within the cell by an elaborate process requiring a large number of proteins and other complex molecules.

For example, one step in this process is carried out by structures called ribosomes that in *Escherichia coli* have a molecular weight of about 3 million, and can be broken down into 55 distinct protein subunits.[31] All these proteins are themselves coded in DNA, and they are manufactured by the same process in which they play an essential role.

Eigen's problem is to show how a stable self-reproducing system could begin to operate before the development of this elaborate machinery, and then show how the machinery could gradually evolve by mutation and natural selection. Dixon and Webb[32] summarize some of the many difficulties that must be overcome in such an attempt, and Smith[33] gives a critique of Eigen's theory. Here we will simply observe that Eigen's theoretical framework is not adequate for his task. In a model based on reaction-diffusion equations, each chemical compound is represented by a continuous function describing its distribution in space and time. In such models there is no direct way to describe three-dimensional geometrical structures composed of molecules, even though such structures are very important in living cells.

For this reason, evolutionary models based solely on reaction-diffusion equations are necessarily incomplete. Such models cannot readily simulate processes involving such three-dimensional structures as ribosomes or cell membranes, and they are even less suited to showing how such structures may have evolved. At present, there seem to be no mathematical models of biochemical processes that are both reasonably complete and easy to handle. Hence we have based the analysis in this chapter on the laws of quantum mechanics, even though these laws are difficult to apply in practical calculations, and are also subject to a number of theoretical drawbacks.

As a final point we note that an analysis of evolution on the basis of information theory has been carried out independently by Hubert Yockey. Yockey considered the problem of chemical evolution in a primordial soup, and he has given estimates for the information content of proteins such as cytochrome-c.[34]

5.4 Complex Form and the Frustration of Empiricism

In this chapter we have used information theory to study the hypothesis that life has originated and evolved through the action of natural processes governed by the known laws of chemistry and physics. There are a number of ways of interpreting this analysis. Some of the more important of these are the following:

(1) The universe *is* characterized by simple natural laws and simple initial conditions. Adequate descriptions of living organisms *do* require

large amounts of information, and the evolution of such organisms is indeed exceedingly improbable. Yet this is what happened—simply by chance.

(2) Adequate descriptions of organisms have a high information content, and this information is built into the boundary conditions or initial conditions of the universe. Evolution is thus a process whereby pre-existing information is transformed from one form to another.

(3) Considerable amounts of information are required to describe living organisms, and this information is built into the fundamental laws of the universe. These laws correspond to the absolute reality underlying the flux of transient phenomena, and thus life, or at least the information for life, can be regarded as absolute.

(4) Detailed descriptions of living organisms may seem highly complex, but actually they have a low information content. We cannot see how to define such descriptions with simple programs, but this is nonetheless possible, and thus evolution may take place with high probabilities in simple systems.

(5) It is hopeless to speculate on these topics, for we cannot arrive at any satisfactory or reliable conclusions.

Let us begin by discussing interpretation (1). Evolution is often presented in popular accounts as an inexorable, progressive development that advances inevitably from primitive to advanced forms. Evolutionists frequently emphasize that chance enters the theory of evolution only as a source of necessary variations, and that the deterministic mechanisms of natural selection provide systematic guidance for the development of species.[35] Intelligence in particular is often seen as an inevitable product of evolution, and many scientists, such as the astronomer Carl Sagan, speculate on the possible development of human or superhuman intelligence on other planets.[36]

Yet, a number of evolutionists have expressed a contrary view. The evolutionary theorist Stephen J. Gould has recently popularized the idea that sheer randomness plays an important part in the origin and development of life.[37] This point had been elaborated previously by Theodosius Dobzhansky[38] and George G. Simpson, who both maintained that the evolution of man or manlike beings has a probability of zero. Simpson's arguments are as follows:

> The factors that have determined the appearance of man have been so extremely special, so very long continued, so incredibly intricate . . . and every-

> thing we learn seems to make them even more appallingly unique. If human origins were indeed inevitable under the precise conditions of our actual history, that makes the more nearly impossible such an occurrence anywhere else. I therefore think it extremely unlikely that anything enough like us for real communication of thought exists anywhere in our accessible universe.[39]

Simpson's reasoning is based on his intuition that natural selection is not an independent guiding force, but merely a collocation of innumerable special factors that just happen, in this case, to produce human beings when added together. Since he can see no reason for the pre-existence of these particular factors, Simpson concludes that our existence is an irreproducible consequence of sheer chance.

Simpson's ideas about the improbability of human evolution seem completely incompatible with the general understanding of evolution as a progressive process. Of course, one might try to reduce this incompatibility by limiting Simpson's observations to man, while maintaining that higher life in general is still likely to evolve. Yet the analysis given here implies that Simpson's conclusions must apply to all features of life characterized by descriptions of high information content. This includes everything from the complex structures of cells to highly abstract aspects of human personality. In a system operating under simple physical laws and initial conditions, such patterns of organization can arise only with a probability of nearly zero. (See Section 5.3.)

Now, one might assert that this is exactly what has happened. This is indeed the message conveyed by Jacques Monod in his book *Chance and Necessity:*

> The thesis I shall present . . . is that the biosphere does not contain a predictable class of objects or of events but constitutes a particular occurrence, compatible indeed with first principles, but not *deducible* from these principles and therefore essentially unpredictable.[40]

Monod is proposing that life in all its diverse manifestations constitutes a unique phenomenon that has arisen simply by chance. Monod believes, of course, that life follows physical laws, and that organisms must be constructed in accordance with the dictates of these laws. (Thus land animals cannot exceed a certain size, for example.) But apart from this he regards life as completely unpredictable.

Monod's view is consistent with the analysis presented here, but this view is the antithesis not only of the theory of evolution, but of any effort to scientifically explain the origins of life. In effect, Monod says that science can do no more to explain the origins of life than simply to state the obvious: Life is possible, and has originated.

The theory of information shows, in fact, that a complex form can be "explained" only by a statement of equal or greater complexity that includes the information in the original form. Such a statement can amount to little more than a description in some language of the original form—a mere assertion of the form's existence. Thus complex form constitutes a barrier of ultimate frustration for those who are seeking simple explanations of nature.

We cannot avoid this frustration by adopting the hypothesis that the information for living beings was encoded in the initial or boundary conditions of the universe. This hypothesis suggests that the information for life must have originated beyond the boundary of the universe, or at a time before the universe existed. Yet nothing can lie beyond the spatial or temporal boundaries of a truly universal model, and if we envision a succession of models of greater and greater extent, then we are stuck with an infinite regress.

As long as we adhere to a strictly quantitative theoretical approach, we will have to regard the information for life (or, indeed, any complex information) as simply inexplicable. One possible option, however, is to suppose that the boundary of our model represents the point at which mathematical description must be given up and replaced by a nonreductionistic understanding of reality. This opens up the possibility that the origin of complex information may be understandable in a higher context that transcends purely numerical considerations. This option is actually not at all unreasonable *a priori,* but it may appear unpalatable to a person strongly committed to the quantitative method of studying nature.

Let us therefore leave this option aside for the moment, and consider interpretation (3). We have pointed out in Section 5.1 that the idea of complex natural laws is not compatible with the predominant world view of modern science. Physicists have traditionally sought to explain natural phenomena using the simplest laws possible, and scientists in general have tended to assume that the accepted laws of their time were final and universal. Yet we have also seen that it is very difficult to even formulate, much less verify, an adequate representation of the laws of nature. (See Appendix 2 and also Chapter 3.)

On closer inspection it becomes apparent that our knowledge of the laws of nature is not final. Indeed, some eminent scientists have proposed that the known laws may represent only a negligible fraction of the natural laws and principles that remain to be discovered. For example, the physicist David Bohm has observed that "the possibility is always open that there may exist an unlimited variety of additional properties, qualities, entities, systems, levels, etc. to which apply correspondingly new kinds of laws of nature."[41]

Now, what is really meant by a "law of nature"? We have treated such laws as mathematical equations, and from a strictly empirical viewpoint they are simply numerical regularities in the welter of measurable phenomena.[42] Yet many scientists have tended to imagine that these laws represent a fundamental stratum of reality underlying the world of appearances that confronts our senses. They have thus tended to construct a world view in which such things as electrons and quantum fields constitute actual reality, while such things as mountains, trees, and people are simply transient combinations of these underlying ingredients. These scientists have been trying to understand the absolute basis of reality, and they have hoped that this ultimate foundation would be disclosed through the study of physical laws.

We might therefore ask, "What is the absolute reality corresponding to the laws of nature?" We can be sure that whatever this is, it does not consist of numbers, "bits," or mathematical operations. If the laws of nature can be expressed in simple formulas, then we might hope to visualize this reality vaguely in terms of some kind of abstract curves and surfaces. But this is not possible if the laws of nature encompass large amounts of mathematically irreducible information specifying an elaborate hierarchy of biological forms. Due to their very irreducibility, such laws cannot be visualized in terms of simple mathematical constructs. From the quantitative, empirical point of view, the reality corresponding to such laws could only be regarded as completely enigmatic.

Purely empirical arguments cannot carry us very far beyond these rather limited and unsatisfactory conclusions. It may be worthwhile, however, to briefly consider some other approaches to our subject matter that people have pursued in the past. One of the most prominent of these approaches was widely known in Darwin's time as natural theology. According to natural theology, the presence of highly complex order in nature can be interpreted as evidence of intelligent direction. The proponents of this view depart radically from the quantitative school of thought by proposing that the absolute foundation of nature is a primordial sentient being lying completely outside the realm of mathematical describability.

In Darwin's time and earlier, many scientists accepted the argument that complex design in living organisms implies the existence of a transcendental designer.[43] With the introduction of Darwin's theory of evolution, however, this argument was weakened. Darwin's principle of natural selection appeared to provide an explanation of the origin of biological form that could be based completely on simple natural laws. This explanation seemed to involve fewer inexplicable elements than the hypothesis of a primordial creator, and many people therefore came to accept it as scientifically superior.

The analysis presented here removes this objection to natural theology. We have seen that the origin of complex order can be explained neither by natural selection nor by any other principle based on simple natural laws. Natural structures and patterns of high information content are inherently inexplicable by the reductionistic methods of quantitative analysis. The hypothesis that these structures have been generated by a transcendental intelligent being is therefore in no way inferior to our alternative interpretations (1), (2), and (3) as a theoretical explanation. In addition, this hypothesis opens up the possibility that if the ultimate foundation of reality is a sentient being, then it may be possible to acquire absolute knowledge directly from this transcendental source.

At this point the objection might be raised that this hypothesis is not proven by our analysis, and that, indeed, we have not rigorously *proven* that biological form is characterized by high information content. If the forms of organisms only seem complex, but actually have low information content, then our analysis does not rule out the possibility that they might evolve with relatively high probabilities. Thus, by adopting interpretation (4), we may be able to save the idea of progressive evolution in a comprehensible universe governed by simple natural laws.

This approach to the theory of evolution has been adopted by the information theorist Gregory Chaitin. According to Chaitin, the fundamental goal of theoretical biology is

> to set up a nondeterministic model universe, to formally define what it means for a region of space-time in that universe to be an organism. . . , and to rigorously demonstrate that starting from simple initial conditions, organisms will appear and evolve . . . in a reasonable amount of time and with high probability.[44]

This program requires living organisms to have low information content, and Chaitin has therefore proposed that an organism is "a highly interdependent region, one for which the complexity of the whole is much less than the sum of the complexities of its parts."[45]

In order to elucidate Chaitin's proposal, let us refer again to the analysis presented in Sections 5.2 and 5.3. We showed with inequalities (18), (20), and (22) of Section 5.3 that no pattern with an information content of more than 101,392 (= 100,800 + 326 + 266) bits is likely to evolve in our model system. Our upper estimate in Section 5.2 for the number of proteins in a cell was 210,000. For the sake of argument, let us suppose that a list of 210,000 proteins has an information content of no more than 101,392 bits. Then inequalities (12) and (13) of Section 5.2 imply that each successive protein can be specified in terms of the preceding proteins in the list by the addition of only 1.5 bits of new information on the average.[46] In fact, (13) and (14) imply that for at least $210{,}000-101{,}392 = 108{,}608$ values of n, we will have $F(1,X_{n-1})=Y_n$. In other words, 108,608 of these proteins must be exactly determined by the preceding proteins in the list.

Chaitin and his colleague C.H. Bennett are suggesting that relationships of this kind indeed exist, but that they are hidden from our vision. Their argument runs as follows: If structure has a low information content, then, by definition, it can be specified by a short program. Yet even though a program is short, it may run for a very long time before finishing its calculations.[47] Bennett has suggested that biological structures do have very low information content, but can be defined by short programs only if these programs have very long running times. This means that extensive interrelationships must run through all biological structures, but it will not be possible for us to demonstrate this.

If this approach is to save the idea of progressive evolution, it must be consistently applied to the entire spectrum of biological form. All significant symbolic descriptions of organic form must have a low information content. This means that these descriptions and their subdivisions can be systematically transformed into one another using the generating function F. With the addition of small amounts of information, a description of, say, the visual processes of a mammal can be converted into a description of the mitotic machinery of cells; this in turn can be converted into a description of abstract features of human mental ability; and so on. Yet if Bennett's ideas are correct, it will be impossible to show these relationships by any means of analysis that could conceivably be carried out by human beings.[48]

We can conclude that the empirical method of investigation leads us into a frustrating impasse when we try to use it to understand the nature and origin of life. Our effort to rigorously analyze the theory of evolution has led us to consider the generating function F. It seems highly implausible that this simple function—which is defined in a few lines in Appendix 1—can effect the remarkable transformations we have described. There is also no direct evidence that complex designs of organic mechanisms can be automatically generated by the execution of simple computational routines. Yet the possibility remains that this can be done by routines with such long running times that we cannot test them.

At this point some persons might feel inclined to adopt alternative (5), and conclude that speculation on these topics is futile. We can agree that such a conclusion is not at all unreasonable, but we should stress that it entails abandoning all confidence in the theory of evolution as an established understanding of the origin of life. One might advocate, of course, that we should admit our present ignorance in this area, while still maintaining the hope that some day we will show how evolution proceeds by simple laws. We should realize, however, that biological form may well be characterized by high information content, as we argued in Section 5.2. If this is indeed the case, the empirical approach will never be able to provide a simple explanation of life's origins. At best, this approach will be able to produce only a complex description of natural order. Such a description cannot be satisfying as an explanation, and, as Bennett's ideas indicate, it can never be possible to actually prove that the description is final.[49]

These conclusions may seem to be completely negative, but we should not end this discussion without pointing out that they also have a positive side. If nature is indeed simple and comprehensible, then it is hard to imagine any other method of studying nature than the empirical method of experiment and calculation. But by showing that nature may not be so simple, we are opening up the possibility that there may be other valid methods of obtaining knowledge. If the absolute foundation of reality is a reservoir of irreducible and inconceivable qualities, then the possibility arises that we may be able to approach the absolute by methods other than dissection and measurement. Our empirical analysis of evolutionary theory cannot prove *rigorously* that this is so, and it cannot disclose how such an alternative approach could be practically realized. However, it does show that empirical reasoning is capable of pointing beyond itself.

We have mentioned the conclusion of natural theology, that the presence of complex order in nature implies the existence of an absolute intelligence. Although this conclusion is consistent with the results of our information-theoretic analysis, it is certainly not proven by this analysis. Nonetheless, the ideas of natural theology are valuable, for they suggest an alternative to the empirical method of acquiring knowledge. If the absolute basis of nature is a sentient being and we ourselves are products of this absolute source, then it is possible that we may be able to relate personally with the absolute.

In this chapter we will not discuss the ramifications of this possibility, but we mention it simply as a concrete example of the options opened up by our analysis. If it is to be of real interest, such an approach to absolute knowledge must be verifiable by tangible, reproducible experience, for otherwise it amounts to nothing more than empty speculation. Yet the practical means of accomplishing this cannot be established by quantitative analysis, and so they lie beyond the scope of the present discussion. Here we must stop at the boundaries of the empirical realm.

Notes

1. Weinberg, "Conceptual Foundations of the Unified Theory of Weak and Electromagnetic Interactions," pp. 1212–1218.
2. Hawking and Israel, eds., *General Relativity,* p. 21.
3. Slater, *Quantum Theory of Molecules and Solids,* Vol. 1, p. *vii.*
4. Watson, *Molecular Biology of the Gene,* p. 54.
5. *Newton's Principia,* p. *lxviii.*
6. Helmholtz, *Über die Erhaltung der Kraft,* p. 6.
7. These quantum mechanical equations are taken from von Neumann, *Mathematical Foundations of Quantum Mechanics,* and Messiah, *Quantum Mechanics.*
8. Fisher, *The Genetical Theory of Natural Selection.*
9. For example, see Oparin, *The Origin of Life,* and Orgel, *The Origins of Life.*
10. Layzer, "The Arrow of Time," p. 206.
11. This is discussed in Tolman, *The Principles of Statistical Mechanics.*
12. von Neumann, *Theory of Self-Reproducing Automata.*
13. The data for *E. coli* are taken from Watson, chap. 3.
14. Watson, p. 69.
15. Watson, p. 498.
16. Watson, p. 677.
17. Crick, "Split Genes and RNA Splicing," pp. 264–271.
18. Watson, p. 499.
19. Watson, p. 404.
20. The F in equation (11) contains a parameter of $l=10{,}000$ specifying the lengths of the intervals Y_j. In this application of F we have to change this parameter to $l=16{,}800$ bits/page.

21. Watson, p. 76.

22. Satir, "How Cilia Move," pp. 44–52.

23. Staehelin and Hull, "Junctions between Living Cells," pp. 141–152.

24. Winston, "The MIT Robot."

25. According to a famous conjecture of Sir Arthur Eddington, there are exactly $136 \times 2^{256} \approx 1.6 \times 10^{79}$ protons in the universe. (Eddington, *The Philosophy of Physical Science,* p. 176.) Of course, this should not be taken very seriously. The important point here is that $\log_2 T$ will be fairly small, even if the total number of atoms in the system is very large.

26. Macbeth, *Darwin Retried,* p. 47.

27. Here is a brief outline of a simpler but more specialized answer. We have estimated that the DNA coding of a higher animal will contain at least 6×10^5 bits of significant information. Suppose that this coding also contains N bits of random noise. The random noise should not duplicate the significant information, and thus the total information content of the DNA coding should be at least $6 \times 10^5 + N$. The probability that a particular animal with this coding will evolve is therefore bounded by $p = 2^{-N}\ 10^{-150,000}$, according to inequality (18). Now, let P be the probability of the evolution of at least one animal with a genome containing this fixed significant information plus N bits of arbitrary noise. This P could be at most 2^N times as large as p, since there are only 2^N possibilities for N bits of information. This means that $P \leq 2^N p \leq 10^{-150,000}$, which is the same bound as in inequality (20).

28. Prigogine, Nicolis, and Babloyantz, "Thermodynamics of Evolution," pp. 23–28.

29. Eigen and Schuster, "The Hypercycle," in three parts.

30. Cozzarelli, "DNA Gyrase and the Supercoiling of DNA," pp. 953–960.

31. Watson, pp. 316–317.

32. Dixon and Webb, *Enzymes,* pp. 656–663.

33. Smith, "Hypercycles and the Origin of Life," pp. 445–446.

34. Yockey, "A Calculation of the Probability of Spontaneous Biogenesis by Information Theory," pp. 377–398, and "On the Information Content of Cytochrome c," pp. 345–376.

35. Julian Huxley is one well-known proponent of the idea that evolution is a progressive process directed by natural selection. See Huxley, *Evolution in Action*.

36. Shklovskii and Sagan, *Intelligent Life in the Universe*.

37. Gould, "Chance Riches," pp. 36–44,

38. Dobzhansky, "Darwinian Evolution and the Problem of Extraterrestrial Life," p. 173.

39. Simpson, *This View of Life,* p. 268.

40. Monod, *Chance and Necessity,* p. 43.

41. Bohm, *Causality and Chance in Modern Physics,* p. 133.

42. This viewpoint is expounded by the logical positivists, who hold that one can speak meaningfully only of sense perceptions, and that all other categories are mere verbiage. This philosophy is summarized by the physicist Yehudah Freundlich as follows: "To us, the statement that trains have wheels when they are not in the station (when we are not sensing them) *means* that at the station they will have wheels. This is, to us, a very satisfying solution, for having thus defined existence we proceed to speak of wheels on the train even when it is not in the station. In general, attributing a property to a system means that certain predictions about the system can be made." (Freundlich, "Mind, Matter, and Physicists," pp. 130–131.) According to this doctrine, the statement "Man evolved from a primate ancestor" *means* that certain bones may be seen in certain museums. This is far from a satisfying solution to us and, we believe, to many others. Generally, scientists have sought to acquire insight into the nature of what really exists. If empirical science is indeed unable to provide such insight, we can only conclude that its pretensions to universality are greatly overblown.

43. Gillespie, *Charles Darwin and the Problem of Creation*.

44. Chaitin, "Algorithmic Information Theory," p. 357.

45. Chaitin, p. 357.

46. This number refers to the average value of $l(w_n)$. By definition, $w_n \geq 1$, and the choice $w_n = 0$ is excluded. Therefore a w_n of x bits really can convey only $\log_2(2^x - 1)$ bits of information. This is .87 bits if $x = 1.5$.

47. Computer languages have provisions for iterating computational steps

a specified number of times. If the number of iterations in a program is in the millions or even billions, then it may be possible to run the program on existing computers. However, in a simple program we can easily specify very large numbers of iterations, such as 10^{100} or $10^{10^{100}}$ It is not possible to gain practical experience with such programs, since they would not complete their calculations in billions of years on the fastest imaginable computer. Experience with simple programs involving moderate numbers of iterations gives us no reason to suppose that such programs can generate detailed descriptions of life as we know it. Should we suppose that such programs *will* generate descriptions of life if their calculations are prolonged over, say, $10^{1,000,000}$ iterations?

48. Mathematicians have shown that some statements can be neither proven nor disproven, even though they have a sensible meaning and presumably must be either true or false. These are called undecidable statements. There are also statements, called practically undecidable, which can be proven true, but only by proofs of such length that human beings cannot hope to deal with them. As we might expect, complex statements tend to be undecidable. The statement $L(X) \geqslant N$ is always undecidable if it is true and N is large enough. If it is false, then the opposite statement, $L(X) < N$, is often practically undecidable. It is interesting that we are naturally led to consider statements of this kind when we try to rigorously formulate the theory of evolution. (For the undecidability of $L(X) \geqslant N$ see Chaitin, "Algorithmic Information Theory," pp. 350–359. A general account of undecidability is given in Jones, "Recursive Undecidability—An Exposition," pp. 724–738.)

49. This would require a formal proof of $L(X) \geqslant N$. See note 48.

Chapter 6

Chance and The Unity of Nature

Throughout human history, philosophers and seekers of knowledge have sought to discover a single fundamental cause underlying all the phenomena of the universe. Since the rise of Western science in the late Renaissance, many scientists have also felt impelled to seek this ultimate goal, and they have approached it from their own characteristic perspective. Western science is based on the assumption that the universe can be understood mechanistically—that is, in terms of numbers and mathematical formulas—and Western scientists have therefore searched for an ultimate, unified mathematical description of nature.

This search has gone through many vicissitudes, and many times scientists have felt that a final, unified theory was nearly within their grasp. Thus in the beginning of the nineteenth century Pierre Simon de Laplace could contemplate Newton's laws and declare that "All the effects of nature are only the mathematical consequences of a small number of immutable laws."[1] By the turn of the century many new concepts and discoveries had been incorporated into the science of physics, and Laplace's simple picture of the laws of nature had become superannuated. At about this time, however, Albert Einstein embarked on a much more sophisticated and ambitious program of unification. His goal was to explain all the phenomena of the universe as oscillations in one fundamental "unified field."

But even while Einstein was working on this project, revolutionary developments in the science of physics were rendering his basic approach obsolete. For several decades a bewildering welter of new discoveries made the prospect of finding an ultimate theory seem more and more remote. But the effort to find a unified theory of nature has continued, and in 1979 three physicists (Sheldon Glashow, Abdus Salam, and Steven Weinberg) won the Nobel Prize in physics for their effort in partially tying together some of the disparate elements of current physical theories. On the basis of their work, many scientists are now optimistically anticipating the development of a theory that can explain the entire universe in terms of a single quantum field governed by a universal force law.

The scientists' search for a unified explanation of natural phenomena begins with two main hypotheses. The first of these is that all the diverse phenomena of nature derive in a harmonious way from some ultimate, unified source. The second is that nature can be fully explained in terms of numbers and mathematical laws. As we have pointed out, the second of these hypotheses constitutes the fundamental methodological assumption of modern science, whereas the first has a much broader philosophical character.

Superficially, these two hypotheses seem to fit together nicely. A simple system of equations appears much more harmonious and unified than a highly complicated system containing many arbitrary, unrelated expressions. So the hypothesis that nature is fundamentally harmonious seems to guarantee that the ultimate mathematical laws of nature must be simple and comprehensible. Consequently, the conviction that nature possesses an underlying unity has assured many scientists that their program of mechanistic explanation is feasible.

We will show in this chapter, however, that these two hypotheses about nature are actually not compatible. To understand why this is so, we must consider a third feature of modern scientific theories—the concept of chance.

As we carefully examine the role chance plays in mechanistic explanations of nature, we shall see that a mechanistic theory of the universe must be either drastically incomplete or extremely incoherent and disunited. In mechanistic models of reality there is, in fact, a fundamental conflict between unity and diversity, and many scientists have attempted to resolve this conflict by asserting that diversity arises by chance. Unfortunately, however, the concept of chance as an active agency is fallacious. Once the fallacy is exposed, it becomes clear that we must give up either the goal of mechanistically explaining the universe, or the idea that there is an essential unity behind the phenomena of nature.

At the end of this chapter we will examine the conflict between unity and diversity from a broader philosophical perspective. We observe that even though this conflict cannot be resolved by a mechanistic theory, we are already familiar with a natural phenomenon that simultaneously exhibits the features of both unity and diversity. This is the phenomenon of conscious awareness. We go on to show how the Vedic literature presents a unified nonmechanistic explanation of the phenomenal universe based on the concept of universal consciousness.

6.1 Statistical Laws and Their Role in Modern Physics

In this section we will examine how the concept of chance is employed in mechanistic theories. Such theories are normally formulated in the mathematical language of physics, and they involve many complicated technical details. Yet the basic concepts of chance and natural law in current physical theories readily lend themselves to illustration by simple examples. We will therefore briefly contemplate a few such examples and then draw some general conclusions about universal mechanistic theories.

Since we are interested in universal theories, we will want to consider how the concept of chance is to be understood in the setting of the universe as a whole. We will therefore introduce a simple model "universe" that can be used for posing questions about the nature of chance. Figure 1 depicts this model. The model consists of a box with a window that always displays either a figure 0 or a figure 1. The nature of this box is that during each consecutive second the figure in the window may either remain unchanged or else change exactly once at the beginning of that second. We can thus describe the history of the model universe by a string of zeros and ones representing the successive figures appearing in the window during successive seconds. Figure 2 depicts a sample history.

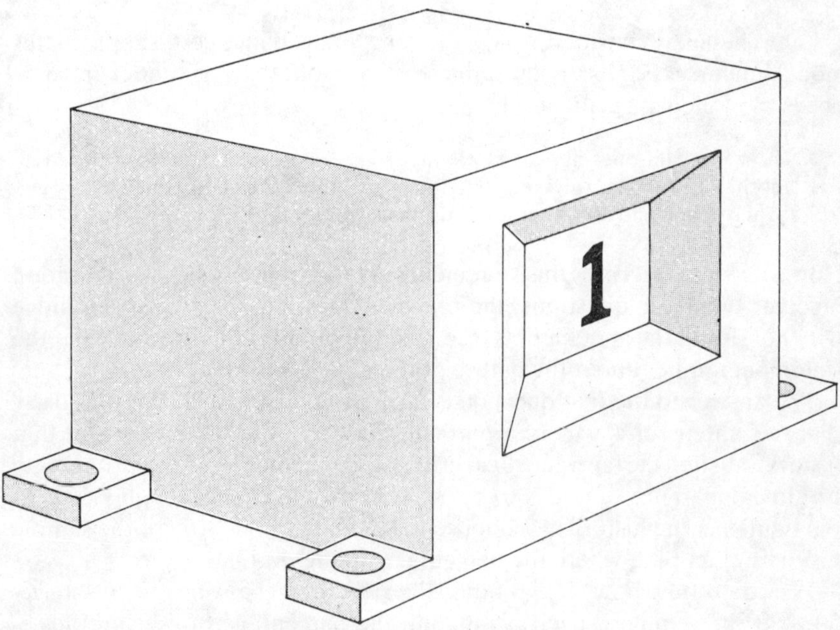

Figure 1. This device displays a figure of zero or one that can change from second to second. We shall regard it as a model "universe" and use it to illustrate the concepts of random events and universal statistical laws.

```
1100101001110110000100111110110100111011001001011001011010
0000001110101000101110110011110001011000100011000000111010
1110011000100010111001110000100100100010110111110100011010
1110111110001000110000001010011010011110110001001111001010
0111001010011100011010100011010111111100110101001100011100
1010011101100011100110010010111011001001011001011010000011
0010100100110001010101111000011100111001011001010101011001
1000001101000001110010101010000110001011111101110011100001
0011100000011111111001010011011111010001101011101111100010
0011000010100000111011101011111110011100100000111001000000
0111010001010100010011111001001001111100011101010111010001
0110000100101110000101100010111010011100110111000111101000
1011101000110001100111001010010011001111101000110101110111
1100010001100001010000011101110101111111101101111110000111
0011101011100000101100101010010101101011100000110001110000
1001011101001100010010100101111000110000011101000111000100
0000010110010101001010111111011011001000001000011001
```

Figure 2. A history of the model universe spanning a total of 979 seconds.

Let us begin by considering how the concept of chance could apply to this model universe. For example, suppose we are told that the model universe obeys the following statistical law:

> The zeros and ones appear randomly in the window, independently of one another. During any given second the probability is 50% that the window will display a one and 50% that it will display a zero.

How are we to interpret this statement? As we shall see, its interpretation involves two basic questions: the practical question of how we can judge whether or not the statement is true, and the broader question of what the statement implies about the nature of the model universe.

The answer to the first question is fairly straightforward. We would say that the statement is true of a particular history of ones and zeros if that history satisfied certain statistical criteria. For example, if the probability for the appearance of one is to be 50%, we would expect roughly 50% of the figures in the historical sequence to be ones. This is true of the sample history in Figure 2, where the percentage of ones is 49.4%.

We could not, however, require the percentage of ones to be *exactly* 50%. If the sequence itself is random, the percentage of ones in the sequence must also be random, and so we would not expect it to take on some exact value. But if the percentage of ones were substantially different from

50%, we could not agree that these ones were appearing in the window with a probability of 50%.

In practice it would never be possible for a statistical analyst to say definitely that a given history does or does not satisfy our statistical law. All he could do would be to determine a degree of confidence in the truth or falsity of the law as it applied to a particular sequence of ones and zeros. For example, our sample history is 979 digits long. For a sequence of this length to satisfy the law, we would expect the percentage of ones to fall between 46.8% and 53.2%. (These are the "95% confidence limits.") If the percentage did not fall within these limits, we could take this failure as an indication that the sequence did not satisfy the law, but we could not assert this as a definite conclusion.

We have seen that the sample history consists of approximately 50% ones. This observation agrees with the hypothesis that this sequence satisfies our statistical law, but it is not sufficient to establish this, for there are other criteria such a sequence must meet. In general, if a sequence is to be considered random or disorderly, we would not expect any particular pattern to appear within the sequence with unusual prominence. This means that for each positive number n, all of the 2^n subsequences of length n should appear in our sequence with nearly equal frequencies.

For example, if the sample history were indeed a random sequence, we would expect each of the subsequences 00, 01, 10, and 11 to appear with a frequency of roughly 25%. In fact, the frequencies of these subsequences are 25.6%, 24.7%, 25.4%, and 24.3% respectively, and these frequencies conform with the hypothesis that our history satisfies the statistical law. As before, we cannot expect the frequency to take on an exact value. We can at most determine a degree of confidence in our statistical hypothesis by measuring how closely the observed frequencies of various subsequences match their expected values.[2]

So in practical terms we can interpret our statistical law as an approximate statement about the relative frequency of various patterns of ones and zeros within a larger sequence of ones and zeros. If statistical laws were never attributed a deeper meaning than this, the concepts of randomness and statistical law might seem of little interest. However, because of an additional interpretation commonly given them, these concepts are actually of great significance in modern science, and particularly the science of physics. This interpretation becomes clear in the following reformulation of our statistical law, as understood from the viewpoint of modern physics:

> The box contains some apparatus that operates according to definite laws of cause and effect and that determines which figures will appear in the window.

> But in addition to its predictable, causal behavior, this apparatus periodically undergoes changes that have *no cause* and that cannot be predicted, even in principle. The presence of a one or a zero in the window during any given second is due to an inherently unpredictable, causeless event. Yet it is also true that ones and zeros are equally likely to appear, and thus we say that their probability of appearance is 50%.

In this formulation, our statistical law is no longer simply a statement about patterns of ones and zeros in a sequence. Rather, it now becomes an assertion about an active process occurring in nature—a process that involves absolutely causeless events. Such an unpredictable process is said to be a "random process" or a process of "absolute chance."

We can bring out the implications of this interpretation of chance by considering the following statement from a standard textbook of probability theory: "The fact that in a number of instances the relative frequency of random events in a large number of trials is almost constant compels us to presume the existence of certain laws, independent of the experimenter, that govern the course of these phenomena."[3] The author of this text is arguing that *because* a sequence exhibits certain regularities, we can conclude that it obeys a statistical law. If we interpret statistical laws as statements about the distribution of ones and zeros in a sequence, then this conclusion is certainly justifiable. But if we view "random events" as inherently causeless and unpredictable natural phenomena, we then find ourselves in the peculiar position of regarding lawlike regularities as evidence for the occurrence of events that, by definition, obey no law at all.

At first glance this second interpretation of the concept of randomness may seem quite strange, even self-contradictory. Nonetheless, since the development of quantum mechanics in the early decades of the twentieth century, this interpretation has occupied a central place in the modern scientific picture of nature. According to quantum mechanics, almost all natural phenomena involve "quantum jumps" that occur by absolute, or causeless, chance. At present many scientists regard the quantum theory as the fundamental basis for all explanations of natural phenomena. Consequently, the concept of absolute chance is now an integral part of the scientific world view.

The role absolute chance plays in the quantum theory can be illustrated by the classical example of radioactive decay. Let us suppose the model universe contains some radioactive atoms, a Geiger counter tube, and some appropriate electrical apparatus. As the atoms decay they trigger the Geiger counter and thereby influence the apparatus, which in turn controls the sequence of figures appearing in the window. We could arrange the apparatus so that during any given second a one would appear in the window if a radioactive decay occurred at the beginning of that second, and otherwise a zero would appear. By adjusting the amount of radioactive substance, we could control the average rate at which the counter was triggered and thus assure that the figure one would appear approximately 50% of the time.

If the apparatus were adjusted in this way, we would expect from observational experience that the sequence of ones and zeros generated by the model universe would satisfy our simple statistical law. Modern physicists interpret this predictable statistical behavior as evidence of an underlying process of causeless chance. Although they analyze the operation of the apparatus in terms of cause and effect, they regard the decay of the atoms themselves as fundamentally causeless, and the exact time at which any given atom decays as inherently unpredictable. This unpredictability implies that the sequence of ones and zeros generated by the model should follow no predictable pattern. Thus the hypothesis of causeless chance provides an explanation of the model's statistical behavior.

If we analyze the above example of a physical system, we can see that it involves a mixture of two basic elements: determinism and absolute chance. In this example we assumed that the electrical apparatus followed deterministic laws, whereas we attributed the decay of the radioactive atoms to absolute chance. In general, the theories of modern physics entail a combination of these two elements. The deterministic part of the theory is represented by mathematical equations describing causal interactions, and the element of chance is represented by statistical laws expressed in terms of probabilities.

When some scientists view natural phenomena in the actual universe as obeying such combined deterministic and statistical laws, they show a strong tendency to suppose that the phenomena are governed by these laws, and by nothing else. They are tempted to imagine that the laws correspond directly to a real underlying agency that produces the phenomena. Once they visualize such an agency, they naturally think of it as the enduring substantial cause, and they regard the phenomena themselves as ephemeral, insubstantial effects.

Thus the physicist Steven Weinberg refers to the theories of physics as "mathematical models of the universe to which at least the physicists give a higher degree of reality than they accord the ordinary world of sensation."[4] Following this line of thinking, some researchers are tempted to visualize ultimate mathematical laws that apply to all the phenomena of the universe and that represent the underlying basis of reality. Many scientists regard the discovery of such laws as the final goal of their quest to understand nature.

Up until now, of course, no one has formulated a mathematically consistent universal theory of this kind, and the partial attempts that have been made involve a formidable tangle of unresolved technical difficulties. Nonetheless, even the most sophisticated theories of modern physics entail statistical laws, and are firmly based on the concept of absolute chance. As we shall see, this simple fact constitutes a fatal flaw in the physicists' program of achieving a complete and unified understanding of nature. The concept of absolute chance is fundamentally fallacious, and any theory based on it must also be fallacious, regardless of how technically sophisticated it may be.

6.2 The Illusion of Absolute Chance

We can uncover the fallacy in the concept of absolute chance by examining the model universe more closely. If we do this we find that the laws of this model adequately describe the deterministic functioning of the electrical apparatus, and also the statistical properties of the sequence of radioactive decays. They do not, however, have anything to say about the details of this sequence. Of course, according to the theory of the model, this sequence cannot be expected to display any meaningful patterns, and thus it might seem pointless to inquire about these details. Nonetheless, for the sake of clarity we should consider the following questions: Can our theoretical description of the model universe really be considered complete or universal? In order for the description to be complete, wouldn't we need to incorporate into it a detailed description of the actual sequence of radioactive decays?

Considering these questions, we note that if we were to augment the theory in this way, then by no means could we consider the resulting enlarged theory unified. It would consist of a short list of basic laws followed by a very long list of data displaying no coherent pattern. Yet, if we did not include the exact sequence of radioactive decays, we would have to admit that the theory was incomplete in that it failed to account for this detailed information. Clearly, we could consider such a theory complete only if we adopted a standard of completeness that enabled us to ignore most of the detailed features of the very phenomena the theory was intended to describe.

Now, when we consider the concept of absolute chance, we see that it seems to provide just such a standard of completeness. The idea that a sequence of events is generated by causeless chance seems intuitively to imply that these events should be disorderly, chaotic, and meaningless. We would not expect one totally random sequence to be distinguishable in any significant way from any of the innumerable other random sequences having the same basic statistical properties. We would expect the details of the sequence to amount to nothing more than a display of pointless arbitrariness.

This leads naturally to the idea that one may consider a theoretical description of phenomena complete as long as it thoroughly accounts for the statistical properties of the phenomena. According to this idea, if the phenomena involve random sequences of events—in other words, sequences satisfying the statistical criteria for randomness—then these sequences must be products of causeless chance. As such, their detailed patterns must be meaningless and insignificant, and we can disregard them. Only the overall statistical features of the phenomena are worthy of theoretical description.

This method of defining the completeness of theories might seem satisfactory when applied to the example of radioactive decay. Certainly the observed patterns of atomic breakdown in radioactive substances seem completely chaotic. But let us look again at the sample history of the model universe depicted in Figure 2. As we have already indicated, this history satisfies many of the criteria for a random sequence that can be deduced from our simple statistical law. It also appears chaotic and disorderly. Yet if we examine it more closely, we find that it is actually a message expressed in binary code.

When we decipher this message it turns out, strangely enough, to consist of the following statement in English:

> The probability of repetition of terrestrial evolution is zero. The same holds for the possibility that if most life on earth were destroyed, the evolution would start anew from some few primitive survivors. That evolution would be most unlikely to give rise to new man-like beings.

What are we to make of this? Could it be that by some extremely improbable accident, the random process corresponding to our simple statistical law just happened to generate this particular sequence? Using the law, we can calculate the probability of this, and we obtain a percentage of .000 . . . (292 zeros) . . . 0001.

The answer, of course, is that we did not actually produce the sequence in Figure 2 by a random process. That a sequence of events obeys a statistical law does not imply that a process of chance governed by this law actually produced the sequence. In fact, the sequence in Figure 2 demonstrates that at least in some situations, the presence of a high degree of randomness in a sequence calls for a completely different interpretation. When we consider the method used to construct this sequence, we see that its apparent randomness results directly from the fact that it encodes a large amount of meaningful information.

We produced the sequence in Figure 2 by a technique from the field of communications engineering known as "data compression." In this field, engineers confront the problem of how to send as many messages as possible across a limited communications channel, such as a telephone line. They have therefore sought methods of encoding messages as sequences of symbols that are as short as possible but can still be readily decoded to reproduce the original message.

In 1948 Claude Shannon established some of the fundamental principles of communications engineering.[5] He showed that each message has a certain information content, which can be expressed as a number of "bits," or binary ones and zeros. If a message contains *N* bits of information, we can encode it as a sequence of *N* or more ones and zeros, but we cannot encode it as a shorter sequence without losing part of the message. When we encode the message as a sequence of almost exactly *N* ones and zeros, its density of information is maximal, and each zero or one carries essential information.

Shannon showed that when encoded in the shortest possible sequence, a message appears to be completely random. The basic reason for this is that if patterns of ones and zeros are to be used in the most efficient possible way to encode information, all possible patterns must be used with roughly equal frequency. Thus the criteria for maximal information density and maximal randomness turn out to be the same.

Figures 3 and 4 show the effects of information compression for the message encoded in Figure 2. Figure 3 illustrates some of the characteristics of an uncompressed binary encoding of this message. The bar graph in this figure represents the frequency distribution for five-bit subsequences, each representing a letter of the English text. This distribution clearly does not follow the bell-shaped curve we would expect for a random sequence. However, when we encode the message in compressed form, as in Figure 2, we obtain the distribution shown in Figure 4. Here we see that simply by encoding the message in a more succinct form, we have greatly increased its apparent randomness.[6]

We can conclude that it is not justifiable to insist upon absolute chance as an explanation of apparent randomness in nature. If a sequence of events exhibits the statistical properties of randomness, this may simply mean that it contains a large amount of significant information. Also, if a sequence exhibits a combination of random features and systematic features, as with our text before compression, this may reflect the presence of significant information in a less concentrated form. In either case, we would clearly be mistaken to disregard the details of the sequence, thinking them simply products of chance.

In summary, we recall that a sequence of events is generally called random if it satisfies the statistical criterion that all possible subsequences should appear with roughly equal frequency. Many scientists have interpreted the occurrence of random sequences in nature as evidence for the existence of a natural process of causeless chance. Yet we have observed that the criterion for maximal information content in a sequence is the same as the criterion for randomness, and a sequence containing a high density of meaningful information certainly cannot be attributed to absolute chance. Since the idea of inferring lawlessness from lawful behavior seems contradictory anyway, we can only conclude that the concept of absolute chance is fallacious. This concept simply serves to give us an illusion of understanding when we deal with phenomena that we can describe but cannot explain.

6.3 Chance and Evolution

At this point let us consider how these observations bear on the actual universe in which we live. Could it be that while focusing on ultimate mechanistic laws, modern scientists are disregarding some significant information encoded in the phenomena of nature? In fact, this is the implication of the sequence in Figure 2 when we decode it and perceive its higher meaning—namely, as a statement about human evolution. The source of this statement is the prominent evolutionist Theodosius Dobzhansky,[7] who here expresses a view held widely among researchers in the life sciences. Dobzhansky is visualizing the origin of human life in the context of an underlying physical theory that involves combined processes of causation and chance. He is expressing the conviction that although such processes have generated the highly complex forms of human life we know, they nonetheless have a zero probability of doing so.

No one has shown, of course, that the universe as a whole, or even the small part of it we inhabit, really does obey some fundamental mechanistic laws. Yet suppose, for the sake of argument, that it does. In effect, Dobzhansky is asserting that from the viewpoint of this ultimate universal theory, the detailed information specifying the nature and history of human life is simply random noise.[8] The theory will be able to describe only broad statistical features of this information, and will have to dismiss its essential content as the vagaries of causeless chance.

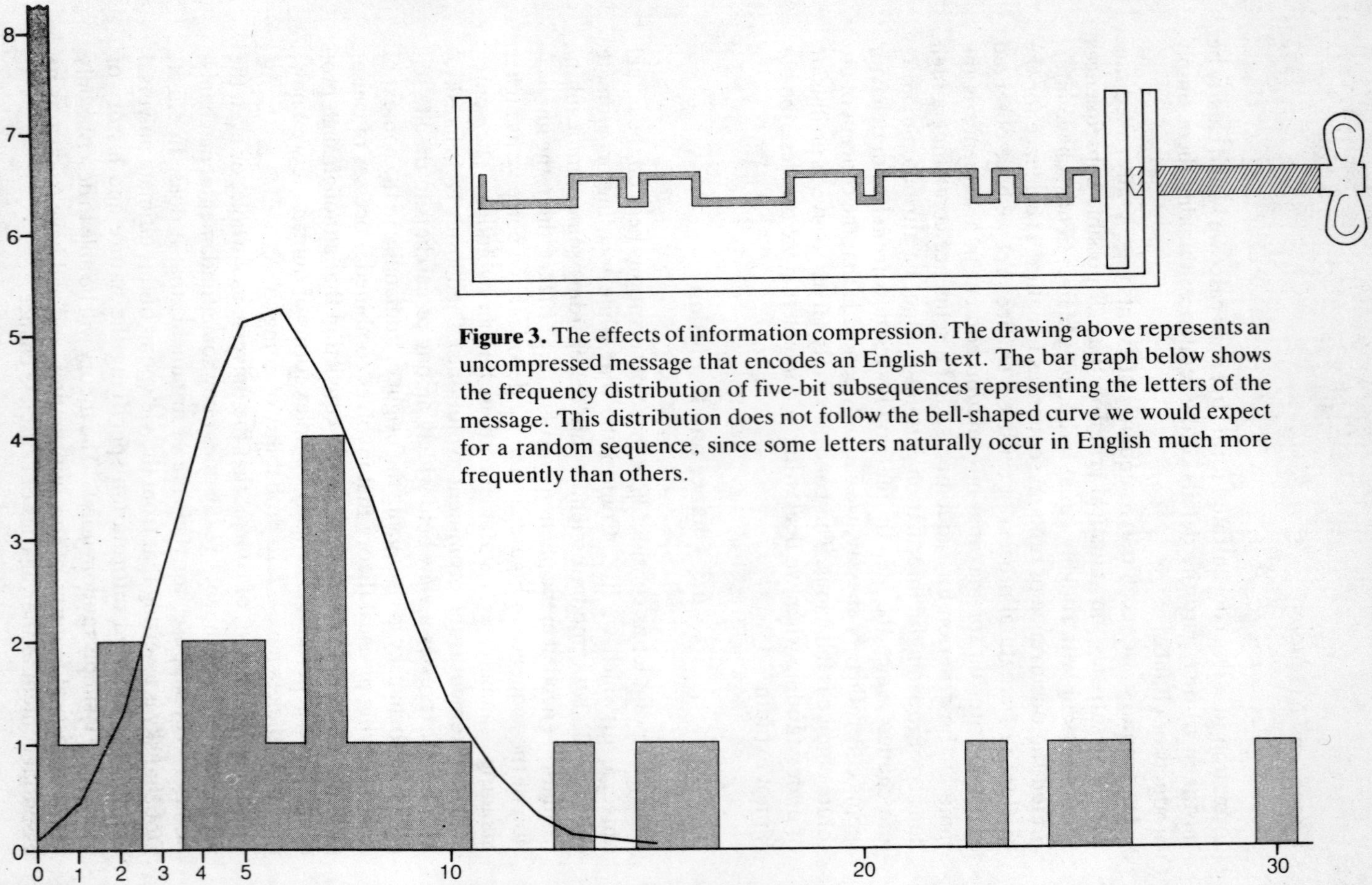

Figure 3. The effects of information compression. The drawing above represents an uncompressed message that encodes an English text. The bar graph below shows the frequency distribution of five-bit subsequences representing the letters of the message. This distribution does not follow the bell-shaped curve we would expect for a random sequence, since some letters naturally occur in English much more frequently than others.

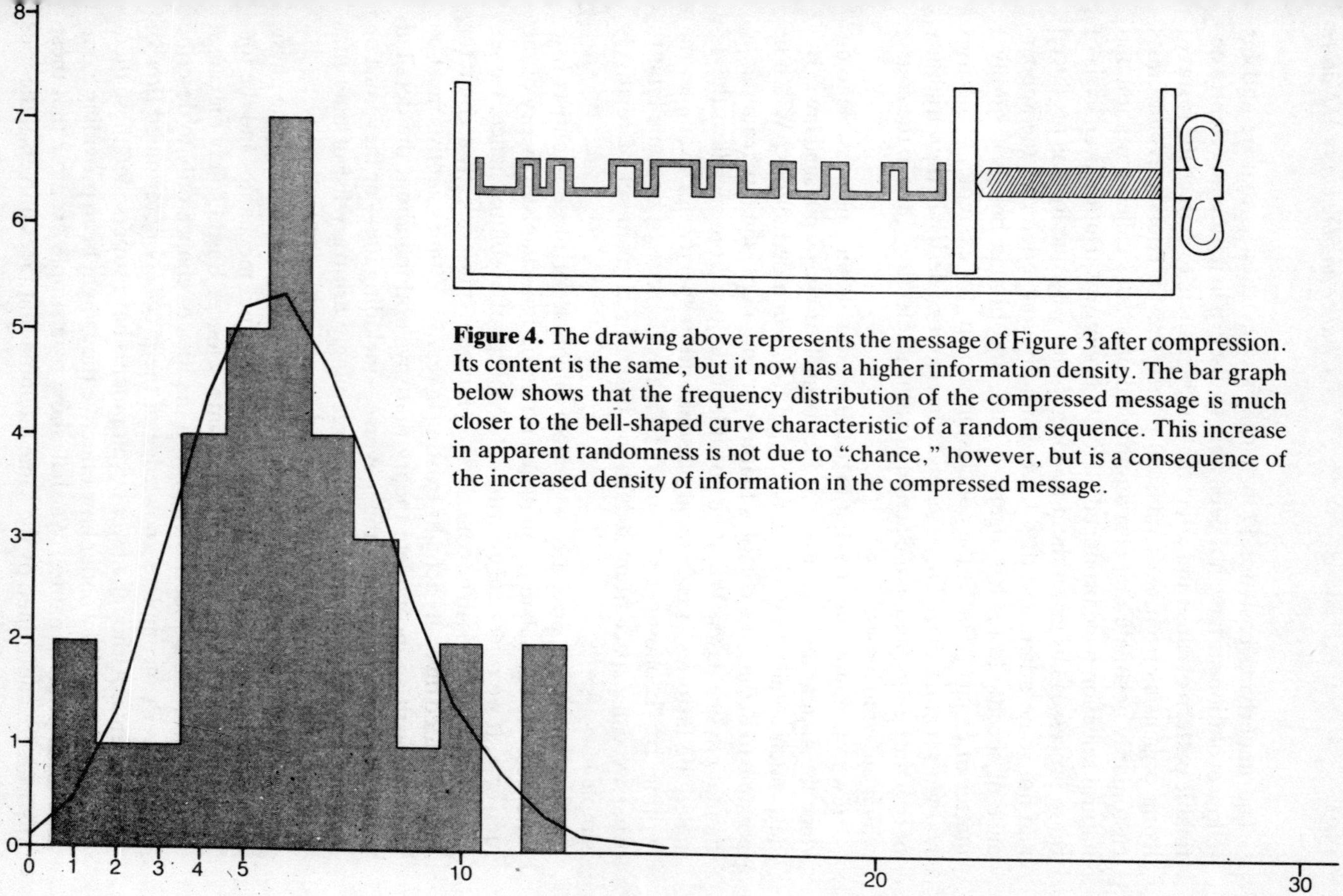

Figure 4. The drawing above represents the message of Figure 3 after compression. Its content is the same, but it now has a higher information density. The bar graph below shows that the frequency distribution of the compressed message is much closer to the bell-shaped curve characteristic of a random sequence. This increase in apparent randomness is not due to "chance," however, but is a consequence of the increased density of information in the compressed message.

The underlying basis for Dobzhansky's conviction is that he and his fellow evolutionists have not been able to discern in nature any clearly definable pattern of cause and effect that enables them to deduce the forms of living organisms from basic physical principles. Of course, evolutionists customarily postulate that certain physical processes called mutation and natural selection have produced all living organisms. But their analysis of these processes has given them no insight into why one form is produced and not some other, and they have generally concluded that the appearance of specific forms like tigers, horses, and human beings is simply a matter of chance. This is the conclusion shown, for example, by Charles Darwin's remark that "There seems to be no more design in the variability of organic beings, and in the action of natural selection, than in the course which the wind blows."[9]

Now, one might propose that in the future it will become possible to deduce the appearance of particular life forms from basic physical laws. But how much detail can we hope to obtain from such deductions? Will it be possible to deduce the complex features of human personality from fundamental physical laws? Will it be possible to deduce from such laws the detailed life histories of individual persons and to specify, for example, the writings of Theodosius Dobzhansky? Clearly there must be some limit to what we can expect from deductions based on a fixed set of relatively simple laws.

These questions pose a considerable dilemma for those scientists who would like to formulate a complete and unified mechanistic theory of the universe. If we reject the unjustifiable concept of absolute chance, we see that a theory—if it is to be considered complete—must directly account for the unlimited diversity actually existing in reality. Either scientists must be satisfied with an incomplete theory that says nothing about the detailed features of many aspects of the universe—including life—or they must be willing to append to their theory a seemingly arbitrary list of data that describes these features at the cost of destroying the theory's unity.

We can further understand this dilemma by briefly considering the physical theories studied before the advent of quantum mechanics and the formal introduction of absolute chance into science. Based solely on causal interactions, these theories employed the idea of chance only to describe an observer's incomplete knowledge of the precisely determined flow of actual events. Although newer developments have superseded these theories, one might still wonder how effective they might be in providing a unified description of nature. We shall show by a simple example that these theories are confronted by the same dilemma that faces universal theories based on statistical laws.

Figure 5 depicts a rectangular array of evenly spaced spheres. Let us suppose that the positions of these spheres are fixed and that the array extends in all directions without limit. We shall consider the behavior of a single sphere that moves according to the laws of classical physics and rebounds elastically off the other spheres. We can imagine that once we set the single sphere into motion, it will continue to follow a zigzag path through the fixed array of spheres.

Figure 5 illustrates how a slight variation in the direction of the moving sphere can be greatly magnified when it bounces against one of the fixed spheres. On successive bounces this variation will increase more and more,

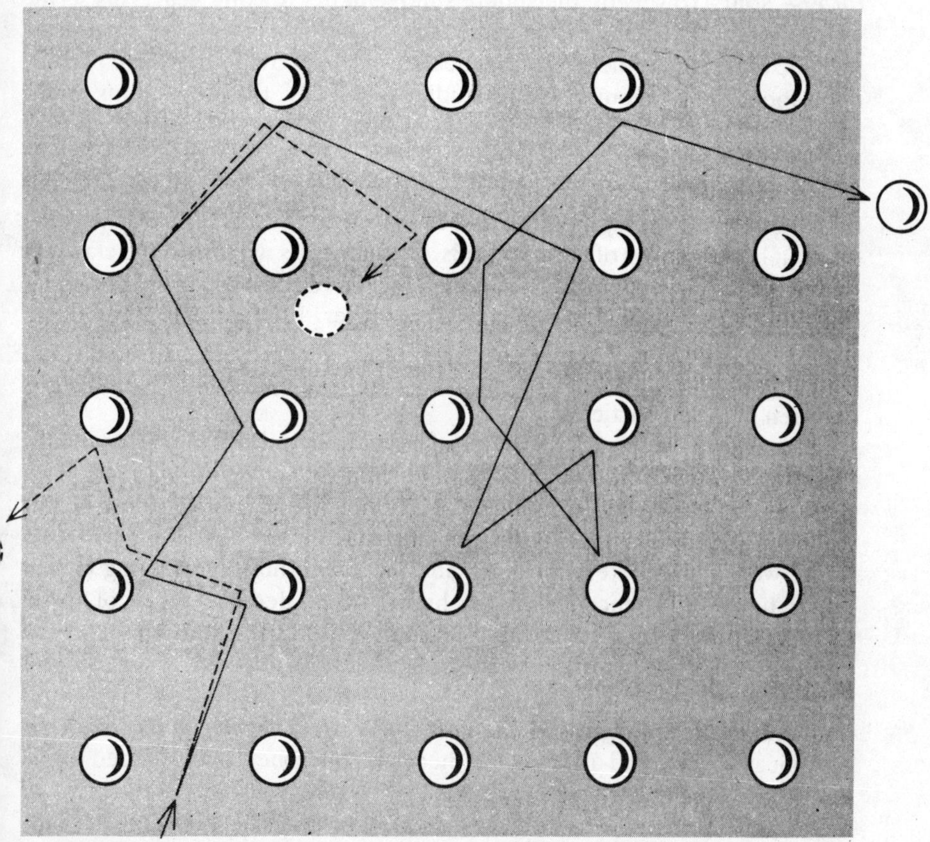

Figure 5. An example illustrating a simple deterministic theory. The moving sphere bounces elastically against fixed spheres in an infinite rectangular array. A slight variation in the direction of the moving sphere is quickly amplified into a large change in the sphere's path.

and we would therefore have to know the sphere's initial direction of motion with great accuracy to predict its path correctly for any length of time. For example, suppose the moving sphere is going sixty miles per hour, and the dimensions of the spheres are as shown in the figure. To predict the moving sphere's path from bounce to bounce for one hour, we would have to know its original direction of motion (in degrees) with an accuracy of roughly two million decimal places.[10] We can estimate that a number with this many decimal digits would take a full 714 pages to write down.

In effect, the number representing the initial direction of the sphere constitutes a script specifying in advance the detailed movements of the sphere for one hour. To specify the sphere's movements for one year, this script would have to be expanded to more than six million pages. We can therefore see that this simple deterministic theory can provide complete predictions about the phenomena being studied—namely, the movements of the sphere—only if a detailed description of what will actually happen is first built into the theory.

We can generalize the example of the bouncing sphere by allowing all the spheres to move simultaneously and to interact not merely by elastic collision but by force laws of various kinds. By doing this we obtain the classical Newtonian theory of nature mentioned by Pierre Simon de Laplace in the quotation cited at the beginning of this chapter. Laplace and many other scientists of his time wished to account for all phenomena by this theory, which was based entirely on simple laws of attraction and repulsion between material particles.

Let us therefore consider what this theory implies about the origin of life. Although it is more complicated than our simple example, this theory has some of the same characteristics. To account for life as we know it, the theory would have to incorporate billions of numbers describing the state of the world at some earlier time, and the entire history of living beings would have to be encoded in the higher-order decimal digits of those numbers.[11] Some of these decimal digits would encode the blueprints for a future rhinoceros, and others would encode the life history of a particular human being.

These digits would encode the facts of universal history in an extremely complicated way, and as far as the theory is concerned this encoded information would be completely arbitrary. This might tempt an adherent of the theory to abandon the idea of strict determinism and say—perhaps covertly—that the encoded information must have arisen by absolute chance (see note 8). Yet we have seen that this is a misleading idea, and it certainly has no place in a theory based solely on causal interactions. All we can realistically say in the context of this theory is that the facts of universal history simply are what they are. The theory can describe them only if a detailed script is initially added to it.

We can conclude that the prospects for a simple, universal mechanistic theory are not good. Once we eliminate the unsound and misleading idea of absolute chance, we are confronted with the problem of accounting for an almost unlimited amount of detailed information with a finite system of formulas. Some of this information may seem meaningless and chaotic, but a substantial part of it is involved with the phenomena of life, and this part includes the life histories of all scientific theorists. We must regard a theory that neglects most of this information as only a partial description of some features of the universe. Conversely, a theory that takes large amounts of this information into account must be filled with elaborate detail, and it can hardly be considered simple or unified.

6.4 The Paradox of Unity and Diversity

It seems that on the platform of finite mathematical description, the ideal of unity is incompatible with the diversity of the real world. To account for diversity, a mechanistic theory has to contain a large amount of irreducible, detailed information. This is certainly true of diversity that we might consider unimportant, such as the particular pattern of waves on the surface of the ocean, or the swirling patterns of leaves blowing in the wind. It is also true of patterns of diversity to which we tend to attach more significance, such as the complex bodily designs of living organisms, or the productions of advanced human culture.

There is always the hope that one may be able to reduce the apparent complexity of a pattern by discovering a simple underlying law that can be used to compute the pattern. The discovery of such laws has been the goal of physics since the days of Galileo and Newton, and such discoveries can be viewed as instances of data compression, in which large masses of raw data are represented by codes consisting of a few formulas and some initial and boundary conditions. Yet we have seen in this chapter and in Chapter 5 that we cannot expect the total information describing the real world to be unlimitedly compressible. We have every reason to suppose that the information describing complex phenomena—such as the phenomena of life—can be compressed only to a certain degree, leaving a large residue of information that cannot be represented in simpler terms.

If we examine the concepts of unity and diversity, we can see that in modern science unity has figured as an underlying philosophical goal, whereas diversity is an undeniable, observable feature of the world. And so we might conclude that the goal of finding unity is a mere chimera—and simply resign ourselves to accepting that the world contains a large amount of incomprehensible complexity that can be described but not explained. Unfortunately, this conclusion would bar us from ever understanding the most important features of life, and of human life in particular.

Here we shall set aside the mechanistic paradigm of modern science and pursue a different approach to the problem of finding a unified cause underlying the phenomena of nature. Our starting point is the observation that we are already familiar with a phenomenon that simultaneously exhibits the features of both unity and diversity. This is the phenomenon of conscious awareness.

Consider what happens when we look out through a window and observe a distant scene. We are simultaneously aware of distinct elements of the scene—such as buildings, trees, and clouds—and we are also aware of our accompanying thoughts and feelings. It is true that our awareness of the details of the scene may be quite imperfect. (Certainly our memory is imperfect, for if we are asked to describe the scene after seeing it, we may be able to give only a very incomplete and distorted account.) Nonetheless, it must be admitted that while we are observing the scene, our conscious awareness does *simultaneously* encompass many separate features.

It may be argued that the eye scans quickly from one part of the scene to another, and that the apparent unity of the picture we perceive is simply due to the rapid blending together of numerous distinct picture elements. However, it is just as hard to account for the unified conscious perception of events in a temporal sequence as it is to account for the simultaneous perception of different parts of a picture.

A photograph of the scene consists of many distinct colored grains that are not tied together in a unified way. The sequence of electrical pulses emerging from a television camera may represent the scene as a temporal pattern, but these pulses are also not unified. If the information representing the scene is processed by a computer, it can be transformed within the computer's memory into a variety of different forms, and these can succeed one another at a rapid rate. Yet neither these representations nor their pattern of succession in time will ever exhibit real unity.[12] As we have observed, information can be compressed only to a certain degree, and the residue of incompressible information represents intractable diversity that cannot be treated mechanistically in a unified way.

It is evident that our conscious awareness possesses features of simultaneous unity and diversity that are paradoxical from the mechanistic point of view. We have already observed in Part I that consciousness is a feature of reality that cannot be explained in mechanistic terms. There we introduced a nonmechanistic understanding of consciousness based on the *Bhagavad-gītā* and other texts from the Vedic literature of India. Here we would like to introduce another element of the world view of the *Bhagavad-gītā*. As we shall see, the *Bhagavad-gītā* does provide a description of how the variegated phenomena of the universe arise from a single unified source. This is done by introducing the nonmechanistic concept of universal consciousness.

According to the *Bhagavad-gītā,* conscious personality is the irreducible basis of reality. The ultimate source of all phenomena is understood to be a single Supreme Personality, who is known by many personal names such as Kṛṣṇa, Mādhava, and Hṛṣīkeśa. This primordial person is fully endowed with consciousness, senses, knowledge, will, and all other personal features. According to the *Bhagavad-gītā,* all these attributes are absolute and transcendental to matter. It is not possible to reduce them to the mathematically describable interaction of some simple entities that can be represented by sets of numbers. Rather, all the variegated phenomena of the universe, including the phenomenon of life, are manifestations of the energy of the Supreme Person, and they can be fully understood only in relation to this original source.

We should stress immediately that the Supreme Person, as portrayed in the *Bhagavad-gītā,* can be neither investigated nor adequately understood by empirical research based on ordinary sense data and conducted within the framework of mechanistic thought. We do not maintain that the empirical arguments presented in this chapter and in Chapter 5 *prove* the existence of such a transcendental being. Rather, these arguments disclose some insurmountable barriers blocking the path of conventional scientific investigation, and they give some hints as to what may lie beyond.

These arguments show that the forms of living beings and the patterns of human culture are inexplicable from the mechanistic point of view. They also suggest that the information for these highly complex forms and patterns is just as much a part of reality as the information for the simple natural laws studied by physicists. Now, if these complex patterns are indeed manifestations of a single, unified whole, what can we say about the nature of that whole? Such a mechanistically impossible entity would constitute an absolute, unified source of irreducible information pertaining to life and personality. This at least suggests that the world has been generated by a supreme intelligent being.

It is therefore interesting to consider the idea that a universal conscious being may constitute the unified foundation of reality. To elucidate this idea, we shall briefly discuss the characteristics of the Supreme Person, as understood in the Vedic literature. We shall begin by considering the first *śloka* of the *Īśopaniṣad.*

oṁ pūrṇam adaḥ pūrṇam idaṁ
pūrṇāt pūrṇam udacyate
pūrṇasya pūrṇam ādāya
pūrṇam evāvaśiṣyate

"The Personality of Godhead is perfect and complete, and because He is completely perfect, all emanations from Him, such as this phenomenal world, are perfectly equipped as complete wholes. Whatever is produced of the complete whole is also complete in itself. Because He is the complete whole, even though so many complete units emanate from Him, He remains the complete balance."[13]

This conception of completeness is reminiscent of certain ideas in the mathematical theory of sets, wherein we find that one infinite set can be taken away from another infinite set without depleting it. For example, if we take the set of all odd integers away from the set of all integers, we obtain the set of even integers. If these are then divided by two, we are left once again with the set of all integers.

The theory of infinite sets can also be used to illustrate, in an approximate way, the idea of an entity that is simultaneously differentiated and unified. We can regard a finite set of, say, one hundred points as essentially disunited, since any part of it has fewer points than the whole and is therefore different from the whole. In this sense, the only unified finite set is the set consisting of exactly one point. In contrast to this, consider a continuous line one unit in length. If we select any small segment of this line, no matter how short, then the entire line can be obtained by expanding this segment. Thus, the line has unity in the sense that it is equivalent to its parts. If we consider the reason for this, we can see that it depends on the fact that the line has infinitely many parts.

Although this is a crude example, it will serve as a metaphor to illustrate the difference between the Supreme Person and the hypothetical physical processes depicted in mechanistic theories. A mechanistic theory based on a finite system of mathematical expressions can be truly unified only if it can be reduced to one symbol—a single binary digit of "0" or "1." Of course, a theory that described the world in this way would say nothing at all, and theorists have had to settle for the goal of seeking the simplest possible theory that can adequately describe nature. Unfortunately, we have seen that the simplest adequate theory must be almost unlimitedly complex.

It follows that the fundamental basis of nature could possess no unity if it truly could be described by a mechanistic theory. In contrast, the Supreme Person is understood in the Vedic literature to be a complete unit, for even though He possesses unlimited variegated features, He is nondifferent from His parts. This is indicated by the following description of Kṛṣṇa from the *Brahma-saṁhitā*.

> *eko 'py asau racayituṁ jagad-aṇḍa-koṭiṁ*
> *yac-chaktir asti jagad-aṇḍa-cayā yad-antaḥ*
> *aṇḍāntara-stha-paramāṇu-cayāntara-sthaṁ*
> *govindam ādi-puruṣaṁ tam ahaṁ bhajāmi*

"He is an undifferentiated entity, in that there is no distinction between the potency and the possessor thereof. In His work of creation of millions of worlds, His potency remains inseparable. All the universes exist in Him, and He is present in His fullness in every one of the atoms that are scattered through the universe, at one and the same time. Such is the primeval Lord whom I adore."[14]

These characteristics of Kṛṣṇa are dimly reflected in our example of the line, but there is a significant difference. The equivalence of the line to its parts depends on an externally supplied operation of expansion, and thus the unity of the line exists only in the mind of an observer (as does the line itself, for it is only an abstraction). In contrast, the identity of Kṛṣṇa with His parts is inherent in the reality of Kṛṣṇa Himself, and therefore His unity is natural and complete. We cannot, of course, conceive of this in terms of mathematical examples, but we may obtain some inkling of what it means by considering the idea of universal consciousness.

We should emphasize the distinction between universal and individual consciousness. It is stated in the Vedic literature that just as a drop of salt water is qualitatively the same as the ocean, so the consciousness of the individual person is qualitatively the same as the universal consciousness of Kṛṣṇa. However, there must be a tremendous quantitative difference, for what person can honestly say that he is conscious of the entire universe and whatever lies beyond?

Nonetheless, some philosophers and scientists have declared that individual and universal consciousness are one and the same. One notable scientist who has come to this conclusion is the physicist Erwin Schrödinger, who said that "I—I in the widest meaning of the word . . . —am the person, if any, who controls the 'motion of the atoms' according to the Laws of Nature."[15] Schrödinger believed that matter behaves strictly in accordance with the "Laws of Nature," and he reconciled this with his perception of himself as an active conscious being by identifying himself with the universal consciousness underlying all phenomena. He supported his assertion by saying that according to the *Upaniṣads,* "the personal self equals the omnipresent, all-comprehending eternal self."[16] We note, however, that while the *Upaniṣads* and other Vedic literatures do assert the qualitative equality of the supreme conscious being and the individual conscious selves, they do not maintain that they are identical.[17]

Since Schrödinger and others have found the relationship between the Supreme Person and the laws of nature to be a source of perplexity, let us consider this relationship in greater detail. As we have indicated, the philosophy of the *Bhagavad-gītā* holds that the final cause underlying all phenomena is the Supreme Person, Kṛṣṇa. According to the *Bhagavad-gītā,* the matter and energy studied in modern physics originally emanate from Kṛṣṇa, and their actions and transformations are completely determined by His will. All phenomena are under direct conscious control, but since the consciousness of Kṛṣṇa is unlimited, only an infinitesimal fraction of His attention is required to run the material universe.

At first glance, this might seem to be incompatible with our knowledge of physics. Some phenomena of nature do appear to follow rigid, deterministic laws, and this might seem to rule out the possibility that they are under direct conscious control. However, there is no real contradiction here. From a mechanistic viewpoint, the actions of an intelligent being must appear as patterns in the phenomena of nature. Just as a human being can create architectural designs exhibiting simple patterns, so the Supreme Person can easily impose simple patterns on the behavior of matter in the universe.

Furthermore, on the basis of our knowledge of physics, we cannot rule out the appearance of highly complex patterns reflecting the willful exercise of higher intelligence. Such patterns might exhibit complex regularities representing the execution of higher-order laws, or they might correspond to unique and seemingly capricious displays of free will. As we have pointed out in Chapters 3 and 5, scientists actually know very little about the laws of nature, and they have found it very difficult to apply the known laws to complex phenomena. Our present knowledge is certainly compatible with the idea that nature is directed by higher intelligence.

Here the objection might be raised that if all the phenomena of the universe are arising from the will of a supremely intelligent being, then why do so many of these phenomena appear chaotic and meaningless? Part of the answer to this question is that meaningful patterns may appear random if they contain a high density of information. We have seen that such complex patterns tend to obey certain statistical laws simply as a consequence of their large information content. Thus a complex, seemingly random pattern in nature may actually be meaningful, even though we do not understand it. Another part of the answer is that meaningless patterns can easily be generated by the transformation of meaningful patterns. This is illustrated by the fact that many meaningful conversations, when heard simultaneously in a crowded room, merge together into a meaningless din. Such meaningless patterns will inherit the statistical properties of their meaningful sources, and will appear as undecipherable "random noise."

These considerations enable us to understand how apparent meaninglessness and chaos can arise in nature, but they tell us nothing about the definition of meaning itself. Thus far, no one has been able to give a satisfactory definition of meaning or purpose within the framework of the mechanistic world view. However, such a definition is provided by the *Bhagavad-gītā.* As we shall see, the ultimate meaning of the universe can be understood by first understanding the nature of the individual conscious beings, and the nature of their relationships with both material nature and the Supreme Person. We will discuss these matters step-by-step in the chapters that follow.

Notes

1. Bell, *Men of Mathematics,* p. 172.
2. We should note that for large n, the number of possible subsequences, 2^n, becomes much larger than the length of our sequence, and so most of these subsequences will not appear at all. This means that when we deal with a finite amount of data, as we must in practice, we have no basis for saying definitely whether or not a sequence of events obeys a statistical law.

   Many different methods of formulating statistical laws have been studied, and here we have briefly introduced the most widely used of these, which is known as the method of relative frequency. For a detailed discussion of the most important methods of defining probabilities and statistical laws, see Fine, *Theories of Probability.* After an exhaustive analysis, Fine ascertains that none of these formulations is satisfactory, and he concludes that, "Conceivably, probability is not possible." (p. 248).
3. Gnedenko, *Theory of Probability,* p. 55.
4. Weinberg, "The Forces of Nature," p. 175.

5. Shannon, "A Mathematical Theory of Communication," p. 379.

6. This sequence was encoded using the method of Huffman, "A Method for the Construction of Minimum Redundancy Codes," p. 1098. As it stands the sequence is highly random, but since it still contains the redundancy caused by the repetition of words such as "evolution," it is not fully so. Thus further compression and consequent randomization are possible.

7. Dobzhansky, "From Potentiality to Realization in Evolution," p. 20.

8. We should note that in his article Dobzhansky does not clearly define his conception of the ultimate principles underlying the phenomena of the universe. He says that evolution is not acausal, that it is not due to pure chance, and that it is due to many interacting causal chains. Yet he also says that evolution is not rigidly predestined. He says that the course of evolution was not programmed or encoded into the primordial universe, but that primordial matter had the potential for giving rise to all forms of life, including innumerable unrealized forms. He speaks of evolution in terms of probabilities and stresses that the probability of the development of life as we know it is zero.

   It appears that Dobzhansky is thinking in terms of causal interactions that include, at some point, some mysterious element of absolute chance. We can only conclude that his thinking is muddled. We suggest that the reason for this is that although he needs the concept of absolute chance in order to formulate his evolutionary world view, at the same time he recognizes the illogical nature of this concept and would like to avoid it. Thus, he is caught in a dilemma.

9. Darwin, *The Life and Letters of Charles Darwin,* p. 20.

10. Assume that the diameter of the spheres is ¼ inch. If there is an average movement of about 2 inches between bounces, then a slight variation in direction will be magnified by an average of at least 16 times per bounce. Consequently, an error in the nth decimal place in the direction of motion will begin to affect the first decimal place after about $.83n$ bounces.

11. We should note that the unpredictable behavior of the bouncing ball in our example is a common feature of many nonlinear dynamical models. See, for example, Ruelle, "Strange Attractors," pp. 126–137.

12. The relation between computer operations and self-referential consciousness can be further elucidated by the following thought experi-

ment. Suppose that a given computer, by virtue of its programming, is actually able to experience the consciousness of Joe Smith contemplating a sunny summer afternoon. We might imagine that the computer is able to do this by rapidly going through various loops representing Joe's awareness of his own awareness. The question is: What happens if the computer is slowed down, or even "single stepped" by the operator at a very slow rate? The pattern of computer operations remains the same, but is the same consciousness still there, stretched out over time? Is the same consciousness still "there" if the computer is made to execute one step per year? The absurdity of this is an indication that consciousness cannot be represented in terms of computer operations.

13. A.C. Bhaktivedanta Swami Prabhupāda, *Śrī Īśopaniṣad,* p. 1.
14. Bhakti Siddhanta Saraswati Thakur, *Shri Brahma Samhita,* pp. 99–100.
15. Schrödinger, *What Is Life? and Mind and Matter,* p. 93.
16. Schrödinger, p. 93.
17. This point is discussed in detail, with many references to the history of Indian philosophy, in Kavirāja, *Śrī Caitanya-caritāmṛta, Ādi-līlā,* Vol. 2, chap. 7.

Chapter 7

On Inspiration

In this chapter we will examine how human beings acquire knowledge in science, mathematics, and art. Our focus shall primarily be on the formation of ideas and hypotheses in science and mathematics, since the formal nature of these subjects tends to put the phenomena we are concerned with into particularly clear perspective. We will show that the phenomenon known as inspiration plays an essential part in acquiring knowledge in modern science and mathematics and the creative arts (such as music). We will argue that the phenomenon of inspiration cannot readily be explained by mechanistic models of nature consistent with present-day theories of physics and chemistry.

To give a positive alternative to these models, we will continue the project of outlining the nonmechanistic theoretical system of the *Bhagavad-gītā*. Thus far we have introduced the concept of the conscious self or *jīvātmā* as an entity distinct from the material body (Chapters 1 and 2), and we have also introduced the concept of the all-pervading superconscious being or *paramātmā*. The *Bhagavad-gītā* shows how the idea of the *paramātmā* can be used to construct a model of the interaction between the conscious self and the material body. As we shall see, this model accounts for the phenomenon of inspiration in a direct and striking way.

Modern scientists acquire knowledge, at least in principle, by what is called the hypothetico-deductive method. Using this method, they formulate hypotheses and then test them by experimental observation. Investigators consider hypotheses valid only insofar as they are consistent with the data obtained by observation, and they must in principle reject any hypothesis that disagrees with observation. Much analysis has been directed toward the deductive side of the hypothetico-deductive method, but the equally important process of hypothesis formation has been largely neglected. So we ask, "Where do hypotheses come from?"

It is clear that scientists cannot use any direct, step-by-step process to derive hypotheses from raw observational data. To deal with such data at all, they must already have some working hypothesis, for otherwise the data amount to nothing more than a bewildering array of symbols (or sights and sounds), which is no more meaningful than a table of random numbers. In this connection Albert Einstein once said, "It may be heuristically useful to keep in mind what one has observed. But on principle it is quite wrong to try grounding a theory on observable magnitudes alone. In reality the opposite happens. It is the theory which determines what we can observe."[1]

Pure mathematics contains an equivalent of the hypothetico-deductive method. In mathematics, instead of hypotheses there are proposed systems of mathematical reasoning intended to answer specific questions. And instead of the experimental testing of a hypothesis there is the step-by-step process of verifying that a particular proof, or line of mathematical reasoning, is correct. This verification process is straightforward and could in principle be carried out by a computer. However, there is no systematic, step-by-step method of generating mathematical proofs and systems of ideas, such as group theory or the theory of Lebesque integration.

If hypotheses in science and systems of reasoning in mathematics are not generated by any systematic procedure, then what is their source? We find that they almost universally arise within the mind of the investigator by sudden inspiration. The classic example is Archimedes' discovery of the principle of specific gravity. The Greek mathematician was faced with the task of determining whether a king's crown was solid gold without drilling any holes in it. After a long period of fruitless endeavor, he received the answer to the problem by sudden inspiration while taking a bath.

Such inspirations generally occur suddenly and unexpectedly to persons who had previously made some unsuccessful conscious effort to solve the problem in question. They usually occur when one is not consciously thinking about the problem, and they often indicate an entirely new way of looking at it—a way the investigator had never even considered during his conscious efforts to find a solution. Generally, an inspiration appears as a sudden awareness of the problem's solution, accompanied by the conviction that the solution is correct and final. One perceives the solution in its entirety, though it may be quite long and complicated when written out in full.

Inspiration plays a striking and essential role in the solution of difficult problems in science and mathematics. Generally, investigators can successfully tackle only routine problems by conscious endeavor alone. Significant advances in science almost always involve sudden inspiration, as the lives of great scientists and mathematicians amply attest. A typical example is the experience of the nineteenth century mathematician Karl Gauss. After trying unsuccessfully for years to prove a certain theorem about whole numbers, Gauss suddenly became aware of the solution. He described his experience as follows: "Finally, two days ago I succeeded . . . Like a sudden flash of lightning, the riddle happened to be solved. I myself cannot say what was the conducting thread which connected what I previously knew with what made my success possible."[2]

We can easily cite many similar examples of sudden inspiration. Here is another one, given by Henri Poincaré, a famous French mathematician of the late nineteenth century. After working for some time on certain problems in the theory of functions, Poincaré had occasion to go on a geological field trip, during which he set aside his mathematical work. While on the trip he received a sudden inspiration involving his researches, which he described as follows: "At the moment when I put my foot on the step the idea came to me, without anything in my former thoughts seeming to have paved the way for it, that the transformations I had used . . . were identical with those of non-Euclidean geometry."[3] Later on, after some fruitless work on an apparently unrelated question, he suddenly realized, "with just the same characteristics of brevity, suddenness, and immediate certainty,"[4] that this work could be combined with his previous inspiration to provide a significant advance in his research on the theory of functions. Then a third sudden inspiration provided him with the final argument he needed to complete that work.

Although inspirations generally occur after a considerable period of intense but unsuccessful effort to consciously solve a problem, this is not always the case. Here is an example from another field of endeavor. Wolfgang Mozart once described how he created his musical works: "When I feel well and in good humor, or when I am taking a drive or walking, . . . thoughts crowd into my mind as easily as you could wish. Whence and how do they come? *I do not know and I have nothing to do with it* . . . Once I have a theme, another melody comes, linking itself with the first one, in accordance with the needs of the composition as a whole . . . Then my soul is on fire with inspiration, if however nothing occurs to distract my attention. The work grows; I keep expanding it, conceiving it more and more clearly until I have the entire composition finished in my head, though it may be long . . . It does not come to me successively, with its various parts worked out in detail, as they will be later on, but it is in its entirety that my imagination lets me hear it."[5] (Italics added.)

From these instances we discover two significant features of the phenomenon of inspiration: first, its source lies beyond the subject's conscious perception; and second, it provides the subject with information unobtainable by any conscious effort. These features led Poincaré and his follower Hadamard to attribute inspiration to the action of an entity which Poincaré called the "subliminal self," and which he identified with the subconscious or unconscious self of the psychoanalysts. Poincaré made the following interesting observations about the subliminal self: "The subliminal self is in no way inferior to the conscious self; it is not purely automatic; it is capable of discernment; it has tact, delicacy; it knows how to choose, to divine. What do I say? It knows better how to divine than the conscious self, since it succeeds where that has failed. In a word, is not the subliminal self superior to the conscious self?"[6] Having raised this question, Poincaré then backs away from it: "Is this affirmative answer forced upon us by the facts I have just given? I confess that for my part, I should hate to accept it."[7] He then offers a mechanical explanation of how the subliminal self, viewed as an automaton, could account for the observed phenomena of inspiration.

7.1 The Mechanistic Explanation

Let us carefully examine the arguments for such a mechanical explanation of inspiration. This issue is of particular importance at the present time, because the prevailing materialistic philosophy of modern science holds that the mind is nothing more than a machine, and that all mental phenomena, including consciousness, are nothing more than the products of mechanical interactions. The mental machine is specifically taken to be the brain, and its basic functional elements are believed to be the nerve cells and possibly some systems of interacting macromolecules within these cells. Many modern scientists believe that all brain activity results simply from the interaction of these elements according to the known laws of physics.

No scientist has yet formulated an adequate explanation of the difference between a conscious and an unconscious machine, or even indicated how a machine could be conscious at all. In fact, investigators attempting to describe the self in mechanistic terms concentrate exclusively on the duplication of external behavior by mechanical means; they totally disregard the individual person's subjective experience of conscious self-awareness. (See Chapter 2.) This approach to the self is characteristic of modern behavioral psychology. It was formally set forth by the British mathematician Alan Turing, who argued that since whatever a human being can do a computer can imitate, a human being is merely a machine.

For the moment we will follow this behavioristic approach and simply consider the question of how the phenomenon of inspiration could be duplicated by a machine. Poincaré proposed that the subliminal self must put together many combinations of mathematical symbols by chance until at last it finds a combination satisfying the desire of the conscious mind for a certain kind of mathematical result. He proposed that the conscious mind would remain unaware of the many useless and illogical combinations running through the subconscious, but that it would immediately become aware of a satisfactory combination as soon as it was formed. He therefore proposed that the subliminal self must be able to form enormous numbers of combinations in a short time, and that these could be evaluated subconsciously as they were formed, in accordance with the criteria for a satisfactory solution determined by the conscious mind.

As a first step in evaluating this model, let us estimate the number of combinations of symbols that could be generated within the brain within a reasonable period of time. A very generous upper limit on this number is given by the figure 3.2×10^{46}. We obtain this figure by assuming that in each cubic Ångstrom unit of the brain, a separate combination is formed and evaluated once during each billionth of a second over a period of one hundred years. Although this figure is an enormous overestimate of what the brain could possibly do within the bounds of our present understanding of the laws of nature, it is still infinitesimal compared to the total number of possible combinations of symbols one would have to form to have any chance of randomly hitting a proof for a particular mathematical theorem of moderate difficulty.

If we attempt to elaborate a line of mathematical reasoning, we find that at each step there are many possible combinations of symbols we can write down, and thus we can think of a particular mathematical argument as a path through a tree possessing many successive levels of subdividing branches. This is illustrated in the figure below. The number of branches in such a tree grows exponentially with the number of successive choices, and the number of choices is roughly proportional to the length of the argument. Thus as the length of the argument increases, the number of branches will very quickly pass such limits as 10^{46} and 10^{100}. For example, suppose we are writing sentences in some symbolic language, and the rules of grammar for that language allow us an average of two choices for each

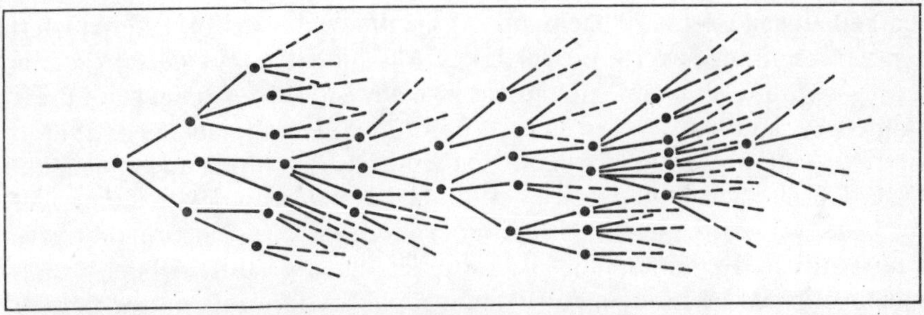

Figure 1. The relationship between different possible lines of mathematical reasoning can be represented by a tree. Each node represents a choice among various possibilities that restricts the further development of the argument.

successive symbol. Then there will be approximately 10^{100} grammatical sentences of 333 symbols in length.

Even a very brief mathematical argument will often expand to great length when written out in full, and many mathematical proofs require pages and pages of highly condensed exposition, in which many essential steps are left for the reader to fill in. Thus there is only an extremely remote chance that an appropriate argument would appear as a random combination in Poincaré's mechanical model of the process of inspiration. Clearly, the phenomenon of inspiration requires a process of choice capable of going more or less directly to the solution, without even considering the vast majority of possible combinations of arguments.

7.2 Some Striking Examples

The requirements that this process of choice must meet are strikingly illustrated by some further examples of mathematical inspiration. It is very often found that the solution to a difficult mathematical problem depends on the discovery of basic principles and underlying systems of mathematical relationships. Only when these principles and systems are understood does the problem take on a tractable form. Therefore difficult problems have often remained unsolved for many years, until mathematicians gradually developed various sophisticated ideas and methods of argument that made their solution possible. However, it is interesting to note that on some occasions sudden inspiration has completely circumvented this gradual process of development. There are several instances in which famous mathematicians have, without proof, stated mathematical results that later investigators proved only after elaborate systems of underlying relationships had gradually come to light. Here are two examples:

The first example concerns the zeta-function studied by the German mathematician Bernhard Riemann. At the time of his death, Riemann left a note describing several properties of this function that pertain to the theory of prime numbers. He did not give any proof for existence of these properties, and many years elapsed before mathematicians were able to find existence proofs for all but one of them. The remaining question is still unsettled, though an immense amount of labor has been devoted to it over the last seventy-five years. Of the properties of the zeta-function that *have* been verified, the mathematician Jacques Hadamard said, "All these complements could be brought to Riemann's publication only by the help of facts which were completely unknown in his time; and, for one of the properties enunciated by him, it is hardly conceivable how he can have found it without using some of these general principles, no mention of which is made in his paper."[8]

The work of the French mathematician Evariste Galois provides us with a case similar to Riemann's. Galois is famous for a paper, written hurriedly in sketchy form just before his death, that completely revolutionized the subject of algebra. However, the example we are considering here concerns a theorem Galois stated, without proof, in a letter to a friend. According to Hadamard this theorem could not even be understood in terms of the mathematical knowledge of that time; it became comprehensible only years later, after the discovery of certain basic principles. Hadamard remarks "(1) that Galois must have conceived these principles in some way; (2) that they must have been unconscious in his mind, since he makes no allusion to them, though they themselves represent a significant discovery."[9]

It would appear, then, that the process of choice underlying mathematical inspiration can make use of basic principles that are very elaborate and sophisticated and that are completely unknown to the conscious mind of the person involved. Some of the developments leading to the proof of Riemann's theorems are highly complex, requiring many pages (and even volumes) of highly abbreviated mathematical exposition. It is certainly hard to see how a mechanical process of trial and error, such as that described by Poincaré, could exploit such principles. Yet, if other, simpler solutions exist that avoid the use of such elaborate developments, they have remained unknown up to the present time, despite the extensive research devoted to these topics.

The process of choice underlying mathematical inspiration must also make use of selection criteria that are exceedingly subtle and hard to define. Mathematical work of high quality cannot be evaluated simply by the application of cut-and-dried rules of logic. Rather, its evaluation involves emotional sensibility and the appreciation of beauty, harmony, and other delicate aesthetic qualities. Of these criteria Poincaré said, "It is almost impossible to state them precisely; they are felt rather than formulated."[10] This is also true of the criteria by which we judge artistic creations, such as musical compositions. These criteria are very real but at the same time very difficult to define precisely. Yet evidently they were fully incorporated in that mysterious process which provided Mozart with sophisticated musical compositions without any particular effort on his part and, indeed, without any knowledge on his part of how it was all happening.

If the process underlying inspiration is not one of extensive trial and error, as Poincaré suggested, but rather one that depends mainly on direct choice, then we can explain it in terms of current mechanistic ideas only by positing the existence of a very powerful algorithm (a system of computational rules) built into the neural circuitry of the brain. However, it is not at all clear that we can satisfactorily explain inspiration by reference to such an algorithm. Here we will briefly discuss two major problems entailed by the brain-algorithm hypothesis.

(1) *Origins*. If mathematical, scientific, and artistic inspirations result from the workings of a neural algorithm, then how does the pattern of nerve connections embodying this algorithm arise? We know that the algorithm cannot be a simple one when we consider the complexity of the automatic theorem-proving algorithms that have been produced thus far by workers in the field of artificial intelligence.[11] These algorithms cannot even approach the performance of advanced human minds, and yet they are extremely elaborate. But if our hypothetical brain-algorithm is extremely complex, how did it come into being? It can hardly be accounted for by extensive random genetic mutation or recombination in a single generation, for then the problem of random choice among vast numbers of possible combinations would again arise. One would therefore have to suppose that only a few relatively probable genetic transformations separated the genotype of Mozart from those of his parents, who, though talented, did not possess comparable musical ability.

However, it is not the usual experience of those who work with algorithms that a few substitutions or recombinations of symbols can drastically improve an algorithm's performance or give it completely new capacities that would impress us as remarkable. Normally, if this were to happen with a particular algorithm, we would tend to suppose that it was a defective version of another algorithm originally designed to exhibit those capacities. This would imply that the algorithm for Mozart's unique musical abilities existed in a hidden form in the genes of his ancestors.

This brings us to the general problem of explaining the origin of human traits. According to the theory most widely accepted today, these traits were selected on the basis of the relative reproductive advantage they conferred on their possessors or their possessors' relatives. Most of the selection for our hypothetical hidden algorithms must have occurred in very early times, because of both the complexity of these algorithms and the fact that they often must be carried in a hidden form. It is now thought that human society, during most of its existence, was on the level of hunters and gatherers, at best. It is quite hard to see how, in such societies, persons like Mozart or Gauss would ever have had the opportunity to fully exhibit their unusual abilities. But if they didn't, then the winnowing process posited by the theory of evolution could not effectively select these abilities.

We are thus faced with a dilemma: It appears that it is as difficult to account for the origin of our hypothetical inspiration-generating algorithms as it is to account for the inspirations themselves.

(2) *Subjective experience.* If the phenomenon of inspiration is caused by the working of a neural algorithm, then why is it that an inspiration tends to occur as an abrupt realization of a complete solution, without the subject's conscious awareness of intermediate steps? The examples of Riemann and Galois show that some persons have obtained results in an apparently direct way, while others were able to verify these results only through a laborious process involving many intermediate stages. Normally, we solve relatively easy problems by a conscious, step-by-step process. Why, then, should inspired scientists, mathematicians, and artists remain unaware of important intermediate steps in the process of solving difficult problems or producing intricate works of art, and then become aware of the final solution or creation only during a brief experience of realization?

Thus we can see that the phenomenon of inspiration cannot readily be explained by means of mechanistic models of life consistent with present-day theories of physics and chemistry. In the remainder of this chapter we will explore the nonmechanistic approach of the *Bhagavad-gītā.*

7.3 The Interaction Between Consciousness and Matter

In the first part of this book we discussed consciousness and, drawing from the *Bhagavad-gītā,* introduced the conception of the conscious self as a nonphysical entity. In the second part we discussed biological form and the problem of finding a unified description of nature. We concluded that it is not possible to construct a unified quantitative theory that can give a satisfactory account of the origin of complex forms, such as the bodily structures of living organisms. But turning once again to the *Bhagavad-gītā,* we showed how an intuitively reasonable, unified picture of nature can be based on the nonquantifiable idea of universal consciousness.

Thus far we have not given any indication of how the conscious self, or *jīvātmā,* influences the behavior of the material body. As we observed in Chapter 2, philosophers have not been able to solve this problem, and many have responded either by denying the existence of consciousness or by trying to explain it as a byproduct of brain activity. Nonetheless, a simple solution does exist. The *Bhagavad-gītā* indicates that the interplay between the conscious self and the material body is indirect, and depends on the interaction between the localized self and universal consciousness. This explanation of the relationship between the *jīvātmā* and matter resolves many of the problems that have perplexed philosophers, and it also directly accounts for the phenomena of inspiration. Most importantly, this explanation entails a direct method of obtaining verifiable knowledge about both localized and universal consciousness.

The description of the interaction between the *jīvātmā* and the material body given in the first part of the *Bhagavad-gītā* may seem perplexing: "The bewildered spirit soul, under the influence of the three modes of material nature, thinks himself to be the doer of activities, which are in actuality carried out by nature."[12] Or again: "The embodied spirit, master of the city of his body, does not create activities, nor does he influence people to act, nor does he create the fruits of action. All this is enacted by the modes of material nature."[13] Apparently, these statements support the viewpoint that nature is working entirely in accordance with certain fixed laws, and that the conscious self can at best be an epiphenomenon affected by the actions of the material body but unable to affect them in turn.

The *Bhagavad-gītā* confirms that nature is indeed working according to laws. But the key to the solution of the mind-body problem lies in understanding the *character* of these laws. Physicists tend to conceive of the laws of nature as a closed set of immutable rules that can be specified by a few simple equations. According to the *Bhagavad-gītā,* however, the laws of nature are like the laws of human society promulgated by a head of state. Like the laws of the physicists, these laws can also be represented in symbolic terms, but unlike them they tend to be highly complex. And since the laws of nature are actually under personal control, they are always subject to interference and modification.

In the *Bhagavad-gītā* the Supreme Person, Kṛṣṇa, describes the laws of nature in the following terms: "This material nature is working under My direction, O son of Kuntī, and it is producing all moving and nonmoving beings. By its rule this manifestation is created and annihilated again and again."[14] Thus although the physicists are right that the material energy is acting according to rules, they fail to see that these rules have their ultimate source in a personal director.

We can visualize these rules in terms of a hierarchy. On the lowest level are the relatively simple laws governing the gross behavior of matter. These are studied to some extent by physicists and chemists. On the next level are higher-order laws governing the complex behavior of the living beings. These laws, sometimes referred to as the laws of *karma* (action), are discussed in the *Bhagavad-gītā* in some detail. Finally, on the highest level are the direct interventions of the Supreme Person in the course of natural events. We have discussed in Parts I and II how one can extend the world view of modern science to encompass such an open-ended hierarchy of natural laws. In such a hierarchy the laws on each level are not, of course, absolute. They are merely approximations subject to refinement and modification in accordance with higher laws and, ultimately, the unconstrained will of the Supreme Person.

From the mechanistic viewpoint, such an "unconstrained will" is at best nothing more than a name for the arbitrary and the inexplicable. Yet the *Bhagavad-gītā* describes some additional nonquantifiable factors that can give us greater insight into the will of the Supreme Person. One of these factors is the personal interaction between the Supreme and the localized conscious selves.

In the *Bhagavad-gītā* Kṛṣṇa states, "The Supreme Lord is situated in everyone's heart, O Arjuna, and is directing the wanderings of all living entities, who are situated on a machine made of the material energy."[15] As we have already mentioned, the materially embodied *jīvātmā* is in an essentially passive state, unable directly to influence the actions of the material body. Yet the *jīvātmā* is conscious of the bodily situation and filled with desires relating to the outcome of various bodily activities. According to the *Bhagavad-gītā,* the Supreme Person perceives the desires of the embodied beings and responds to these desires by appropriately controlling the bodily machinery.

The manifestation of the Supreme Person within the heart of every living being is known as the *paramātmā,* or Supersoul. "Although the Supersoul appears to be divided," says the *Bhagavad-gītā,* "He is never divided. He is situated as one."[16] This is another illustration of the simultaneous oneness and multiplicity of the Supreme Person, which we discussed in Chapter 6. Since the Supreme Person possesses unlimited consciousness, He is able to attend simultaneously to innumerable material situations without becoming confused.

The Supreme Person, as understood from the *Bhagavad-gītā,* is not remote from the material world. Rather, He is all-pervading in space and time and is also transcendental to space and time. This idea may seem paradoxical, but we should note that a similar problem arises when we try to visualize the reality underlying the laws of nature as conceived in modern physics. These laws are postulated as spatially and temporally invariant; but what is it that pervades all space and time and determines that gravitation, for example, will operate according to a certain universal force constant, G?

In our day-to-day experience we desire to perform various physical actions, and we generally find that the body immediately acts in accordance with our desires. Although we do not understand how our will gives rise to action, this seems to happen automatically, and we normally take it for granted and think, "I am doing this." According to the *Bhagavad-gītā*, what is actually happening is that the Supersoul is perceiving our desires and translating them into action. He does this through the manipulation of the laws of nature on a sophisticated level. As a consequence, our actions seem to conform to the known physical laws, even though, if we could analyze these actions thoroughly enough, we would find no fixed system of laws ultimately able to account for them.

The philosophy of the *Bhagavad-gītā* thus provides us with a simple explanation of the phenomenon of inspiration—the very explanation, alas, that Poincaré, after analyzing his own mathematical inspirations, felt he would hate to accept. In each of the cases we have discussed, a person initially desired very strongly to carry out a difficult mental task, such as finding the proof of a mathematical theorem. Generally, the person spent some time fruitlessly endeavoring to execute the task, and then he suddenly and unexpectedly became aware of the solution to his problem. (The example of Mozart shows, however, that an initial period of frustrating failure is not always involved.) We have seen that in many instances such unexpected realizations cannot be satisfactorily explained as byproducts of known physical processes. But we can readily understand experiences of sudden illumination as the responses of the Supersoul to the desires of the embodied living being.

We should note that different persons will generally have different experiences of inspiration. Even if two people desiring to solve the same problem are of similar ability and education, one may find the solution and the other may not. The *Bhagavad-gītā* explains this variance as a consequence of *karma,* or the accumulated byproducts of past actions. The Supersoul does not direct the actions of the material body solely in accordance with the immediate desires of the living being. Rather, He determines these actions by systematically evaluating both the living being's current desires and his past activities. He bases these judgements on an established set of higher-order laws—the laws of *karma*—which provide an absolute standard for universal justice and morality. These laws are just as real as the "natural laws" of physics and chemistry. But they are much more complex than these laws, and they are directly involved with the phenomenon of life.

The *Bhagavad-gītā* deals primarily with the means whereby the individual conscious being can become free from the bondage of past *karma.* A living being acting under the laws of *karma* is more or less a helpless spectator of an elaborate drama of actions and reactions stemming from past and present desires. In this state the living being tends to identify fully with his physical body and to be completely unaware of the role played by the Supersoul in the affairs of his life.

Under the laws of *karma*, the relationship between the individual *jīvātmā* and the Supreme Person is essentially impersonal and legalistic. Yet it is possible for the *jīvātmā* to become directly aware of the Supreme Person and reciprocate with Him in a personal relationship. In such a state of consciousness, the *jīvātmā* is freed from karmic reactions to past activities and becomes fully aware of his own nature as a nonphysical being.

Inspiration plays an essential role in the attainment of this state of consciousness. In the *Bhagavad-gītā* Kṛṣṇa declares, "To those who are constantly devoted and worship Me with love, I give the understanding by which they can come to Me. Out of compassion for them, I dwelling in their hearts, destroy with the shining lamp of knowledge the darkness born of ignorance."[17] The purport of this statement is that direct knowledge of the Supreme Person is available to any person willing to approach the Supreme with a positive, favorable attitude. Normally, Kṛṣṇa supplies the embodied *jīvātmā* only with information relating to his particular material desires, but if the *jīvātmā* approaches Kṛṣṇa with love and without underlying material motives, then Kṛṣṇa will directly reveal Himself.

This is the conclusion of the *Bhagavad-gītā's* philosophy, and it constitutes the only real means of verifying the truth of this philosophy. By analyzing empirical arguments, we can identify some of the shortcomings of mechanistic theories and show how the philosophy of the *Bhagavad-gītā* can supply important elements now missing from the prevailing scientific world view. But if we remain within the framework of mechanistic thought, we can neither prove that this philosophy is true nor practically apply it. We can verify transcendental subject matter only if we are able to actually function on the transcendental platform.

In the discussion thus far we have indicated that according to the *Bhagavad-gītā*, such transcendental consciousness is theoretically attainable. The individual self is always in contact with the Supersoul and is capable, in principle, of relating with the Supersoul on the level of direct personal exchange. In Chapter 9 we will discuss the epistemology of transcendental knowledge and indicate briefly how this theoretical possibility might be practically realized.

Notes

1. Brush, "Should the History of Science be Rated X?" p. 1167.
2. Hadamard, *The Psychology of Invention in the Mathematical Field*, p. 15.

3. Poincaré, *The Foundations of Science*, pp. 387–388.
4. Ibid.
5. Hadamard, p. 16.
6. Poincaré, p. 390.
7. Poincaré, p. 391.
8. Hadamard, p. 118.
9. Hadamard, p. 120.
10. Poincaré, p. 390.
11. Weizenbaum, *Computer Power and Human Reason*, chap. 9.
12. A.C. Bhaktivedanta Swami Prabhupāda, *Bhagavad-gītā As It Is*, text 3.27, p. 192.
13. Ibid., text 5.14, p. 286.
14. Ibid., text 9.10, p. 457.
15. Ibid., text 18.61, p. 830.
16. Ibid., text 13.17, p. 640.
17. Ibid., texts 10.10–11, pp. 506–508.

Chapter 8

The Doctrine Of Evolution

"All reputable evolutionary biologists now agree that the evolution of life is directed by the process of natural selection, and by nothing else."[1] With these words Sir Julian Huxley summed up the consensus of learned opinion at the Darwin Centennial Celebration in 1959.

Among the eminent biologists and evolutionists attending the celebration, great confidence prevailed that the origin of living species was now almost fully understood. Evolutionists had clearly established that all living organisms had gradually evolved through small variations in form and function, slowly accumulating, generation by generation, over a vast span of geological time. Geneticists had shown that all biological variations arose from random genetic accidents called mutations. Evolutionary theorists, building on this finding, had clearly identified Darwinian natural selection as the sole guiding force that sorted out these variations and thereby molded the diverse forms of living beings. Although many minute details certainly remained to be worked out, scientists believed they had arrived at an essentially complete understanding of life and its historical development.

With this striking unanimity of established scientific opinion reached little more than two decades ago, perhaps we are surprised to hear that the theory of evolution has recently become the focus of a great controversy among evolutionists themselves. The last few years have seen the established theory of mutation and natural selection increasingly challenged by critical studies and dissenting interpretations of the evidence. The theory has clearly shown itself unsound, although scientists have thus far been unable to devise an acceptable new theory to replace it.

Recently this controversy became a near battle, when some 150 prominent evolutionists gathered at Chicago's Field Museum of Natural History to thrash out various conflicting hypotheses about the nature of evolution. After four days of heated discussions (closed to all but a few outside observers), the evolutionists remained convinced that evolution is a fact. Unfortunately, however, they could not reach a clear understanding of just what this fact *is*. According to a report from *The New York Times*, the assembled scientists were unable either to specify the mechanism of evolution or to agree on "how anyone could establish with some certainty that it happened one way and not another."[2]

Why this shift from unanimity and certainty to controversy and indecision? We shall try to answer this question by examining some basic features of the modern theory of evolution. We shall try to identify the reasons why many scientists have sought an evolutionary explanation of life, and we shall also point out some of the problems that have impeded their efforts.

Finally, we shall argue that the theory of evolution has been motivated more by philosophical misunderstanding than by the strength of empirical evidence. One of the most persistent themes of evolutionary argumentation has been that evolution is the only viable alternative to certain stereotyped conceptions of divine creation. The theory of evolution can thus be seen as an effort to enlist natural evidence in support of an alternative to an unwanted and unsatisfactory spiritual world view. We propose that this effort is futile, and that the underlying philosophical problems can be solved only if we take advantage of a direct, scientific approach to spiritual knowledge.

8.1 Evolution: an Invisible Process

When Charles Darwin originally set forth his evolutionary theory, he maintained that the forms of living organisms change slowly and continuously from generation to generation, and that over many millions of years these changes bring about new species and higher categories of organisms. One immediate implication of this theory was that the fossil record of ancient plant and animal life should display a continuum of fossilized life forms, ranging from the most primitive to the most advanced. Given that organisms tend to leave occasional fossilized remains, scientists naturally expected to find a petrified motion picture of evolutionary history entombed in the earth's sedimentary rocks.

But in Darwin's time it was well known that the fossil record did not actually reveal such a picture. On the contrary, paleontologists had observed that distinct plant and animal species tended to appear abruptly in the fossil strata without recognizable antecedents. Each species remained essentially unchanged throughout the strata bearing its fossilized remains. Fossils yielded practically no evidence of gradual change from one species to another.

Darwin admitted that the fossil evidence, far from supporting his theory, seemed directly to contradict it. He responded by proposing that the fossil record was drastically incomplete. The innumerable intermediate life forms required by his theory must have existed, but they had left no recognizable traces in the fossil deposits known in his time. Darwin suggested that further research would undoubtably uncover many of these missing forms, and their discovery would vindicate his theory.

For many years orthodox evolutionary opinion has adhered to Darwin's basic views. But dissenting voices have increasingly been heard. At the recent meeting of evolutionists in Chicago, Niles Eldridge, a paleontologist from the American Museum of Natural History in New York, declared, "The pattern we were told to find for the last 120 years does not exist."[3] Despite intense effort, several generations of paleontologists have found few examples in which one fossil species seems to transform gradually into another, and some researchers say none at all have been found.

As a result, Eldridge, Steven J. Gould, and several other prominent paleontologists now propose that species have not actually arisen by a slow process of transformation. As an alternative, they have devised what they call the theory of "punctuated equilibrium."[4] According to this theory, evolutionary changes take place in short bursts separated by long periods during which the forms of living organisms remain static. A typical species will arise from an earlier species in a "geological microsecond"—a period of a few thousand years that appears like an instant from the multimillion-year perspective of geological time. Also, a species will not arise through a gradual modification of its parent population. Rather, it will arise when a

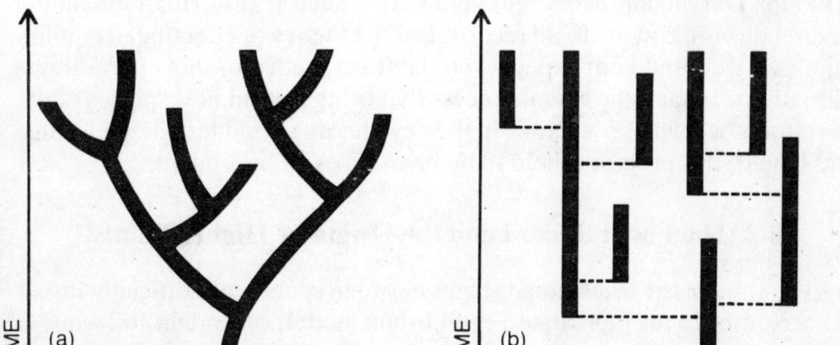

Figure 1. The Darwinian theory of evolution states that species have developed gradually, as illustrated by the branching tree pattern (a). But the fossil record does not substantiate this pattern of development. As a result, some paleontologists have introduced the "punctuated equilibrium" model, shown in (b), in which the transitions between species are officially invisible.

tiny group that has been isolated from the main population, perhaps by a geographical barrier, is rapidly transformed.

One consequence of the theory of punctuated equilibrium is that it makes the evolution of species officially invisible. On one hand, we cannot expect the fossil record to show how a new species evolved, for the evolution takes place in a tiny population during a geological "microsecond." On the other hand, we cannot expect to see a new species evolve within the recorded span of human history, for a geological microsecond of 10,000 to 50,000 years is still immensely long when measured in human lifetimes.

Of course, we may possibly observe small-scale changes in organisms, like those produced through controlled breeding, or like the famous change in color exhibited by the peppered moths of industrial England. Yet such changes are known to be reversible, and at most they result in only minor variations within a species. For example, settlers introduced domesticated rabbits into Australia in 1788, and some escaped and flourished in the wild. Despite the effects of breeding by humans, these domesticated rabbits were still classed as rabbits, and today their descendants have reverted to their ancestral form: they look exactly like wild rabbits.[5]

Explaining superficial variations of this kind is not the real problem confronting evolutionists. The real problem is explaining how higher forms of plants and animals have arisen from lower forms, and how these in turn have arisen from inanimate matter. No large-scale transformations of this kind have ever been observed within the brief span of human history. The orthodox Darwinian theory maintained that such transformations should be directly visible in the fossil record. But the theory of punctuated equilibrium says we should not expect even the fossil record to show these transformations. In fact, the actual process that brings about new species of life has *always* been invisible. Now, in the new theory propounded by Eldridge and Gould, this process is held to be invisible even in principle.

8.2 The Fossil Record and the Origin of Higher Plants

Even though the transitional stages between species are officially invisible according to the punctuated equilibrium model, one might still wonder whether or not the fossil record shows a large-scale progression from primitive to advanced life forms that appears reasonably continuous. When we examine a half-tone picture under a magnifying glass, we see an array of disconnected dots; but when we view the picture at a distance, these dots seem to merge together to form a continuous image. Similarly, we might expect the disjointed succession of life forms in the fossil record to merge into an unbroken evolutionary continuum when viewed from a sufficiently broad perspective.

If we examine the published descriptions of the fossil record, however, we find that this is not the case. The fossil record is characterized by abrupt appearances and disappearances on every level of morphological classification from species to phyla. It is not possible for us to see an evolutionary continuum by standing back, so to speak, and taking into account only the most significant features of organisms. Even such important general patterns as the basic vertebrate body plan are seen to appear suddenly in the fossil record without recognizable antecedents. It would certainly be misleading to claim that the fossil record demands an evolutionary interpretation. Indeed, some features of this body of data can be made to appear consistent with such an interpretation only by the introduction of artificial, *ad hoc* hypotheses.

There are many examples of such features, but here we shall restrict ourselves to considering only one—the paleontological history of the flowering plants. (This history is represented graphically in Figure 2.) We will briefly discuss the implications of this history after first introducing some necessary background information about the geological time scale.

Geologists and paleontologists divide the history of the earth into a series of time intervals that they correlate with successive strata of sedimentary rock in the earth's surface. Table 1 summarizes the standard geological time scale.[6] Geological time is divided into successively finer intervals called eras, periods, and epochs. Dates have been assigned to these intervals by a complex process involving radiometric dating and various methods of analyzing and correlating sedimentary strata. In Table 1 the epochs making up each period are designated by numbers. These epochs vary considerably in length, but their average length is about six million years.

In Figure 2 the numbers along the horizontal axis represent the first 40 epochs in the geological time scale, and the triangles mark the boundaries of the first five geological periods. For each epoch, we can read from the graph the number of families of flowering plants that paleontologists have found in the strata corresponding to that epoch.[7]

The most striking feature of this graph is that in epochs 20 and 19, the Cenomanian and Albian epochs of the Cretacious period, the number of families rises abruptly from 0 to about 50. If we interpret the record literally, this means that at the end of the Cenomanian epoch (about 100 million years ago), there existed hundreds of species of angiosperms, or flowering plants, including many familiar modern trees and herbs. From this time

Era	Period	Epoch numbers	Period boundaries in millions of years
Cenozoic	Quaterniary	1–2	0–2
	Tertiary	3–13	2–65
Mesozoic	Cretacious	14–25	65–136
	Jurassic	26–35	136–190
	Triassic	36–42	190–225
Paleozoic	Permian	43–47	225–280
	Carboniferous	48–53	280–345
	Devonian	54–60	345–395
	Silurian	61–63	395–435
	Ordovician	64–69	435–500
	Cambrian	70–72	500–570
Pre-Cambrian	Varangian	73	above 570
	Pre-Varangian	74	—

Table 1. The geological time scale.

onward, the angiosperms have been the dominant land plants throughout the world.

In contrast, in the strata antedating the Albian epoch paleontologists have found very little unambiguous evidence for the existence of flowering plants. There are some fossils, which suggest that angiosperms may have existed in the Jurassic and Triassic periods.[8] However, the compilers of the standard reference used to draw Figure 2 apparently did not feel that this evidence justified the inclusion of Jurassic or Triassic angiosperms in their list of fossil families. In fact, according to this reference, two families of angiosperms date from epochs 23 and 21, and all other families appear in epoch 20 or later.

Here we seem to have "punctuated equilibrium" with a vengeance. In a span of some 12 million years, the flowering plants rise from a position of complete insignificance to one of world dominance. Could this be due to an exceedingly intense burst of evolutionary diversification? In fact, the general opinion of paleontologists is that the angiosperms could not have evolved so quickly. The prevailing view is that the angiosperms must have gradually evolved in some part of the world where, for many millions of years, they left no significant fossil remains. Then in the late Cretacious

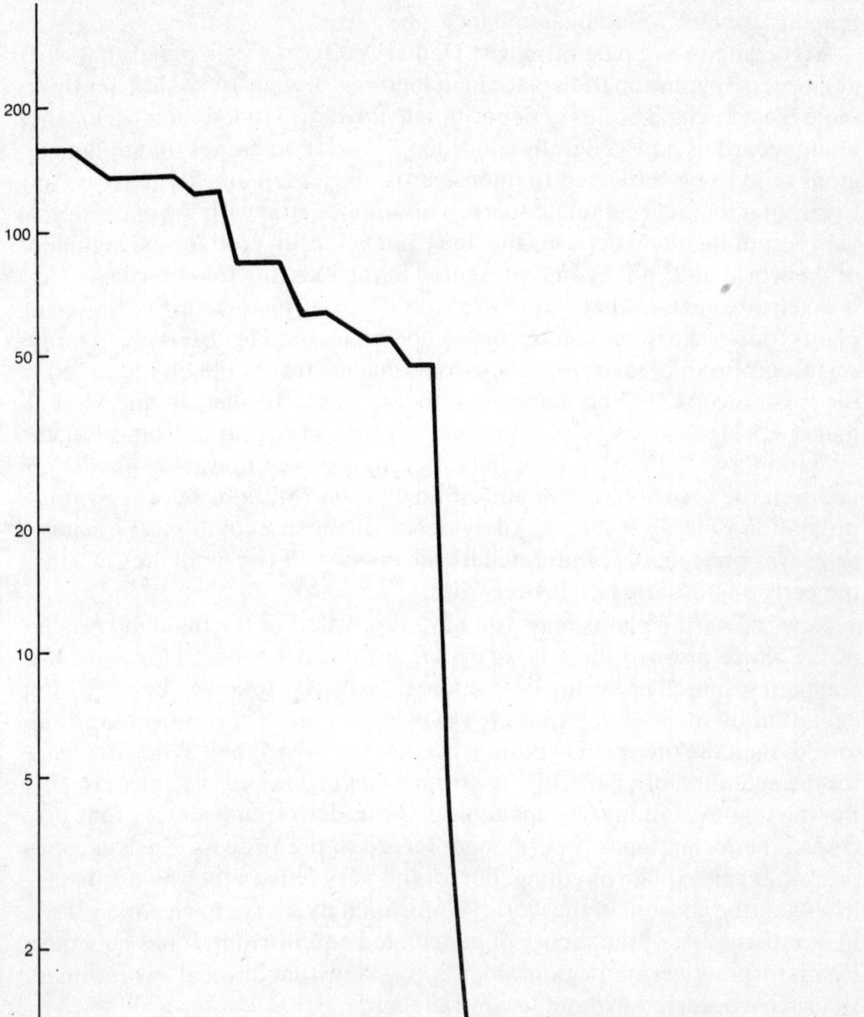

Figure 2. The number of families of flowering plants as a function of time. The numbers on the horizontal axis represent geological epochs. The graph depicts the number of families of flowering plants that paleontologists have discovered in the strata corresponding to these epochs. In epochs 19 and 20 (the Cenomanian and Albian divisions of the Cretacious period) the number of families shoots up abruptly from zero to about 50.

period they suddenly migrated en masse into the regions where their remains are now found in abundance.

According to the paleontologist Daniel Axelrod, "The belief that early angiosperm evolution took place in upland regions, in areas sufficiently remote from lowland basins of deposition to have precluded their occurrence in the record, is now generally conceded."[9] Axelrod argues that upland regions tend to be subjected to intense erosion, which quickly destroys any fossils that might accumulate there. This implies that with the exception of very recent highland deposits that have not yet been eroded, the highlands of the world have not been represented in the existing fossil record.

Axelrod suggests that the entire evolutionary history of the flowering plants took place in these unrecorded upland areas. He observes, "The ancestral group that gave rise to angiosperms has not yet been identified in the fossil record, and no living angiosperm points to such an ancestral alliance."[10] He also notes that the fossil record gives no indication of the evolutionary relationship between different types of flowering plants: "In addition the record has shed almost no light on relations between taxa at ordinal and family level."[11] All evidence of these evolutionary relationships was presumably obliterated by the erosion of the highlands in which the early angiosperms exclusively lived.

Now, flowering plants may well have flourished in the highland regions of the world prior to the Albian epoch of the Cretacious. However, it is completely unscientific for paleontologists to try to save the theory of evolution by maintaining that they evolved there. If this procedure is allowed, then the theory of evolution becomes unfalsifiable. When evidence for the evolution of a particular life form is lacking, it is easy to propose that the missing evolutionary steps took place under circumstances that precluded the formation of a permanent record of the process. Such vacuous proposals can explain anything, but for this very reason they have no place in a scientific account of the world. Unfortunately, as we have already seen in our discussion of the theory of punctuated equilibrium, it has become a standard practice for paleontologists to claim that critical evolutionary steps have occurred without leaving a record.

Now that we have identified one unscientific practice of the evolutionists, it may not be out of place here to point out a complementary practice that is also unscientific. This is the procedure of setting aside and ignoring evidence that does not fit into a particular evolutionary scheme. For example, many paleontologists believe that the angiosperms must have had a long evolutionary history prior to the Cretacious period, and thus they would be willing to accept earlier fossil evidence of flowering plants. But what would they say about evidence for the existence of flowering plants, say two billion years ago?

According to the standard scenario presented in textbooks[12] and popular accounts[13], all higher vascular plants, including the angiosperms, evolved from the psilophytes, an extremely primitive type of plant that flourished in the upper Silurian and lower Devonian periods. The preceding periods of the Paleozoic era are represented in the fossil record only by marine deposits, and evolutionists generally suppose that life had not yet emerged from the seas during these periods. Prior to the Cambrian period, the fossil record is very scanty, and evolutionists maintain that throughout most of this time, life existed only in the form of single-celled organisms such as algae and bacteria.[14]

Yet there is evidence that flowering plants may have existed during this time. According to a report in *Nature*, angiosperm pollen has been found in Pre-Cambrian rock on the frontier between Venezuela and British Guiana.[15] This rock has been dated by radiometric methods, and has been assigned ages of 2,090 million[16] and 1,710 million[17] years.

If this report can be taken at face value, it completely upsets the accepted scientific picture of the origin and evolution of life. If flowering plants were existing at a time far antedating all known remains of higher organisms, then the standard evolutionary interpretation of the fossil record must be mistaken. The obvious implication is that there must have existed Pre-Cambrian continental regions that were occupied by many different types of higher organisms, but that were totally destroyed in the course of time. Such regions can, of course, be compared with the "highlands" posited by Axelrod to explain the sudden appearance of the angiosperms in the more recent portion of the fossil record. In this case the evidence directly implies the existence of such regions, but it still leaves us in the dark as to the mode of origin of the higher organisms that lived there.

It is perhaps not surprising that evolutionists do not accept evidence that so blatantly contradicts their theories. Yet the report we have just discussed is not an isolated instance. There are, in fact, many reports of pollen and spores from sedimentary formations antedating the periods in which the evolution of higher plants is commonly believed to have taken place. Indeed, there are evolutionists who have accepted some of this evidence and have tried to incorporate it into various modified evolutionary schemes.

An example of this is provided by a paper by Axelrod that appeared in the journal *Evolution* in 1959.[18] Therein he cites several reports of spores and fragments of wood that have been assigned to the Cambrian period.

Some of these spores were found in Kashmir and have been identified as pteridophytes (ferns), pteridosperms (seed ferns), and gymnosperms (the category of plants including the conifers, or pine trees).[19] Axelrod uses this and other evidence to completely overturn the standard theory that higher plants have evolved from Silurian and Devonian psilophytes. He argues that the different groups of higher plants must all have evolved independently from algal ancestors in the Cambrian or earlier. (Axelrod does not mention, by the way, that angiosperm pollen has also been reported in the Cambrian strata of Kashmir.[20])

These proposals have apparently not found widespread acceptance, for current textbooks still expound the psilophyte theory. This becomes especially interesting when we consider one particular piece of evidence that Axelrod cites to disprove this theory. According to him, some of the early Devonian psilophyte fossils are accompanied by fossils of *Callixylon* logs that are up to three feet in diameter.[21] *Callixylon* is a type of conifer. One would think that this fact, if true, would certainly cast doubt on the theory that all higher plants are descended from these psilophytes.

We can conclude that there is considerable uncertainty and ambiguity in our current knowledge of the origin and ancient history of the higher plants. The fossil record can only be made to support an evolutionary interpretation by the introduction of unverifiable hypotheses. There are also cases where evidence conflicting with established evolutionary scenarios seems to have been ignored, or even suppressed. We note that similar points can also be made about the fossil record of past animal life, although we do not have enough space to discuss this here.

8.3 The Enigma of Biological Form

If we cannot hope to find direct evidence delineating the development of major new forms of life, we might at least expect the theory of evolution to provide us a convincing explanation of how, in principle, such developments might take place. Since the Darwinian theory asserts that small variations in organic form gradually accumulate, we might expect evolutionary theorists to provide us with plausible evolutionary sequences leading from lower to higher forms of life. In such evolutionary sequences, each organism should be fit to live in its particular environment, and the differences between successive organisms in the chain should be of the kind we would expect from random mutation.

When we examine the literature of evolutionary theory, we do indeed encounter many explanations of this kind, but in every case they are disappointingly vague and incomplete. Typical is this statement by the prominent evolutionist Ernst Mayr: "The evolution of the eye ultimately hinges on one particular property of certain types of protoplasm—photosensitivity. . . . Once one admits that the possession of such photosensitivity may have selective value, all else follows by necessity."[22] Mayr does not, and indeed *cannot,* specify the particular steps leading from a photosensitive speck to a fully developed eye. His account of the evolution of the eye is typical of theoretical evolutionary explanations, for it relies on an abiding faith in the power of natural selection and mutation to effect transformations in organic form that evolutionists themselves cannot even imagine, much less observe.

Although evolutionists have adhered to this mode of explanation for many years, there is now evidence that its appeal is beginning to wane. According to a report in *Science,* the predominant view among the evolutionists assembled at the recent meeting in Chicago was that the gradual selective accumulation of small variations cannot account for the appearance of new species.[23]

What has happened is that many evolutionists are now openly acknowledging one of the fundamental problems confronting evolutionary theory—the problem posed by the complex networks of structure and function that are characteristic of living organisms. Generally, each component of such a network is essential for the proper functioning of the whole. How, then, could the complete arrangement have arisen through a finely graded series of functional intermediate forms? In the past many evolutionists have been content to accept on faith that such sequences of intermediate stages must always be possible. But now a number of prominent evolutionists are openly admitting that in many significant cases the required intermediate stages simply may not exist.

To illustrate this problem in evolutionary theory, we shall consider a simple example provided by a type of flatworm called the *microstomum.*[24] This flatworm is equipped with a kind of defensive cell called a nematocyst, which can fire a poisonous barbed thread. When the flatworm is attacked by a predator, the nematocysts, situated just beneath the surface of the worm's back, are discharged, thereby stinging the assailant and driving it away.

The most interesting aspect of this arrangement is that the nematocysts are not produced from the tissues of the flatworm itself. Rather, they are stolen from the hydra, an aquatic organism on which the flatworm preys. The hydra has tentacles armed with several kinds of nematocysts, which it uses to subdue and capture the small animals on which it feeds. Some of these cells fire poisonous barbs, and others discharge various types of coiled and sticky threads that enable the hydra to hold on to its prey.

These flatworms generally avoid hydras. But biologists have observed that when one of them needs more nematocysts, it will eat hydras and digest all of their tissues except these particular cells. The nematocysts are neither damaged nor discharged, but are enclosed within certain of the flatworm's cells, which carry them toward the worm's back. The nematocysts that fire coiled or sticky threads are then digested, but those that fire poisonous barbs are transported to sites just beneath the outer layer of the worm's back.

There the nematocysts are oriented so that their stings will fire upward. The epithelial cells which form the worm's outer layer become very thin just above the newly positioned nematocysts, thus providing portholes for the firing of the stings. Finally, the cells that have encapsulated the nematocysts undergo extensive changes that enable these cells to act as trigger mechanisms. (The hydra's original trigger mechanism is contained in a type of cell called a cnidoblast, which the flatworm digests.)

Let us consider whether or not these defensive arrangements of the *microstomum* could have evolved step by step. An evolutionary scenario would have to begin with an ancestral flatworm that ate hydras but did not make use of their nematocysts. In such a worm, what would be the first evolutionary step leading to the eventual exploitation of the nematocysts as defensive weapons? Unless the nematocysts were actually used as weapons, for the worm to manipulate them internally would be useless. Indeed, it would be dangerous, since the flatworm can easily be killed by the discharge of the hydra's stings.

Yet each step in the internal processing of the nematocysts is essential for their eventual use as weapons. If they were not transported to the flatworm's back, they could not be usefully deployed. If transported to the back but oriented incorrectly, they would be useless or even dangerous. If they were oriented beneath epithelial cells of normal thickness, the discharged sting would lose its momentum while passing through the epithelium, and the worm would sting itself.

There is also a further problem. Evidently the nematocysts are not triggered simply by pressure applied to the worm's back. Rather, their firing is governed by a complex control mechanism within the worm. Without this trigger mechanism the whole arrangement would be useless, even if the nematocysts were properly oriented beneath epithelial "portholes."

When examined closely, each step in the internal manipulation of the nematocysts resolves into a complex of substeps. For example, for a nematocyst to be transported to the back of the flatworm, one of the worm's cells must first recognize it, and then the cell must initiate a process of motion that specifically carries the nematocyst to the worm's dorsal region. These are both complex procedures. Yet for the flatworm to take advantage of the hydra's nematocysts, it would seem that many complex arrangements of this kind must be present simultaneously.

It is hard to see how complicated, interlocking arrangements such as the *microstomum's* defensive system could have evolved by many small steps in the traditional Darwinian manner. Darwin himself maintained, "If it could be demonstrated that any complex organ existed which could not possibly have been formed by numerous, successive, slight modifications, my theory would absolutely break down."[25] Yet what possible sequence of intermediate forms could span the gap between an ordinary flatworm and a flatworm capable of deploying stolen nematocysts for its own defense? It would seem that we are confronted with one of two alternatives: either (1) some of these hypothetical intermediate forms must have useless or deleterious features, or (2) some of these forms must be separated by large gaps corresponding to many simultaneous modifications. It is quite possible that a series of intermediate forms of the kind required by Darwin simply does not exist.

Many organs are so complex that we do not clearly understand how they work. One might think that evolutionists would refrain from offering evolutionary explanations for such organs. Unfortunately, it is precisely in these cases, where our understanding is vague and incomplete, that evolutionists seem most eager to explain origins by waving the wand of Darwinian natural selection. For example, one prominent exponent of the evolutionary viewpoint has argued in a popular presentation that a mere increase in size can transform an ape's brain into a human brain.[26] He claims this could be accomplished by the natural selection of a series of slight prolongations of the period of foetal brain growth. But can a mere increase in brain size account for the difference in mentality between human beings and apes? It is possible to entertain such fantasies only because we are now almost entirely ignorant of how the brain works.

Simpler organs are easier to analyze, and we can frequently see, as we did in the case of *microstomum,* that they are not amenable to explanation by traditional evolutionary concepts. To illustrate this, we will briefly consider three additional examples of simple organ systems.

Our first example is provided by the statocyst of a certain species of shrimp.[27] The statocyst is a hollow, fluid-filled sphere built into the shrimp's shell. It is lined with cells bearing pressure-sensitive hairs, and it contains a small weight. The weight tends to sink and press against the downward portion of the sphere, thus enabling the shrimp to tell up from down. Curiously, the weight is a small grain of sand that the shrimp picks up with its claws and inserts into the statocyst through a small hole in its shell. Since the statocyst is built into the shell, the shrimp has to do this every time it moults.

Now, by what intermediate stages could the shrimp's statocyst have arisen? Both the statocyst and the behavioral pattern involved in picking up the grain of sand are quite complex, and neither is of any use without the other. Even if the statocyst had evolved with a built-in weight and then had lost this feature by a mutation, the appearance of the insertion behavior would require a leap involving the coordination of many variables.

For our second example we turn to the bacterium *Escherichia coli,* an organism that is thought to be very low on the evolutionary scale. Each *E. coli* bacterium possesses several long, helically curved fibers (called flagella) that enable it to swim.[28] Each flagellum is connected at one end to a kind of motor built into the bacterial cell wall. When these motors rotate in a certain direction, the flagella rotate in unison and act as propellers to drive the bacterium forward through the water. When the motors rotate in the opposite direction, the flagella separate and change the orientation of the bacterium by pulling in various ways. By systematically alternating between these two modes of operation, the bacterium is able to swim from undesirable to desirable regions of its environment.

Some investigators have proposed that the motors are driven by a flux of protons flowing into the cell.[29] According to them, each motor consists of a ring of sixteen protein molecules attached to an axle and a stationary ring of sixteen proteins built into the cell wall. Protons are steadily pumped out of the cell by its normal metabolic processes. As some of these protons flow back into the cell through the pairs of rings, they impart a rotary motion to the movable ring. Since the motor can operate in forward or reverse, there must be some mechanism that adjusts the configuration of the molecules in the rings so as to reverse the torque produced by the flow of ions.

Although the exact details of the *E. coli's* molecular motors have not yet been worked out, we can see that their operation depends on the precise, simultaneous adjustment of many variables. Even though these motors are fairly simple in structure, it is very hard to imagine a continuum of useful forms spanning the gap between a motorless cell and a cell with a fully functional motor. It is quite possible that no such continuum of forms exists, or that such a continuum must involve intermediate structures much more complicated than the existing molecular motors. In any event, we presently have no idea how the *E. coli's* motors could have evolved. Indeed, the problem becomes even more difficult when we consider that these motors are useless without their control systems, and the control systems are useless without the motors.

For our final example we consider a kind of marine invertebrate called a sea slug. Certain of these sea slugs are able to steal the nematocysts from sea anemones (a marine creature similar to the hydra) and use them for their own defense.[30] Their system is quite similar to that of *microstomum*, except that instead of transporting the nematocysts by special migratory cells, the sea slugs move them into position by sweeping them through narrow ciliated tubes that pass from their stomachs to their backs.

Now, the sea slug is a mollusc, and therefore cannot be closely related to the flatworm, *microstomum*. Evolutionists customarily explain the existence of similar traits in ostensibly unrelated organisms by invoking the idea of convergent evolution. According to this idea, the forces of evolution will automatically produce similar effects in similar circumstances. But the problem we face here is that by the hypothesis of gradual evolutionary change, we cannot explain the origin of the defensive system of either the sea slug or *microstomum*.

8.4 The Resurrection of the Hopeful Monster

Clearly we must reject the standard evolutionary theory of gradual change through the natural selection of many small variations. How, then, can the origin of species be explained? At the conference in Chicago, there were signs that at least some evolutionists are trying to resurrect a theory that was greeted with almost universal scorn and derision when first proposed in the 1940s.[31] This is the theory of the "hopeful monster," devised by the geneticist Richard Goldschmidt.

The key to this theory is the idea that the genetic systems of organisms must be so arranged that a single mutation can produce, in one stroke, an elaborate systematic change in biological structure and function. Almost all known mutations result in gross defects, and a few result in small modifications that can be useful for the organism under suitable environmental conditions. According to Goldschmidt, however, there must exist a special type of mutation capable of generating new complex structures, such as functional legs, wings, or lungs. Most of these macromutations, as he called them, would result in bizarre monstrosities completely unfit for survival. But a few macromutations would produce "hopeful monsters," novel creatures that just happened to be adapted to a totally new mode of existence.[32]

This theory is now at a very tentative and speculative stage, and many evolutionists still view it with suspicion. Nonetheless, it represents an important trend in current evolutionary thought, and it illustrates the desperate extremes to which evolutionists have been forced to go in their efforts to construct a workable evolutionary theory. We shall therefore briefly consider some of the reasoning underlying the theory of the hopeful monster.

In its present recension, this theory relies on the concepts of regulative and structural genes.[33] Biologists define a structural gene as a sequence of DNA coding that defines a specific structural element of a living organism. An example is the gene for hemoglobin, the oxygen-carrying pigment of the red blood cells. In contrast, a regulative gene is a sequence of DNA coding that controls the timing and order of expression of other genes. We can envision an interacting system of regulative and structural genes that acts as a kind of genetic computer program. Such a program might be capable of expressing and repressing various combinations of structural genes in a complex and systematic way. The hopeful monster theory proposes that small changes in such genetic programs might result in the systematic large-scale changes in biological organization that evolutionary theorists need.

Biologists cite certain kinds of mutations as evidence for the existence of regulatory genes. For example, sometimes horses are born with three-toed feet. One might tentatively explain this variation by saying that although the genetic system of the horse always has the structural information for a multitoed foot, in normal horses a regulatory gene suppresses the genes for all the toes but one. When a mutation disables this regulatory gene, the latent genetic information is expressed, and a multitoed horse is born.

A certain mutation of fruit flies provides another possible example of the interaction of regulative and structural genes. In this mutation, known as aristapedia, a fully developed leg grows from the head of the fly in the position where the antenna normally grows. Scientists explain this anomaly by proposing that the regulative and structural genes for the leg comprise a kind of "subroutine" that is set in motion under the control of other regulatory genes. These regulatory genes may store information specifying the location of the leg, and if this information is disrupted by a mutation, the leg may form in an abnormal place.

Although the theory of regulative genes is still highly speculative, it does not seem unreasonable as a way of explaining certain types of mutation. But how this theory can account for Goldschmidt's hypothetical "macromutations" that produce complex, finely coordinated organs in a single stroke is not at all clear.

We shall try to illustrate the potentialities and limitations of systems of regulatory genes by constructing a simple artificial example. We can regard the following array of symbols as a "genetic" system for a series of English sentences.

> I am in (2); the orthodox (1) in (3). I believe I am in (9) as an (8) would be in if set to learn (5). The (8) (1) it was (7); ( ) yet I cannot keep out of (4).
>
> 1—would say; 2—thick mud; 3—fetid abominable mud; 4—the question; 5—the first book of Euclid; 6—and I am in much the same mind; 7—no manner of use; 8—old gorilla; 9—much the same frame of mind.

The code used in this genetic system is almost self-explanatory. To produce the encoded English statements, simply replace each number in parentheses with the corresponding numbered phrase. The result is the following statement made by Charles Darwin about the mechanism of large-scale evolution.

> I am in thick mud; the orthodox would say in fetid abominable mud. I believe I am in much the same frame of mind as an old gorilla would be in if set to learn the first book of Euclid. The old gorilla would say it was no manner of use; yet I cannot keep out of the question.[34]

In our artificial genetic system, the numbers in parentheses play the role of regulatory genes, and the phrases play the role of structural genes. If we mutate the regulatory gene (4), changing it to (3), we shall observe a change in Darwin's statements similar to the aristapedia mutation of fruit flies. (We invite the reader to try this and observe the effects.) Also, when we examine the genetic system closely, we find that a mutation has changed one regulatory gene to ( ). If we convert this gene to (6), Darwin's statement apparently acquires an entirely new sentence, although all that has actually happened is that the complete text of the original has been restored.

We can thus see that various kinds of large-scale effects result from mutations in the regulatory genes of our artificial system. Yet all of these effects have one thing in common. They all involve the manipulation of material already present in the genetic system. To induce the system to produce something entirely new is a different matter.

For example, we invite the reader to try to find mutations that will expand Darwin's remarks to include the following statement from his *Origin of Species.*

> I can see no difficulty in a race of bears being rendered, by natural selection, more and more aquatic in their habits, with larger and larger mouths, till a creature was produced as monstrous as a whale.[35]

We find ourselves in a quandary. We can gradually build up this additional statement by many small mutations, each of which might occur by "chance" with a reasonably high probability. But the intermediate states will all entail nonsensical sentence fragments that correspond in our analogy to useless or harmful mutant organs. We can also introduce the entire statement by a single random mutation; but then we are confronted by the problem that such a mutation must be exceedingly improbable. The more numerous the letters involved, the more improbable it is that they will fall into place the way you want them. The probability goes down exponentially with the number of variables, and the same can be said in general about multifeatured biological mutations.

Of course, we could devise a genetic system in which a mutation in a single regulatory gene would cause our new statement suddenly to manifest itself. But could we do this without, in effect, building the statement into the system? If not, one might naturally ask how such complex latent information got into the genetic system in the first place.

Questions such as these cannot be avoided in the study of bears, whales, and living beings in general. The point of our artificial example is that the concepts of regulative and structural genes, although suggesting possible ways to explain several kinds of mutations, do not automatically answer these questions. The real problem of evolutionary theory—how to account for the origin of completely new organs and functions—remains as baffling as before. And until evolutionists can provide a convincing solution to this problem, we must conclude that their evolutionary speculations have no sound basis.

As a final observation, we note that the concept of regulatory genes can be used as the starting point of a nonevolutionary theory of the origin of species. Consider the datum that horses are occasionally born with three-toed feet. One explanation of this is that horses are the lineal descendants of multitoed ancestors. According to the latest theories, in the course of the horses's evolutionary history, a series of mutations in regulatory genes must have suppressed the embryonic development of all but the central toe.

An alternative explanation runs as follows: Let us suppose that an intelligent creator wished to devise blueprints for a variety of animal forms. What would be the most economical way for him to go about this? Would it be best for him to design each animal completely from scratch? Or would it be more efficient for him to devise one basic plan that could be modified in various ways to produce various specific animal forms?

We can see that the second strategy would be the most economical, and it is certainly the strategy that a human engineer would choose, if possible. Now, it turns out that the idea of regulative genes provides a means of executing this strategy. Suppose, for example, that a highly intelligent engineer had decided to design the mammals by making modifications in a fundamental five-toed body plan. In that case, when he began to work on the design for a horse, he would be faced with the problem of how to eliminate all but one of the toes of the generalized mammalian foot. Our proposal is that this could easily be done by the manipulation of regulatory genes *if* the engineer had had the foresight to properly design the genetic system of his basic mammalian plan. If the genetic system were properly designed, he could suppress the growth of the unwanted toes simply by throwing a single genetic switch, and thus save himself the effort of completely redesigning the genes for the foot.

We should point out, however, that while such manipulations of the genetic system might simplify the task of designing a horse's foot, they could not be sufficient for the complete execution of this task. Consider the following description of a horse's hoof:

> Such a hoof, which is fitted to the limb like a die protecting the third phalanx, can without rubber or springs buffer impacts which sometimes exceed one ton. It could not have formed by mere chance: a close examination of the structure of the hoof reveals that it is a storehouse of coaptations and of organic novelties. The horny wall, by its vertical keratophyl laminae, is fused with the podophyl laminae of the keratogenous layer. The respective lengths of the bones, their mode of articulation, the curves and shapes of the articular surfaces, the structure of bones (orientation, arrangement of the bony layers), the presence of ligaments, tendons sliding with sheaths, buffer cushions, navicular bone, synovial membranes with their serous lubricating liquid, all imply a continuity in the construction which random events, necessarily chaotic and incomplete, could not have produced and maintained.[36]

The author of this description is observing that the horse's hoof has many complex, intricately interrelated features that can hardly be accounted for by random mutations in either structural or regulatory genes. To design a regulative gene system that would allow for the quick production of such an elaborate structure, much work would be required—perhaps as much work as would be needed to design the hoof completely from scratch. Here our engineer would have no recourse but to directly confront a difficult problem in complex design. This, of course, is possible for an intelligent engineer, but no one has yet shown how it could be accomplished by a blind evolutionary process.

The baleen whales provide another example of how regulative genes could be used to facilitate the production of organic designs. These whales do not have teeth, and their mouths are equipped with an elaborate filter that they use to strain from the seawater the small organisms on which they feed. The embryo of a baleen whale begins to develop teeth, but these are resorbed by the tissues of the mouth at an early stage of development. Evolutionists have argued that these embryonic teeth prove that the baleen whales must have descended from a toothed ancestor.[37]

Yet a different interpretation is possible. Let us suppose, as before, that an intelligent engineer was designing the forms of various mammals by modifying a basic mammalian plan. Such a plan would naturally have specifications for teeth, but if the plan were properly designed, the engineer could suppress the development of the teeth by making simple adjustments in regulatory genes. Such adjustments would not eliminate all of the specifications for teeth from the genetic system, and they might allow for the temporary appearance of teeth in the embryonic stage, as we see in the whale. To produce the baleen filter, however, the engineer would have to introduce many specific, detailed instructions into the genetic system.

We can thus see that the supposedly atavistic teeth of the embryonic whale can also be given a nonevolutionary interpretation as byproducts of the design strategy of an intelligent engineer. The whale's filtration system can also readily be understood as a product of intelligent design, but it is hard to see how it could have evolved by mutation and natural selection.

The hypothesis that living organisms have been designed by an intelligent creator is in agreement with the alternative world view that we have been introducing step-by-step in this book. We cannot conclude, of course, that the structural plans of living organisms were necessarily conceived and executed in the particular way that we have envisioned in this speculative discussion. Our aim was to show that evidence commonly cited as proof of the theory of evolution can often be explained just as convincingly in nonevolutionary terms. However, such speculative explanations cannot actually provide reliable information about the process of creation or the nature of the creator. Our theme has been that such information can only be obtained by a transcendental process that takes advantage of the higher sensory and cognitive capacities of the conscious self.

8.5 Evolution and Negative Theology

We have seen that there is no direct evidence for the evolution of complex organic forms and that some prominent paleontologists maintain that such evidence may never be found. We have also seen that evolutionists do not have an adequate theory of evolutionary change and that they are still groping for such a theory in the realms of speculation and vague conjecture. We are therefore led to ask: In the absence of both observation and theory, what has convinced scientists to accept what we can only call the doctrine of evolution?

One important line of reasoning that has led many persons to adopt an evolutionary point of view could be called the argument by negative theology. Darwin himself used this argument extensively, and since his time it has been a mainstay of evolutionary thought.

In a recent popular book, the paleontologist Steven J. Gould presents one form of the negative theological argument in these words: "Odd arrangements and funny solutions are the proof of evolution—paths that a sensible God would never tread but that a natural process, constrained by history, follows perforce."[38] The general form of the argument can be outlined as follows: "God must have certain characteristics, *X*, and therefore He would have created a certain sort of world. Since the world as we see it is very different from this, it must be that there is no God. Since the only alternative to divine creation that we can think of is evolution, life must have arisen by some kind of evolutionary process."

This argument has two basic forms. One of these is the traditional argument from evil against the existence of God. According to this argument, the existence of many kinds of suffering, both in the human species and in the plant and animal kingdoms, is inconsistent with the idea that the world was created by an all-powerful, benevolent being. In contrast, such suffering seems to fit naturally into the evolutionary world view.

The second form of the argument is that many features of living organisms would not, as Gould says, be designed by a "sensible God" and must therefore be due to evolution. An example of this sort of argument is provided by Darwin's work with orchids. Darwin observed that the petals of these flowers are deployed in many remarkable arrangements, which insure that visiting insects will carry pollen from one flower to another. Yet since modified petals, rather than a completely novel kind of structure, are used in these arrangements, Darwin argued that divine creation was ruled out and that the orchids must therefore be products of evolution. In the words of Gould, "If God had designed a beautiful machine to reflect his wisdom and power, surely he would not have used a collection of parts generally fashioned for other purposes."[39]

What can we say about these arguments? We can immediately dismiss both versions of the negative theological argument as scientifically unsound, for they are based on completely speculative ideas about the purposes of God and the methods He uses to achieve them. We have pointed out before that while reasoning that rests on a finite set of material observations may confirm a given theory about God, such reasoning cannot prove the theory to be true. The same observation can be made about *negative* arguments that depend on a particular theological theory. In the negative theological argument the initial premise, "God must have certain characteristics, *X*," has never even been clearly formulated by the evolutionists, and such a premise has certainly never been proven by them, either by logic or by induction from observations. It is also hardly necessary to point out that the second premise of this argument—the premise that evolution is the only alternative to divine creation—has also never been proven.

The negative theological argument is dependent on a painfully naive and limited conception of God, and it collapses as soon as a more satisfactory conception is introduced. We have already seen an example of this in our discussion of the horse's toes and the embryonic teeth of the whale. Evolutionists argue that a "sensible God" would never produce such aberrations, but we have seen that these bodily structures can readily be interpreted as byproducts of the design strategy of a master engineer. The key to this interpretation is the realization that God does not necessarily intend the material world as an exhibition of His finest worksmanship.

What is the purpose of the material world? The evolutionists have adopted a mechanistic world view that excludes the very idea of purpose, but at the same time some of them cling to a certain conception of what God's purposes would be *if* He existed. Yet theirs is not the only conception that is possible. To demonstrate this, we will outline the understanding of the purpose of the material world presented in the *Bhagavad-gītā*.

According to the *Bhagavad-gītā*, one can understand the purpose of the material creation through the concept of free will. The natural relationship between the *jīvātmā* and Kṛṣṇa is one of loving reciprocal service, and love can exist only for one who has freedom. The *jīvātmā* is free to turn away from his relationship with the Supreme Person and seek to be independent, and Kṛṣṇa creates the material world as a place where the *jīvātmā* can do this. Here the *jīvātmā* becomes temporarily forgetful of his true nature and transmigrates from body to body in various species of life.[40]

Therefore, the material world is a place of suffering. The conditioned living beings, deprived of their central object of devotion, inevitably have clashing interests, and become intense sources of misery for one another. This misery is a byproduct of the more fundamental misery of ignorance and forgetfulness that characterizes the material world, and is exhibited in various degrees of severity in various forms of embodied life.

The bodies of the living species are temporary vehicles designed to accommodate sentient beings in various states of forgetful consciousness.

Since all of these forms represent limitations on the true nature of the *jīvātmā,* it is not surprising that they should be crafted in a rough and ready manner. It is also not surprising that the living species should show systematic similarities in bodily structure. All organic forms correspond to states of consciousness of one fundamental type of being, and, in principle, they can all be understood systematically in psychological terms.

According to the *Bhagavad-gītā,* the miserable conditions in the material world are due neither to malevolence nor to poor design on the part of the creator. Rather, they are consequences of the free will of the *jīvātmā* himself, and they can be alleviated on an individual basis by the proper exercise of free will. In Chapter 9 we will discuss this in greater detail. Here we simply note that the negative theological argument of the evolutionists does not apply to the world system of the *Bhagavad-gītā*—at least, not as the argument stands. Evolutionists would do well to examine the hidden metaphysical assumptions of their argument, and consider whether or not such an argument can serve as the basis for a scientific theory.

If we closely examine the negative theological argument, we find that it seems to originate not from logical considerations, but from a sense of deep dissatisfaction with the theological conceptions that form its real foundation. These conceptions are inherited from Western religious systems that the evolutionists, beginning with Darwin, have emphatically rejected. Presentations of the theory of evolution are often permeated with an attitude of contempt for these religious systems, and the negative theological argument, in particular, often takes the form of an emotional tirade directed against the idea of divine creation.

When we consider the irrational character of such presentations in light of the observational and theoretical weaknesses of evolutionary thought, the "theory" of evolution seems little more than a poorly reasoned intellectual reaction against a spiritual tradition that was perceived as inadequate. Unfortunately, it has also been an entirely futile reaction, for the evolutionists have succeeded neither in providing a genuine alternative source of spiritual knowledge nor in establishing a workable material explanation for the origin of life.

The role the negative theological argument plays in the theory of evolution becomes clear when we consider the historical context in which this theory arose. When Darwin published his *Origin of Species* in 1859, scientific thought in Europe had been dominated for many years by an approach to spiritual knowledge known as natural theology. According to this approach, one can deduce from observations of natural phenomena that the world has been created by a supremely intelligent, benevolent, and all-powerful being. Pointing to the highly organized plans of living beings, the proponents of natural theology evoked the "argument from design," which maintains that these plans imply the existence of an intelligent creator.

This emphasis on natural theology indicated a serious weakness in the philosophical and religious thought of the time. The argument from design was stressed because it seemed to provide definite proof of the existence of God. Yet this argument has two deficiencies—it is not able to actually prove that God exists, and more importantly, it is not able to provide definite information about the nature of God.

The conception of God advocated by the natural theologians was actually derived from the traditional religious systems of Judaism and Christianity. The verifiability of this conception was entirely dependent on the capacity of these religious systems to bring individuals into direct contact with God. The argument from design could only provide confirmation and the illusion of verification, and the fact that it was heavily stressed shows that practical means of attaining genuine spiritual realization were wanting.

To many scientists this state of affairs was disheartening. The argument from design seemed to lock them into a stultifying system of useless, unverifiable doctrines. It could not satisfy their curiosity about the origins of life, it offered no new avenues of scientific investigation, and it provided no tangible spiritual insight. Thus many perceived natural theology as a dead end.

In this context we can understand the initial appeal of Darwin's theory of evolution. Darwin explicitly rejected the sterile arguments of natural theology and introduced an approach to the origin of life based entirely on physical principles. This approach seemed to bring the question of origins into the familiar realms of physics and chemistry, where scientists had had so much success using the experimental method, and thus it held forth the promise of similar success.

Yet we have seen that this promise has never been fulfilled. Although the theory of evolution has become institutionalized as the standard explanation for the origin of species, it has not outgrown its original status as a reaction against an imperfect and restrictive system of theological thought. As such, it is no more valid than the system of natural theology it historically displaced. If speculative reasoning has given rise to an imperfect conception of God, then we certainly cannot expect negative arguments based on this conception to yield a true understanding of life's origins.

How, then, can we obtain a genuine understanding? Our suggestion is that we can reach such an understanding only through a valid spiritual science. Speculation resting on a finite set of material observations is indeed inadequate to provide valid knowledge about a supreme transcendental being. But the answer to this problem is not to deny the existence of such a being and to seek explanations solely in familiar physical principles. This is the fallacy of the drunk who lost his keys near the doorstep of his house but would search for them only under a streetlamp because the light was better there.

Notes

1. Tax and Callender, eds., *Evolution After Darwin,* pp. 265–266.
2. Rensberger, "Recent Studies Spark Revolution in Interpretation of Evolution," p. C3.
3. Ibid.
4. Gould and Eldridge, "Punctuated Equilibria: The Tempo and Mode of Evolution Reconsidered," pp. 115–151.
5. Grasse, *Evolution of Living Organisms,* p. 124.
6. Harland, *et. al.* (eds.), *The Fossil Record.*
7. Ibid.
8. Andrews, *Studies in Paleobotany,* chap. 6.
9. Axelrod, "The Evolution of Flowering Plants," p. 229.
10. Axelrod, p. 230.
11. Ibid.
12. Dodson and Dodson, *Evolution, Process and Product,* p. 141.
13. Valentine, "The Evolution of Multicellular Plants and Animals," pp. 141–158.
14. Glaessner, "Biological Events and the Precambrian Time Scale," pp. 470–477.
15. Stainforth, pp. 292–294.
16. McDougall, Compston, and Hawkes, p. 567.
17. Snelling, p. 1079.
18. Axelrod, "Evolution of the Psilophyte Paleoflora," pp. 264–275.
19. Jacob, Jacob, and Shrivastava, p. 166.
20. Wadia, *The Geology of India,* pp. 141–142.

21. Axelrod, "Evolution of the Psilophyte Paleoflora," pp. 268–269.
22. Mayr, "The Emergence of Evolutionary Novelties," p. 359.
23. Lewin, "Evolutionary Theory Under Fire," p. 883.
24. Kepner, Gregory, and Porter, "The Manipulation of the Nematocysts of Chlorohydra by Microstomum," pp. 114–124.
25. Darwin, *On the Origin of Species,* p. 189.
26. Gould, *The Panda's Thumb,* p. 133.
27. Buddenbrock, *The Senses,* pp. 138–141.
28. Berg, "How Bacteria Swim," pp. 36–44.
29. Hinkel and McCarty, "How Cells Make ATP," p. 116.
30. Wilson, *The Mystery of Physical Life,* pp. 28–31.
31. Adler, "Is Man a Subtle Accident?" pp. 95–96.
32. Goldschmidt, *The Material Basis of Evolution.*
33. Gould, "Hens Teeth and Horse's Toes," pp. 24–28.
34. Cited in Gillespie, *Charles Darwin and the Problem of Creation,* p. 87.
35. Darwin, p. 184.
36. Grasse, p. 51.
37. Gould, *The Panda's Thumb,* p. 29.
38. Ibid., pp. 20–21.
39. Ibid.
40. A.C. Bhaktivedanta Swami Prabhupāda, *Bhagavad-gītā As It Is,* pp. 89, 102, 704–707.

PART III

CONCLUSION

Chapter 9

The Epistemology Of Transcendental Consciousness

In a letter to Max Born, Albert Einstein expressed his faith as a physicist:

> You believe in the God who plays dice, and I in complete law and order in a world which objectively exists, and which I, in a wildly speculative way, am trying to capture. I firmly *believe*, but I hope that someone will discover a more realistic way, or rather a more tangible basis than it has been my lot to do.[1]

Einstein believed that the phenomena of nature were expressions of a unified underlying reality, and he was convinced that this ultimate foundation must be accessible to human understanding. Following the path of modern science, he believed that the fundamental principles of nature could be expressed by mathematical formulas abstracted from experimental data by the power of his mind. According to Einstein, scientists could pin down the unified basis of reality if they could find simple formulas that would account for all the phenomena of the universe.

Yet we have seen in Part II that a quantitative description of nature cannot be both simple and universal. In particular, we have shown that any quantitative description that adequately accounts for the phenomena of life must be exceedingly complex. When a large amount of information is expressed as succinctly as possible, it satisfies the statistical criteria for randomness; thus a truly complex law, if it is reduced to its simplest form, will appear to be a product of lawless chaos. (See Chapters 5 and 6.) It follows that Einstein's method of capturing the world can end only in frustration. In the search for a unified understanding of nature, we must ultimately confront a vast array of irreducibly complex patterns that cannot be specified by a simple universal law or formula, and that must therefore seem extremely arbitrary from a mechanistic point of view.

We encounter such irreducible patterns when we try to explain living form in its various aspects—which range from the metabolic processes of cells to the subtleties of human behavior. In an ultimate sense, such patterns are inexplicable, for any quantitative explanation that is intended to account for them must be just as complex and arbitrary as the patterns themselves.

While the complex bodily structures of living organisms cannot be concisely explained in mechanistic terms, at least they can be quantitatively described. In Part I of this book, however, we discussed another feature of life—the phenomenon of conscious awareness—that is not even touched upon by descriptions of the measurable behavior of matter.

We customarily associate consciousness with certain states of activity in "conscious living bodies," but since we directly perceive our own consciousness, consciousness must be more than just a name for particular patterns of behavior. One may say that this perception is subjective, but if we are to avoid the position of solipsism, we must accept the consciousness of others to be an objective fact of nature. This objectively existing consciousness must be distinguished from the behavior of matter. Indeed, if we analyze the functioning of material systems such as the brain, we see that the contents of our consciousness cannot be correlated in a one-to-one fashion with measurable events in such systems. (See Chapters 2 and 3.) Consciousness is thus a feature of reality that is impossible to capture by mechanistic laws, either simple or complex.

The phenomena of consciousness and complex form stand as insurmountable obstacles blocking any attempt to capture the world by a quantitative theory. To find a successful approach to understanding reality, we must therefore depart from the mechanistic framework of modern science. In this book we have taken a step in this direction by outlining an alternative, nonmechanistic world view based on the *Bhagavad-gītā,* the *Bhāgavata Purāṇa,* and other Vedic literatures of India.

The world view of the *Bhagavad-gītā* is based on the postulate that conscious personality is the ultimate basis of reality. Thus far we have introduced some of the elements of this world view by briefly describing two fundamental categories of conscious beings. The first category has a single member—the unique Supreme Person, Kṛṣṇa, who is the primordial cause of all causes, and who is directly conscious of all phenomena. The second category consists of the innumerable localized conscious beings, or *jīvātmās.* The *jīvātmās* are irreducible conscious persons, and they are qualitatively the same as the Supreme Person. Yet they differ from the Supreme in that they are minute and dependent, whereas the Supreme Person is unlimited and fully independent.

The nature of the *jīvātmās* is discussed in Chapters 1, 2, and 3, and the Supreme Person is described in Chapter 6. Chapter 7 discusses the relationship between the Supreme Person, the *jīvātmās,* and the material energy, and it introduces the solution to the mind-body problem given in the *Bhagavad-gītā*.

We argue in these chapters that the philosophy of the *Bhagavad-gītā* provides a consistent picture of the phenomena of life. It accounts for the origin and continued maintenance of the complex material forms of living organisms. It also clarifies the nature of individual consciousness, and explains the relationship between the conscious self and the body. The objection may be raised, however, that even though this philosophy may provide interesting speculative solutions to certain fundamental scientific problems, we have not yet even begun to prove that it is true.

We agree that nothing we have said so far constitutes proof. The two categories of conscious beings that we have considered lie almost entirely outside the purview of empirical investigation based on reason and ordinary sense perception. Our conscious awareness includes direct perception of itself, but apart from this, our ordinary senses provide us only with information about the configurations of material bodies. On the basis of reasoning, introspection, and ordinary sense perception, we can infer that consciousness must be due to some entity that is distinct from matter as we know it, but we cannot arrive at a truly satisfactory understanding of this entity by these means.

Similar remarks can be made about the problem of proving the existence of a supreme conscious being. Many philosophers and scientists have maintained that the complex order displayed by the bodies of living organisms is evidence for the existence of an intelligent creator. We have argued that this is indeed a reasonable explanation of biological form, and we have shown in Chapters 5 through 8 that scientists of the evolutionary persuasion are still groping unsuccessfully to find a workable mechanistic explanation. Yet observations of biological form convey no clear picture of the creator by themselves, and it is indeed hard to see how a finite number of observations made within a limited region of space and time could prove very much about the nature of an unlimited eternal being.

Arguments for the existence of God from the evidence of nature are usually based indirectly on a conception of God that is derived from other sources. These arguments may show that such a conception is consistent with the facts of nature, but what these facts actually entail is at best an idea of God so vague and general that it is practically useless.

So, if our alternative model of reality cannot be established by standard empirical methods, then how can it be established? We have suggested that the key to verifying our model is provided by the unique nonmechanistic features of the model itself. According to the *Bhagavad-gītā*, the natural senses of the *jīvātmā* are not limited to picking up information from the sensory apparatus of a particular material body. Indeed, a *jīvātmā* in this situation is considered to be in an abnormal condition, and can be compared to a person who has become so engrossed in watching a television program that he has forgotten about his own existence, and has accepted the flickering two-dimensional image on the television screen to be the all in all. The *jīvātmā* is capable of directly perceiving both other *jīvātmās* and the Supreme Person, although in the bodily state of existence, he is prevented from doing this by his preoccupation with the fascinating show presented by the bodily senses.

It follows that our model can be verified if a way can be found to reawaken the full cognitive capacities of the conscious self. In this chapter we will outline a practical method of doing this known as *bhakti-yoga,* or devotional service. We will present this process as a method of obtaining reliable knowledge about aspects of reality that are inaccessible by traditional methods of scientific research. We should note, however, that *bhakti-yoga* is not simply a method of obtaining knowledge. Rather, it is a means whereby each individual conscious self can attain the ultimate goal of his existence.

9.1 The Process of Bhakti-yoga

The process of *bhakti-yoga* involves reawakening the natural relationship that exists between the individual conscious self and the Supreme Person, Kṛṣṇa. We pointed out in Chapter 7 that Kṛṣṇa accompanies each embodied *jīvātmā* as the Supersoul, and that He directs the material body of the *jīvātmā* in accordance with the *jīvātmā's* desires and past *karma*. This means that a relationship is always existing between the *jīvātmā* and the Supreme Person, but in the materially embodied state the *jīvātmā* is not conscious of this relationship, and it is consequently one-sided. In this condition the *jīvātmā* is not directly aware of the Lord, and either ignores Him or appeals to Him as a vaguely conceived supplier of material needs.

The fundamental postulate of *bhakti-yoga* is that this is an abnormal state of affairs. Since the *jīvātmā* and Kṛṣṇa are of the same qualitative nature, there is a natural symmetry between their respective personal characteristics and tendencies. In the *Bhagavad-gītā* it is stated that Kṛṣṇa is constitutionally the dearmost friend of all other conscious beings, and that He is always caring for them out of natural concern for their welfare.[2] Similarly, the *jīvātmā* has a natural tendency to care for the happiness and wellbeing of Kṛṣṇa, and in a state of pure consciousness the *jīvātmā* serves Kṛṣṇa without desire for personal profit. In this state a loving reciprocal relationship develops between the person and Kṛṣṇa. One secondary consequence of this relationship is that by directly contacting the Supreme Person, the person is placed in touch with the source of all knowledge.

The goal of *bhakti-yoga* is to purify the person's consciousness so that his natural relationship with the Supreme can be reawakened. This comes about through the performance of practical devotional service to Kṛṣṇa. Just as a lame person can regain the ability to walk by practicing walking, so a person in material consciousness can revive his relationship of loving service to Kṛṣṇa by actually beginning to practice such service. This can be accomplished if an initial link can be established that enables the person to actually serve Kṛṣṇa through the activities performed by his material body. A number of important considerations are involved in establishing this link, and we will discuss these briefly, one at a time.

First we shall discuss the bearing of a person's inner attitudes on his chances for success in the search for knowledge. The world view of modern science rests on the idea that nature is a product of impersonal processes that lie within the reach of human understanding. Following this idea, many scientists view nature as a passive object of conquest and exploitation, and they try to extract the secrets of nature forcibly by the power of their minds and senses. The theories of modern science are consonant with a domineering and aggressive attitude, and it can be argued that their development has been strongly influenced by a desire to accommodate such an attitude.

In contrast, *bhakti-yoga* is based on the idea that nature is the product of a supreme intelligence that is beyond the understanding of the human mind. The approach of *bhakti-yoga* is not to dominate this intelligence, but rather to cooperate with it. It is not possible for a person to acquire real knowledge about Kṛṣṇa by the power of his limited mind. The key to *bhakti-yoga* is that by the mercy of Kṛṣṇa, such knowledge is readily available to a person who approaches Him with a sincerely favorable attitude.

The quality of this attitude is indicated in the following statement spoken by Kṛṣṇa to Arjuna in the *Bhagavad-gītā:*

> Always think of Me and become My devotee. Worship Me and offer your homage unto Me. Thus you will come to Me without fail. I promise you this because you are My very dear friend.[3]

If a person maintains an inimical or aggressive attitude toward the absolute truth and regards it as a field of conquest for his mind, then he will have to depend completely on his ordinary sensory and mental powers in his search for knowledge. But if the person adopts a genuinely agreeable and favorable attitude toward the absolute, then by the mercy of the absolute, the person's internal and external circumstances will gradually be so adjusted that absolute knowledge becomes accessible to him. The essential element is the change in attitude. In the beginning a person may have only the vaguest conception of what the absolute truth may be, but if he adopts a truly positive attitude toward the absolute, then he will eventually be able to reciprocate personally with the absolute in a mutual relationship of love and trust.

This brings us to our second consideration. If a person is initially limited to his ordinary bodily senses as sources of information, then how can he make the first step in obtaining transcendental knowledge? Also, if his ultimate objective is to serve the transcendental Supreme Person, then how can he do this when his activities are limited to the manipulation of matter? The answer to these questions is that Kṛṣṇa is able to reciprocate with an embodied *jīvātmā* in two important ways—internally as the all-pervading Supersoul, and externally through the agency of another embodied person who is already connected with Him in a transcendental relationship.

Such a person is known as a *guru,* or spiritual master. The *guru* is described in the following way in the *Bhagavad-gītā:*

> Just try to learn the truth by approaching a spiritual master. Inquire from him submissively and render service unto him. The self-realized soul can impart knowledge unto you because he has seen the truth.[4]

Since the *guru* is in direct contact with Kṛṣṇa, he can act as Kṛṣṇa's representative. The *guru* can make information about Kṛṣṇa available to the people in general through the medium of the written and spoken word, and he can also accept service on behalf of Kṛṣṇa. According to the system of *bhakti-yoga,* a person can begin to serve Kṛṣṇa by accepting a genuine *guru,* hearing about Kṛṣṇa from him, and rendering service to him. Service to the *guru* is accepted by Kṛṣṇa as direct service to Himself, and He reciprocates by enlightening the person with the knowledge that he needs to make further advancement on the path of *bhakti-yoga.*

The process of *bhakti-yoga* is summed up by the following statement in the *Caitanya-caritāmṛta:*

> Kṛṣṇa is situated in everyone's heart as *caitya-guru,* the spiritual master within. When He is kind to some fortunate conditioned soul, He personally gives that person lessons in how to progress in devotional service, instructing the person as the Supersoul within and the spiritual master without.[5]

In the initial stages of this process, the aspiring candidate depends almost entirely on the guidance supplied to him externally through the *guru*. However, through service to the *guru,* the candidate's link with Kṛṣṇa is established, and his own natural relationship with Kṛṣṇa is gradually awakened.

9.2 Faith, Subjectivity, and Verifiability

At this point we should make a few observations about the role of faith in *bhakti-yoga.* It is often said that religion is based either on subjective experiences that cannot be verified by other persons, or on received doctrines that cannot be verified at all. The charge is therefore made that religion is a matter of blind faith. We should stress that this charge does not apply to the process of *bhakti-yoga,* for *bhakti-yoga* is based on verifiable observation. It is true that the realizations attained by this process cannot be verified by means of ordinary sense perception. But they can be verified by other persons who are also capable of exercising their higher sensory capacities.

In Chapter 3 we illustrated this point by the example of two seeing persons observing a sunset in the presence of a congenitally blind person. The seeing persons are able to discuss what they see, and each will feel confident that both he and the other person really are witnessing a sunset. If necessary, they can confirm this by consulting other seeing persons. In contrast, the congenitally blind person cannot verify the existence of the sunset, and he is probably unable to form a realistic conception of what it would be like to see it. He can either accept the existence of sunsets on blind faith, reject their existence with equal blindness, or else declare himself to be an agnostic.

One might say that it is unfair for a few people to lay claim to knowledge that can only be obtained by methods not available to people in general. However, this charge is actually more applicable to certain fields of modern science than it is to *bhakti-yoga.* For example, physicists use multi-million-dollar particle accelerators and elaborate techniques of mathematical analysis to demonstrate the existence of certain "fundamental" particles. Yet the common man has no access to such expensive equipment, and he does not have the knowledge needed to properly use it. Since these assets are very difficult to acquire, the common man has no choice but to accept the findings of the physicists on faith. Nonetheless, the physicists are confident that they can verify one another's observations, and they would not accept the charge that their conclusions are invalid because they cannot be checked by laymen.

For a given class of observations to be considered objective, the general rule is that there must be a group of responsible people who are capable of verifying them. These people must agree on a clear theoretical understanding of what observations are to be expected and how they are to be interpreted. Modern physics is based on such a group of experts, and the same can be said of the process of *bhakti-yoga*. The system of *bhakti-yoga* is maintained and propagated by a disciplic succession of teachers, or *gurus*, who have reached a high platform of personal realization. These teachers adhere to a standard body of knowledge that is contained in books such as the *Bhagavad-gītā*, and their conclusions and conduct can be checked by the larger community of realized persons, or *sadhus*. The higher realizations of the process of *bhakti-yoga* can be discussed and evaluated by the qualified *sadhus* just as readily as the findings of experimental physics can be evaluated by expert physicists.[6]

Since *bhakti-yoga* is based on verifiable observation, it is not dependent either on blind faith or on speculative argumentation. Yet faith is required in any difficult undertaking, and the process of *bhakti-yoga* is no exception. For example, before studying modern chemistry the prospective student must have faith that the many experiments on which the subject is based actually work. He cannot know in advance that they will work, but without faith in this he will not be motivated to carry out the arduous work needed to master the subject. Normally, the student will begin with a certain amount of initial faith, and this faith gradually will grow as he acquires more and more practical experience. The same gradual development of faith occurs in *bhakti-yoga*.

Perhaps the main reason for the widespread casting aside of religion as "blind faith" is that many systems of theistic thought are not backed up by any verifiable, direct interaction with the Supreme Person. We may ask why this should be if the Supreme Person is as readily accessible as we have indicated in our discussion thus far. The following statement in the *Bhāgavata Purāṇa* gives an interesting answer to this question:

> The great thinkers can know Him [Kṛṣṇa] when completely freed from all material hankerings and when sheltered under undisturbed conditions of the senses. Otherwise, by untenable arguments, all is distorted, and the Lord disappears from our sight.[7]

One of the most important principles of *bhakti-yoga* is that higher realization is impossible as long as the material senses are not brought under control. In the materially conditioned state of consciousness, the *jīvātmā* is motivated by the desire to enjoy his material situation, and he is completely preoccupied with the barrage of stimuli presented by his material senses. In this state the *jīvātmā's* sensory channels are overloaded, and he is unable to perceive the presence of the Supersoul, even though he is constitutionally capable of doing this. Since the *jīvātmā* with uncontrolled senses has no direct access to the Supreme Person, he is prone to indulge in fanciful speculations that simply lead him further and further from the truth.

9.3 The Brain, the Mind, and the Conscious Self

To understand some of the practical problems involved in controlling the senses, we must introduce the concept of the material mind. We have already pointed out that the *jīvātmā* is a complete, conscious individual and that, as such, the *jīvātmā* is inherently capable of carrying out the mental functions of thinking, feeling, and willing. Yet the machinery of the body includes a psychic subsystem that duplicates some of these functions. This subsystem acts as an intermediate link between the natural senses of the *jīvātmā* and the sensory apparatus of the body. Before reaching the *jīvātmā,* data from the bodily senses pass through this subsystem and are augmented and modified by the addition of information representing various thoughts, feelings, and desires.

This intermediate link consists of two components, one of which is the brain. In modern science the brain is generally held to be the seat of all mental functions. According to the *Bhagavad-gītā,* however, the mind has an additional component which in Sanskrit is called the *manaḥ,* or material mind, and which is distinct from both the brain and the conscious self. This material mind serves as a connecting link between the brain and the self. It is composed of a kind of material energy, and, in principle, it could be studied by ordinary empirical methods. At present there is no widely accepted scientific theory of the material mind, but some of the findings of the parapsychologists may provide the basis for such a theory.

It would take us too far afield to discuss the higher physics of the material mind here, but we will make a few remarks about the functional relationship between the material mind and the brain. According to the *Bhagavad-gītā,* the material mind interacts directly with the brain and body, and the conscious self interacts with the material mind through the agency of the Supersoul. The relationship between the brain and the material mind can be compared with the relationship between a computer and a computer programmer. Consider a businessman who has programmed a computer to process his accounts. The computer can be regarded as an extension of the man's mind that has its own memory and data-processing facilities. Even though the man is a complete person in and of himself, he may come to depend heavily on the computer, and thus his ability to conduct his business affairs may be greatly impaired if the computer is damaged. Similarly, the brain is a computerlike extension of the material mind, and even though this material system can function independently of the brain, it tends to become dependent on the brain for the execution of certain data-processing operations.

Taken together, the material body and mind can be regarded as a kind of false self in which the real self rides as a passenger. This false self is not conscious in its own right. Both the brain and the material mind can be regarded as mechanisms for symbol manipulation comparable with man-made computers. The "thoughts" of the material mind are mere patterns of symbols, and they become represented by actual thoughts only when they are perceived by the *jīvātmā.* The tendency of the embodied *jīvātmā,* however, is to accept the thoughts, feelings, and desires of the material mind as his own, and thereby to falsely identify himself as the dramatic persona represented by these patterns of symbols.

Since the material mind is the director of the material senses, control of these senses can be achieved by controlling the mind. Since most of us have never made a real effort to practice such control, we may tend to underestimate both its importance and the difficulties involved in achieving it. We may obtain some idea of these difficulties if we consider the powerful role that habits of thought and action play in our normal activities. The material mind is a reservoir of elaborate programs that govern everything from gross movements to subtle attitudes, and thus our mental life consists of a succession of conditioned thoughts and feelings that unfold inexorably according to their own internal logic and the stimuli of the senses.

Since we normally tend to identify the material mind with the self, we have no real idea of what it would be like to be free from this endless torrent of mundane images and associations. This is indicated, however, by the following statement in the *Bhagavad-gītā:*

> For one who has conquered the mind, the Supersoul is already reached, for he has attained tranquility. To such a man happiness and distress, heat and cold, honor and dishonor are all the same.[8]

Once the material mind is under control, the natural senses of the *jīvātmā* are free to directly perceive the Supreme Person.

9.4 The Positive and Negative Injunctions of Bhakti

In *bhakti-yoga,* control of the material mind and senses is achieved by the following of certain positive and negative injunctions. The negative injunctions involve the restriction of activities that tend to agitate the material mind and distract the *jīvātmā* from the process of self-realization.

The most fundamental of these injunctions prohibit indulgence in intoxication, meat-eating, illicit sexual affairs, and exploitative business enterprises. We do not have sufficient space here to discuss the psychological dynamics of these activities in detail, but we note that they tend to cause persons who engage in them to become more and more preoccupied with the actions and reactions of their material senses.

In many scientific experiments the physical conditions in the experimental apparatus have to be carefully adjusted if the experiment is to be a success. The process of *bhakti-yoga* is an experiment in which the body and material mind are the experimental apparatus, and in which the negative injunctions are neccessary (but not sufficient) conditions for the experiment's success. These injunctions are essential. If a person neglects them he will not be able to free himself from material entanglement, and his "transcendental" realizations will indeed be nothing more than products of self-deception.[9]

The positive injunctions of *bhakti-yoga* prescribe activities that directly engage the individual in service to the Supreme Person, Kṛṣṇa. The effect of these activities is to awaken the *jīvātmā's* natural love for Kṛṣṇa. As a corollary to this reawakening, the *jīvātmā* automatically loses his attraction to the manifestations of his material mind, for these false theatrical displays are inherently less interesting than the absolute reality of Kṛṣṇa. Thus, by engaging in active service to Kṛṣṇa, the individual is able to attain the goal of mental control, and free his senses for further service to Kṛṣṇa.

The ultimate goal of *bhakti-yoga* is to serve Kṛṣṇa directly, and this can be done if the self is freed from entanglement in the affairs of the material mind and senses. This freedom, in turn, can be readily obtained as a consequence of performing service to Kṛṣṇa. This may seem like a vicious circle, but in practice it corresponds to a gradual process of reciprocal development. First, the material mind must be brought under moderate control by adherence to the negative injunctions of *bhakti-yoga*. Then the individual engages in practical service to Kṛṣṇa under the guidance of the *guru,* and by Kṛṣṇa's mercy he attains some realization of the Lord. As a result, his attachment to the material mind is lessened, and he is able to engage in further service to Kṛṣṇa on a higher platform of realization. This leads the individual to further freedom from material desire, and further realization of his constitutional nature as a servant of Kṛṣṇa. The *Bhāgavata Purāṇa* sums up this process and its results as follows:

> As soon as irrevocable loving service is established in the heart, the effects of nature's modes of passion and ignorance, such as lust, desire, and hankering, disappear from the heart. Then the devotee is established in goodness and he

becomes completely happy. Thus established in the mode of unalloyed goodness, the man whose mind has been enlivened by contact with devotional service to the Lord gains positive scientific knowledge of the Personality of Godhead in the stage of liberation from all material association.[10]

9.5 The Process of Śravaṇam

Service to Kṛṣṇa can take many forms, but of these the most fundamental are the processes of *śravaṇam* and *kīrtanam,* or hearing and chanting. To awaken one's relationship with Kṛṣṇa, it is necessary first to hear about Kṛṣṇa, and this is also a form of devotional service. One of the principle themes of this book has been that the absolute truth is not void, but is full of variegated attributes. The Supreme Person, Kṛṣṇa, possesses unlimited personal qualities, and He also engages in unlimited transcendental activities in reciprocation with innumerable *jīvātmās* who live in His association in a state of pure consciousness. By hearing about the attributes and pastimes of Kṛṣṇa, the materially conditioned *jīvātmā* is reminded of his own natural relationship with Kṛṣṇa. This provokes in him a desire to know more about Kṛṣṇa, and it simultaneously decreases his attachment to the affairs of the material body and mind.

The philosophy of *bhakti-yoga* holds that knowledge of the absolute must descend directly from the absolute. Kṛṣṇa is the original source of all material forms, and He is also the origin of the written information which forms the external subject matter of *bhakti-yoga.* This subject matter exists in the form of scriptures that either are produced directly by Kṛṣṇa Himself, or are written by persons who are directly linked with Kṛṣṇa in a transcendental relationship. The *Bhagavad-gītā* is an example of a scripture of the former type, and the *Bhāgavata Purāṇa* and *Caitanya-caritāmṛta* are scriptures of the latter type. As we have pointed out, the subject matter of *bhakti-yoga* is preserved and disseminated by the community of qualified *gurus* and *sadhus,* whose role in the regulation of knowledge can be compared with that of the community of experts in a scientific field.

Unlimited amounts of information about Kṛṣṇa can be encoded in the form of sequences of symbols. However, since Kṛṣṇa is absolute, information about Him is different from ordinary information describing configurations of matter. In our ordinary experience, patterns of symbols can be arranged according to the conventions of a language, so as to represent certain events in a limited region of time and space. When we perceive this information by hearing or reading, we are able to interpret the coded patterns, and as a result we become aware of a mental image of the events.

This mental image is something quite different from the events themselves. However, when the *jīvātmā* interprets information describing the Supreme Person, the resulting mental images actually bring the *jīvātmā* in direct contact with the Supreme Person. Since Kṛṣṇa is absolute, material images and sounds representing Kṛṣṇa are nondifferent from Kṛṣṇa Himself, and this can be understood directly by the *jīvātmā.* Such understanding cannot, of course, be simply a matter of material symbol manipulation. It directly involves the higher sensory and cognitive facilities of the conscious self.

Since this point is quite important, let us explore it in greater detail. According to the philosophy of the *Bhagavad-gītā,* nothing is different from Kṛṣṇa, yet nothing is Kṛṣṇa except for His own primordial personality. Kṛṣṇa is the cause and the essence of all phenomena, and in this sense all phenomena are identical with Kṛṣṇa. Yet the phenomena of this world are merely external displays projected by Kṛṣṇa's will, and His real nature is His eternal personality. As we argued in Part II, the absolute is highly specific, and therefore Kṛṣṇa can be represented by certain symbolic patterns and not others. By means of these patterns, Kṛṣṇa can introduce Himself to the conditioned *jīvātmā,* and thus these configurations are nondifferent from Kṛṣṇa in a direct personal sense. By perceiving such configurations, the *jīvātmā* is reminded of Kṛṣṇa, and by Kṛṣṇa's mercy he is allowed to see Kṛṣṇa directly by his own higher vision.

This explanation may convey some idea of how the embodied *jīvātmā,* who is normally restricted entirely to material modes of sense perception, can begin to perceive the transcendental Supreme Person. In this initial stage, the *jīvātmā's* perception of Kṛṣṇa may seem to be completely dependent on the interactions of matter, but the essence of his experience is not material. We can begin to understand this by considering the ideas that matter itself is a manifestation of Kṛṣṇa, and that material perception is simply a limited, impersonal way of seeing Kṛṣṇa.

In the highest stage of realization the reciprocation between the *jīvātmā* and Kṛṣṇa has nothing to do with the material manifestation. This relationship is not dependent on the material body of the *jīvātmā* in any way, and it continues after the body has ceased to exist. According to the philosophy of *bhakti-yoga,* the material manifestation represents only a minor aspect of the total reality. There is a higher realm that is inaccessible to material sense perception, but is nonetheless full of variegated form and activity. Here we are concerned with the question of how a materially embodied person can acquire absolute knowledge, and so we will not try to discuss this higher realm in detail.

9.6 The Process of Kīrtanam

The process of *śravanam,* or hearing, is complemented by the process of *kīrtanam,* or glorifying the Lord by singing about His qualities and pastimes, and discussing these with others. We have argued that the process of *bhakti-yoga* is scientific in the sense that it is a practical method of obtaining verifiable knowledge about the absolute truth. In the science of *bhakti-yoga,* however, the researcher approaches the absolute with an attitude of reverence and devotion, in stark contrast to the aggressive and exploitative approach that prevails in modern science. By glorifying Kṛṣṇa, the individual can awaken his natural love for Kṛṣṇa, and once this is done, Kṛṣṇa will be fully accessible to him on a personal level.

One important form of *kīrtanam* is the chanting of the names of Kṛṣṇa. In Chapter 1 we mentioned that *bhakti-yoga* involves the chanting of the *mantra,*

Hare Kṛṣṇa, Hare Kṛṣṇa, Kṛṣṇa Kṛṣṇa, Hare Hare
Hare Rāma, Hare Rāma, Rāma Rāma, Hare Hare.[11]

The Sanskrit term *mantra* refers to a pattern of sound that has a purifying effect on the mind. This particular *mantra* is composed of three names of the Supreme Person. Grammatically, the *mantra* is in the vocative case, and its meaning is to address the Lord by calling out His names.

These names are examples of symbolic patterns that directly represent the Absolute Person, and therefore have an absolute, inherent meaning. According to the philosophy of *bhakti-yoga,* Kṛṣṇa's names are nondifferent from Kṛṣṇa Himself, and by chanting and hearing these names, one is brought into personal contact with Kṛṣṇa. This can be directly appreciated by persons whose higher sensory capacities have been awakened. For others, the chanting of these names purifies their consciousness and thereby brings about this awakening.

The results of chanting the names of the Lord can be obtained by the use of any names that are actually connected with the Supreme Person, and are not mere concoctions of the material imagination. The significance of this chanting was described as follows by Śrī Caitanya Mahāprabhu, the great teacher of *bhakti-yoga* who appeared in India in the fifteenth century:

> O my Lord, Your holy name alone can render all benediction to living beings, and thus You have hundreds and millions of names, like Kṛṣṇa and Govinda. In these transcendental names You have invested all Your transcendental energies. There are not even hard and fast rules for chanting these names. O my Lord, out of kindness You enable us to easily approach You by chanting Your holy names, but I am so unfortunate that I have no attraction for them.[12]

The purport of this statement is that due to the blindness caused by his preoccupation with the material mind and senses, the conditioned *jīvātmā* will initially feel very little attraction to chanting the names of the Lord. Yet by regularly chanting these names and following the regulative injunctions of *bhakti-yoga,* this blindness can gradually be cured, and one can attain the stage of loving reciprocation with Kṛṣṇa.

Since the ultimate goal of this chanting is the development of love, it must be carried out with an inner attitude that is compatible with this emotion. Śrī Caitanya Mahāprabhu goes on to describe this attitude as follows:

> One should chant the holy name of the Lord in a humble state of mind, thinking oneself lower than the straw in the street; one should be more tolerant than a tree, devoid of all sense of false prestige, and ready to offer all respect to others. In such a state of mind one can chant the holy name of the Lord constantly.[13]

It may not be possible for a person who has no direct knowledge of the Supreme Person to immediately understand what it might mean to love the Supreme. However, it is possible for him to lay the groundwork for such understanding by adopting a nonexploitative attitude toward the Supreme Person and His creation. Indeed, this is the key to the process of *bhakti-yoga.* To one who wishes to exploit the Supreme, the Supreme will remain unknowable. But if one truly gives up the desire for such exploitation, then the Supreme Person will reveal Himself by His own mercy.

In the letter quoted at the beginning of this chapter, Einstein declared that his goal was to capture the absolute truth. The absolute truth cannot be captured forcefully by a minute part of the absolute, but according to the philosophy of *bhakti-yoga,* the absolute can be captured by love. Once this love is attained, direct knowledge of the absolute will be readily available, but paradoxically, the development of this love is not compatible with the desire for knowledge or power. Knowledge is indeed a byproduct of the process of *bhakti-yoga,* but it cannot be the goal of that process, for the key to the process itself lies in the fundamental reassessment of one's innermost goals.

Although this reassessment may be superficially simple to describe, to carry it out requires a deep insight into one's own psychology. By bringing the inner self into personal contact with the absolute, the process of *bhakti-yoga* enables one to attain this insight. By this means the absolute can be captured—once all desire to conquer the absolute has been forsaken.

Notes

1. French, ed., *Einstein*, pp. 275–276.
2. A.C. Bhaktivedanta Swami Prabhupāda, *Bhagavad-gītā As It Is*, text 5.29, pp. 303–304.
3. Ibid., text 18.66, p. 834.
4. Ibid., text 4.34, p. 259.
5. Kavirāja, *Śrī Caitanya-caritāmṛta, Madhya-lila,* Vol. 8, text 22.48, p. 351.
6. The regulation of the process of *bhakti-yoga* in the society of realized *sadhus* is vividly described in the *Śrī Caitanya-caritāmṛta.* This should be compared with the regulation of scientific research in the scientific community.
7. A.C. Bhaktivedanta Swami Prabhupāda, *Śrīmad-Bhāgavatam,* Canto 2, Vol. 1, text 2.6.41, p. 347.
8. A.C. Bhaktivedanta Swami Prabhupāda, *Bhagavad-gītā As It Is,* text 6.7, p. 315.
9. We stress this point because there are many watered-down systems of *yoga* or meditation in which even the most basic rules for sense control are neglected. Seeking self-realization through such systems is comparable to trying to ignite firewood while simultaneously pouring water on it.
10. A.C. Bhaktivedanta Swami Prabhupāda, *Śrimad-Bhāgavatam,* Canto 1, Vol. 1, texts 1.2.19–20, pp. 116–118.
11. The chanting of this *mantra* is recommended in the *Kalisantaraṇa Upaniṣad.* (See A.C. Bhaktivedanta Swami Prabhupāda, *Teachings of Lord Caitanya,* pp. 203–204.)
12. A.C. Bhaktivedanta Swami Prabhupāda, *Śrimad-Bhāgavatam,* Canto 1, Vol. 1, pp. 41–42.
13. Ibid., p. 41.

Appendix 1
A Discussion of Information Theory

The measure of information content used in Chapter 5 is the subject of a field of study called algorithmic information theory. In this appendix we will discuss the definitions and theorems from this field that we used in Sections 5.2 and 5.3. We will present a brief summary of important results. Additional details can be found in Thompson, (1980), which contains a study of observation functions from the viewpoint of information theory. A general review of algorithmic information theory can be found in Chaitin, (1977).

To define information content we must first establish a fixed computer, **C**. We assume that **C** accepts as programs bit strings P written in a particular programming language similar to BASIC. Let **R** denote the rational numbers. A program P is said to compute the n-ary function $X: \mathbf{R}^n \longrightarrow \mathbf{R}$ on the computer **C** if the computer calculates $X(Y_1, \ldots, Y_n)$ as output, given values $Y_1, \ldots, Y_n \in \mathbf{R}$ as input. (If $n=0$ then X is a constant and there is no input.)

Any suitably powerful programming language can be used to define a measure of information content. However, we have made certain assumptions about the programming language that simplify the algebra of algorithmic information theory. We will introduce some of these assumptions as we go along, and the remainder can be found in (Thompson, 1980). We will assume that programs are written in an alphabet of 64 characters, each of which can be encoded as a 6-bit string. These include the symbols 0, . . . ,9 and A, . . . ,Z. We assume that the language has a system for encoding any integer $0 \leq x < 2^n$ with a string of no more than $n + 6\log_{10}(n) + 12$ bits. We also assume that the computer can handle rational numbers and integers with arbitrarily many significant digits.

Let $X: \mathbf{R}^n \longrightarrow \mathbf{R}$ be an n-ary function that is computable by **C**. The information content of such a function has been defined by A. I. Kolmogorof (1968), G. Chaitin (1977), and others to be

$$L(X \mid \mathbf{C}) = \min \left\{ l(P) : P \text{ computes } X \text{ on } \mathbf{C} \right\} \tag{25}$$

Here $l(P)$, the length of P, is the number of bits in the bit string P.

We can see from this definition that information content is not an absolute, but is dependent on the particular computer, **C**. Yet for any **C** the vast majority of X's have a large information content. There can be no more than 2^k programs P of length less than or equal to k. It follows that the number of integers $0 \leqslant x < 2^n$ with $L(x\,|\mathbf{C}) \leqslant k$ is no more than 2^k, even though there are 2^n numbers in this range. The conventions of our programming language for the coding of integers imply that

$$L(x\,|\mathbf{C}) \leqslant 36 + 6\log_{10}(n) + n \tag{26}$$

and we can thus conclude that most binary integers of n bits have an information content of approximately n.

The computer **C** can be modified by the addition of m externally supplied functions or constants $F_1, \ldots, F_m$ that can be called on by name in programs. This modified computer can be called $\mathbf{C}(F_1, \ldots, F_m)$, and we write $L(X\,|F_1, \ldots, F_m) = L(X\,|\mathbf{C}(F_1, \ldots, F_m))$ and also $L(X) = L(X\,|\mathbf{C})$. $L(X\,|F_1, \ldots, F_m)$ is a measure of the amount of additional information needed to specify X, given that $F_1, \ldots, F_m$ are known. The programming language is designed so that

$$L(X\,|F_1, \ldots, F_{m+1}) \leqslant L(X\,|F_1, \ldots, F_m) \tag{27}$$

and

$$L(X\,|F_1, \ldots, F_m) \leqslant L(X\,|F_1, \ldots, F_{m+1}) + L(F_{m+1}|F_1, \ldots, F_m) \tag{28}$$

The following basic theorem expresses the relationship between information content and the probabilities of events in a mathematical model of a physical system.

Proposition 1.

Suppose that M is a computable function mapping the non-negative integers into the non-negative rational numbers. Suppose that M satisfies

$$\sum_X M(X) \leqslant 2^v \tag{29}$$

for some integer, $v \geqslant 0$. If $L(X\,|M)$, $v < 2^r$ for some integer, $r > 0$, then

$$M(X) \leqslant 2^{c + v - L(X\,|\,M)} \tag{30}$$

where $c = 163 + 5.42r$.

This theorem is proven in Thompson, (1980), and it also holds if we replace $L(X\,|M)$ in (30) by $L(X\,|M, F_1, \ldots, F_m)$.

Corollary 1.

Suppose that M is the same as in Proposition 1. Then, given the same assumptions on X,

$$M(X) \leqslant 2^{c+v+L(M)-L(X)} \tag{31}$$

This corollary follows from Proposition 1 and (28) with $m=0$ and $F_1=M$. Inequality (18) of Section 5.3 follows from (31) with $r=30$. The requirement that $r=30$ simply means that (18) applies only for $L(X)<2^{30}\approx 10^9$.

Let $X_1, \ldots, X_m$ be non-negative integers, and let G be a function mapping non-negative integers to non-negative integers. Suppose that $G(X_1)= \ldots =G(X_m)=Y$. In Section 5.3 we explained how G could be interpreted as a process of observation, and how Y could be interpreted as a description of common observed features shared by all the X_j's. There we also pointed out that $L(Y|G)$ could be taken as a measure of the amount of observable information that is derived by G from the X_j's, but is not simply an artifact of G. We shall define the amount of information shared by $X_1, \ldots, X_m$ to be

$$J(\mathbf{X}) = \max_{Y,G\,:\,G(X_1)=\ldots=G(X_m)=Y} L(Y|G) \tag{32}$$

Here $\mathbf{X}$ stands for the set, $\{X_1, \ldots, X_m\}$.

$J(\mathbf{X})$ represents the maximum amount of information that can be observed in each of the X_j's by some process of observation. We can similarly define $J(\mathbf{X}|F_1, \ldots, F_n)$ by using $L(Y|G,F_1, \ldots, F_n)$ in place of $L(Y|G)$ in (32). This represents the amount of shared information in the X_j's that is independent of $F_1, \ldots, F_n$.

Proposition 2.

Let M be a probability measure on the integers, $0\leqslant x<N$. Suppose that M takes on rational values, and that N can be expressed in 15 or fewer characters.

If $\mathbf{X}$ is a set of integers, $0\leqslant X_1, \ldots, X_m<N$, and $J(\mathbf{X}|M)<2^r$ for some integer $r>0$, then

$$M(\mathbf{X}) \leqslant 2^{c'-J(\mathbf{X}|M)} \tag{33}$$

where $c'=337+3.62r$.

This is proven in Thompson, (1980), and it also holds with $J(\mathbf{X}|M,F_1, \ldots, F_n)$ in place of $J(\mathbf{X}|M)$.

Corollary 2.

With the same assumptions as in Proposition 1,

$$M(\mathbf{X}) \leqslant 2^{c'+L(M)-J(\mathbf{X})} \tag{34}$$

This corollary also follows using (28). Inequalities (24) and (22) in Section 5.3 follow directly from (33) and (34). (Again, we choose $r=30$.) In Thompson, (1980) the properties of $J(\mathbf{X})$ are analyzed, and a number of examples of observation functions are discussed.

In Section 5.2 we argued that if a long bit string has a low information content, then there must exist a strong interdependence among its parts. Now we shall show how this can be formally established. Let X_m be a bit string of length hm, and suppose that X_m is divided into substrings $Y_1, \ldots, Y_m$ of length h. If we treat the Y_k's as binary numbers we can write $X_0=1$ and

$$X_{k+1} = 2^h X_k + Y_{k+1} \tag{35}$$

for each $0 \leq k < m$. (Since X_m may begin with leading zeros, we place a 1 in front of it to convert it into a binary number.)

Let N be a very large fixed number. We say that the bit string X is an *initial segment* of the bit string X' if X' consists of X followed by $n \leq 0$ additional bits. We define $I(X)$ to be the number of bit strings X' such that $L(X') \leq N$ and X is an initial segment of X'.

Now let w be a bit string (which may have leading zeros). We define $F(h,w,X)$ to be the wth integer Y in numerical order for which $0 \leq Y < 2^h$ and

$$I(2^h X+Y) > 2^{-l(w)} I(X) \tag{36}$$

This F can be called the generating function. (F was used in Section 5.2 with the parameter h suppressed for convenience.)

Our application of F in equation (11) of Section 5.2 was based on the following proposition.

Proposition 3.

Let $Y_1, \ldots, Y_m$ be as in (35), and suppose that $L(X_m) \leq N$. Then there are bit strings $w_1, \ldots, w_m$ such that

$$\sum_{n=1}^{m} (l(w_n)-1) \leq L(X_m) \tag{37}$$

and for each $1 \leq n \leq m$,

$$Y_n = F(h,w_n,X_{n-1}) \tag{38}$$

Proof. Define

$$K_n = \min\left\{K\colon I(X_n) \geq 2^{-K}\, I(X_{n-1})\right\} \tag{39}$$

It follows that

$$I(X_m) \leq 2^{\sum_{n=1}^{m}(1-K_n)}\, I(X_0) \tag{40}$$

From the definition of $I(X)$,

$$\sum_{Y=0}^{2^h-1} I(2^h X+Y) \leq I(X) \tag{41}$$

Therefore, at most $2^{K_n}-1$ Y's from 0 to 2^h-1 can satisfy

$$I(2^h X_{n-1} + Y) > 2^{-K_n} I(X_{n-1}) \tag{42}$$

According to (39), inequality (42) is satisfied by $Y=Y_n$. Therefore Y_n is the wth number from 0 to 2^h-1 satisfying (42), where w lies in the interval, $1 \leq w \leq 2^{K_n}-1$. We can produce the desired bit string w_n by adding leading zeros to this w, if necessary, so that its length equals K_n. Then (38) will be satisfied.

To show (37), note that $I(X_0)$ is no greater than the number of strings X' with $L(X') \leq N$, and that this is no greater than 2^N. Now let $n=L(X_m) \leq N$. There must be a program P of length n that computes X_m. The conventions of our programming language can be arranged so as to allow us to construct a program Q of the form $Q=PA$, where A is an arbitrary string of $N-n$ bits. The idea here is that when executing Q, the computer will refer only to the instructions in P, and will never refer to A. Thus A can be chosen in any of 2^{N-n} different ways, and it follows that,

$$I(X_m) \geq 2^{N-n} \tag{43}$$

We obtain (37) by combining (43), (40), and $I(X_0) \leq 2^N$. Q.E.D.

We have seen that the generating function F can be defined very simply. However, an inspection of the definition will show that it is not possible to compute F in practice. In fact, as matters stand, F cannot be computed at all. It can be shown that even though $L(X)$ is a precisely defined function, there does not exist an algorithm that will compute $L(X)$ for any value of X. (This is discussed in (Chaitin, 1977).) This means that $L(X)$ is what is known as an uncomputable or "nonrecursive" function. Since F is defined in terms of L, it is not surprising that F is also uncomputable.

It is interesting that we can unambiguously define numbers and functions that are theoretically impossible to compute. We will not have to consider the implications of this here, however, for we can easily modify our definitions in such a way that F becomes computable. One way of doing this is to place a very large cutoff on the running time of programs on our computer, **C**. If we stipulate that any program running over this limit immediately prints a 0 and stops, then both L and F become formally computable, and all our considerations in Sections 5.1, 5.2, and 5.3 remain essentially unaffected. (We must set the cutoff high enough so that the program for $M(X)$ can complete its calculations.)

Nonetheless, even though F is rendered computable by this device, the number of steps needed to calculate F is so large that we cannot hope to carry them out in practice. One might therefore ask, "What is the value of considering F if this function cannot be computed?" In brief, our answer is as follows: If we choose an appropriate cutoff on the running time of programs on **C**, we can write a very simple program that will calculate F (but not within the time limit imposed by this cutoff). This program involves a few simple arithmetical operations that are repeated over and over again according to a simple pattern. Now, suppose that a detailed description of biological form has a low information content. Then we can apply Proposition 3 and show that successive sections of this description can be generated by applying F to successive code strings $w_1, \ldots, w_n$. As we described in Section 5.2, very elaborate segments of the biological description can be generated in this way by the addition of miniscule amounts of information in the form of the strings w_j.

Our question is, "How can the function F reel off successive descriptions of complex organs and biological processes under the guidance of such minute amounts of information?" If we suppose that F can do this, then we must conclude that the mere repetition of a few simple computational steps, if prolonged over a long enough period, will generate the kind of complex patterns found in living organisms. Furthermore, given the direction provided by the w_j's, the specific patterns of life as we know it will be produced, and no others. This would seem to attribute very remarkable powers to the elementary operations of arithmetic. Although we cannot rigorously prove that F does not have these remarkable properties, we think it worth our while to seriously consider the consequences that follow if, in fact, it does not have them.

Appendix 2
Information Content of the Laws of Chemistry

In this appendix we shall discuss the information content of the physical laws thought to govern both chemical reactions and the interactions between matter and electromagnetic radiation. We will be particularly concerned with the laws of nonrelativistic quantum mechanics summarized in Figure 1 of Chapter 5. These laws apply to a physical system containing M particles with position coordinates $\mathbf{Q}_1, \ldots, \mathbf{Q}_M$. The particles consist of electrons plus several different species of atomic nuclei. We can assume that the particles are situated within a very large box containing a radiation field characterized by the parameters q_n (n=1, 2, 3, . . .).

In Figure 1, equation (a) is the Schrödinger equation, and Ψ is a wave function defining the state of the system. In equation (b), the Hamiltonian H is expressed as a sum of terms representing different kinds of physical interactions. Reading from left to right (and from top to bottom), the first term represents the propagation of electromagnetic radiation in space. The second term represents the kinetic energy of the particles, and the next two terms describe the interaction between the charged particles and the electromagnetic field. The fifth term represents the interaction between the electromagnetic field and the spin, or magnetic moment, of the particles. Finally, the sixth term describes the electrostatic and gravitational interactions of the particles.

To get some idea of the information content of the laws of physics, we have written a program for the numerical solution of the Schrödinger equation using the Hamiltonian of Figure 1. It is not possible, of course, to run such a program on an actual computer, for the required computations would tax the powers of the fastest computers for even a very small number of particles. Nonetheless, it is interesting to see how the laws of physics appear when their abstract definitions are expressed in terms of elementary arithmetical operations.

In Appendix 1 we defined information content in terms of a fixed programming language. This language is written in a 64-character alphabet that includes 0, . . . ,9 and A, . . . ,Z. Special symbols are also included for

IF THEN GOTO FOR TO NEXT PRINT

. : , = ≠ < ≤ ( ) ↑ * / + −

These symbols are adopted from the BASIC programming language, and their meanings and syntactical rules are essentially the same as in that language. There are also a few other symbols for special purposes, including a symbol for the operation, INT, of rounding a number down to an integer. These symbols designate the primitive operations of the language, and all other operations, such as the extraction of roots, must be defined in terms of these elementary symbols. (The language is described in detail in Thompson, (1980).)

In this language, a program for the numerical solution of the equations in Figure 1 can be written in about 1,738 characters, or less than two-thirds of a page. In addition to programming instructions, a table of data is also needed to define various physical constants, such as the charges and masses of the different kinds of atomic nuclei. If we allow 1,062 characters for this data, the total programming for the representation and solution of the quantum mechanical equations comes to one page of 2,800 characters.

In writing this program we have made a number of assumptions. First of all, we assumed that the box containing the physical system has what are known as "periodic" boundary conditions. This makes it possible to expand the electromagnetic vector potential **A** in a standard way as a sum of sine and cosine terms, $\mathbf{A}_n$. We assumed that the box is very large, and that the particles are bound by gravitation near the box's center. (This can be accomplished by introducing a fixed gravitational potential.) These assumptions mean that the boundary of the system can be regarded, in effect, as an infinite vacuum. Since our model does not allow for nuclear interactions, a source of heat and light is necessary, and this can be provided by introducing a fixed source of electromagnetic radiation.

We assumed that electrons have a spin of ½, but we neglected the spins of the nuclei, which were treated as charged point masses. We did not introduce any relativistic correction terms, and we used a cutoff to bound the Coulomb potential, $1/r$, for $r<\varepsilon$. We also introduced a frequency cutoff by using a finite number of modes of oscillation, q_n. Finally, we introduced a finite grid for the approximation of derivatives, and we placed bounds on the number of significant figures to be carried in various calculations.

If we contemplate these assumptions, it becomes clear that our model cannot be taken as a final statement about the laws underlying chemistry. Unfortunately, when we examine the matter closely, we find that it is very difficult to adequately formulate such laws. It is very hard to say whether or not any particular change in our assumptions would significantly affect the validity of our model as a representation of chemical and biological processes. For example, how many significant figures should we include for the charge and mass of an electron? Should we include relativistic effects?

Should we go further and include other physical interactions, such as the weak force? (At least one author has speculated that the weak force may have biologically significant effects.[1])

At present, no mathematically consistent theories have been formulated that take the weak and nuclear forces into account, and there are also serious mathematical difficulties plaguing the relativistic quantum theory of electromagnetism.[2] Even the nonrelativistic quantum theory that we have considered here is beset with controversial problems.[3] Some of these problems are discussed in Chapter 3. Another was raised by the physicist Eugene Wigner, who argued that a self-reproducing organism is not possible in a quantum mechanical system.[4]

These theoretical problems are accompanied by the practical problem that it is very difficult to analyze complex chemical reactions using the quantum theory.[5] As a result, many researchers accept quantum mechanics on faith, but use reaction-diffusion equations to model biochemical systems. Yet as we pointed out in Section 5.3, such models have fundamental drawbacks that make them incapable of adequately representing organisms. Here we have decided to use the quantum mechanical equations of Chapter 5, Figure 1 simply to provide a general idea of the amount of information entailed by the known laws of physics and chemistry.

If we examine the theory of evolution, we find that three basic principles are generally invoked. These are (1) that self-reproducing organisms of great complexity are physically possible, (2) that these organisms can change by random mutation, and (3) that the organisms will be culled by natural selection. One might therefore argue that any laws sufficient to guarantee (1), (2), and (3) could serve as the basis for a model of evolution. As Wigner's arguments indicate, it is not clear at present whether or not these three principles are guaranteed by the known laws of quantum mechanics. However, as we pointed out in Section 5.1, John von Neumann has devised a kind of mathematical model that does provide for (1), (2), and (3). His cellular automata are nonphysical, for they involve many finite-state automata situated in the cells of a two-dimensional lattice. Yet they can represent self-reproducing "organisms" (universal Turing machines) of any degree of complexity.

We have therefore written a program for the $M(X)$ function of a particularly simple cellular automaton model due to E.F. Codd.[6] This model can also represent self-reproducing universal Turing machines, and it can easily be modified to provide for random mutations. The model entails an initially empty lattice that gradually fills up with a "soup" of randomly distributed states. The program for $M(X)$ requires 1,856 characters, or about two-thirds of a page.

As we have pointed out in Section 5.3, the probability for the evolution of recognizable higher forms is practically zero in a model of such low information content. Even if the model were started with an initial population of primitive self-reproducing automata, no higher forms recognizable to us could be expected to evolve. A process of natural selection is to be expected in a population of self-reproducing automata that must compete for space and resources. One might therefore imagine that some kind of "higher intelligence" might gradually evolve. Yet if this happened, the "intelligence" would be so alien that it would be meaningless to call it by this name. In general, no representative of a class of forms is likely to evolve if the class is characterized by a description of high information content.

As a final point, let us consider how $M(X)$ might be defined for our quantum mechanical model. To define $M(X)$ we would first have to devise a coding scheme whereby molecular configurations could be represented by integers, X. A necessary condition for two atoms to be bonded together in a molecule is that their nuclei should be situated within a certain distance of one another. This distance will depend on the types of atoms and the type of bond being considered. The pattern of bonds in a particular molecule can thus be represented as a network of internuclear distances.

Let us suppose that the nuclei in our quantum model have coordinates $\mathbf{Q}_1, \ldots, \mathbf{Q}_N$, where $N<M$. Using our coding scheme, we can define a function $B_X(\mathbf{Q}_1, \ldots, \mathbf{Q}_N)$ which will equal 1 if some subset of the nuclear coordinates $\mathbf{Q}_1, \ldots, \mathbf{Q}_N$ satisfy the spacing requirements for the molecule specified by X. This function will otherwise be set equal to 0.

The function B_X can be used to estimate the probability that the molecule described by X exists within the physical system. If the system is in the quantum mechanical state, Ψ, let

$$M(X,\Psi) = \int |\Psi(\mathbf{Q})|^2 B_X(\mathbf{Q}_1, \ldots, \mathbf{Q}_N)\, d\mathbf{Q} \tag{44}$$

where the integral is taken over all the variables of Ψ. Since B_X defines a necessary (but possibly insufficient) condition for the existence of the molecule X, $M(X,\Psi)$ gives an upper bound on the probability that this molecule exists in the system.

A given arrangement of $\mathbf{Q}_1, \ldots, \mathbf{Q}_N$ can represent only a limited number of molecular configurations. There should be a number T for which

$$\sum_X B_X(\mathbf{Q}_1, \ldots, \mathbf{Q}_N) \leq T \tag{45}$$

for all arrangements of $\mathbf{Q}_1, \ldots, \mathbf{Q}_N$.

To obtain an estimate of T, we shall make a further restriction on B_X. We require that $B_X(\mathbf{Q}_1, \ldots, \mathbf{Q}_N)$ shall equal 1 only if some of these coordinates satisfy the conditions for X but are not within bonding distance of any of the other $\mathbf{Q}_j$'s. Then $B_X=1$ will mean that the molecule represented by X is present, but is not part of a larger molecule. This means that each $\mathbf{Q}_j$ can be part of at most one configuration corresponding to an X with $B_X(\mathbf{Q}_1, \ldots, \mathbf{Q}_N)=1$. Therefore, $T \leq N$.

The function $M(X,\Psi)$ can be specified using (44) and the definition of Ψ in terms of natural laws, initial conditions, and boundary conditions. We can also calculate the probability of finding X in a system described by a mixture of states. If the mixture consists of the states Ψ_j with probability a_j, then this probability is bounded by $\Sigma a_j\ M(X,\Psi_j)$. Thus, the total information content of the function $M(X)$ is given by

$$L(M) \leq L(\text{initial conditions}) + L(\text{boundary conditions}) + L(\text{natural laws}) + L(B) + L(t) + \text{constant}. \tag{46}$$

The B_X we have been considering can be expressed in less than a half page of coding, and thus $L(B)$ need be no more than half a page, or 8,400 bits. In Section 5.2 we allotted a full page for this term so as to allow for a more sophisticated function, B_X.

The constant represents the number of symbols needed to express (44), plus some other odds and ends. The time must be considered in our estimate of $L(M)$ since it enters into the calculation of the state of the system. $L(t)$ will be negligible, however, for times ranging from 0 to billions of billions of years. We have seen that L (natural laws) is about one page in our model. If we allow four pages for the definitions of the initial and boundary conditions, we obtain the upper bound on $L(M)$ given in (16) of Section 5.3.

Notes

1. Garey, "Superweak Interactions and the Biological Time Direction," pp. 1–5.
2. Since its inception in the late 1940s, the theory of relativistic quantum electrodynamics has been beset by serious mathematical difficulties. The standard method of resolving these difficulties has been a procedure called renormalization. This procedure has enabled physicists to make certain calculations that have agreed remarkably well with

experimental measurements. However, renormalization has not eliminated the mathematical difficulties plaguing the theory, and the physicist P. A. M. Dirac has suggested that the renormalization theory "will not survive in the future, and that the remarkable agreement between its results and experiment should be looked on as a fluke." (Dirac, "Evolution of the Physicist's Picture of Nature," p. 50.)

3. Wigner, "Epistemological Perspective on Quantum Theory."
4. Wigner, "The Probability of the Existence of a Self Reproducing Unit," pp. 231–238.
5. Wigner, "Epistemological Perspective on Quantum Theory," p. 374.
6. Codd, *Cellular Automata*.

Bibliography

Adler, J. "Is Man a Subtle Accident?" *Newsweek*, 3 November 1980, pp. 95–96.

Andrews, Henry N. Jr. *Studies in Paleobotany*. New York: John Wiley and Sons, 1961.

Axelrod, Daniel I. "Evolution of the Psilophyte Paleoflora." *Evolution*. Vol. 13, June 1959, pp. 264–275.

Axelrod, Daniel I. "The Evolution of Flowering Plants." In *Evolution After Darwin*. Vol. 1, *The Evolution of Life*. Edited by S. Tax. Chicago: University of Chicago Press, 1960.

Bell, Eric T. *Men of Mathematics*. New York: Simon and Schuster, 1937.

Bell, John S. "On the Problem of Hidden Variables in Quantum Mechanics." *Reviews of Modern Physics*. Vol. 38, no. 3, July 1966, pp. 447–452.

Berg, Howard C. "How Bacteria Swim." *Scientific American*, August 1975, pp. 36–44.

Bhaktivedanta Swami Prabhupāda, A.C. *Bhagavad-gītā As It Is*. Sanskrit text, translation, and commentary. New York: Collier Books, 1972.

Bhaktivedanta Swami Prabhupāda, A.C. *Śrī Īśopaniṣad*. Sanskrit text, translation, and commentary. Los Angeles: Bhaktivedanta Book Trust, 1974.

Bhaktivedanta Swami Prabhupāda, A.C. *Śrīmad-Bhāgavatam of Kṛṣṇa-Dvaipāyana Vyāsa*. Sanskrit text, translation, and commentary. Cantos 1–10 (30 vols.) Los Angeles: Bhaktivedanta Book Trust, 1972–1980.

Bhaktivedanta Swami Prabhupāda, A.C. *Teachings of Lord Caitanya*. Los Angeles: Bhaktivedanta Book Trust, 1974.

Bhaktivedanta Swami Prabhupāda, A.C. *The Nectar of Devotion: A Summary Study of Śrīla Rūpa Gosvāmī's "Bhakti-rasāmṛta-sindhu"*. Los Angeles: Bhaktivedanta Book Trust, 1970.

Bohm, David. *Causality and Chance in Modern Physics*. London: Routledge and Kegan Paul, 1957.

Bohm, David and Bub, J. "A Proposed Solution of the Measurement Problem in Quantum Mechanics by a Hidden Variable Theory." *Reviews of Modern Physics*. Vol. 38, no. 3, July 1966, pp. 453–468.

Brush, Stephen G. "Should the History of Science be Rated X?" *Science*. Vol. 183, 22 March 1974, pp. 1164–1172.

Buddenbrock, Wolfgang von. *The Senses*. Ann Arbor: University of Michigan Press, 1958.

Capra, Fritjof. *The Tao of Physics*. New York: Bantam Books, 1975.

Chaitin, Gregory G. "Algorithmic Information Theory." *IBM Journal of Research and Development*. Vol. 21, no. 4, July 1977, pp. 350–359.

Codd, E. F. *Cellular Automata*. New York: Academic Press, 1968.

Cozzarelli, Nicholas R. "DNA Gyrase and the Supercoiling of DNA." *Science*. Vol. 207, 29 February 1980, pp. 953–960.

Crick, Francis. "Split Genes and RNA Splicing." *Science*. Vol. 204, 20 April 1979, pp. 264–271.

Daneri, A.; Loinger, A.; and Prosperi, G.M. "Further Remarks on the Relations Between Statistical Mechanics and Quantum Theory of Measurement." *Il Nuovo Cimento*. Vol. 44B, no. 1, 1966, pp. 119–128.

Daneri, A.; Loinger, A.; and Prosperi, G.M. "Quantum Theory of Measurement and Ergodicity Conditions." *Nuclear Physics*. Vol. 33, 1962, pp. 297–319.

Darwin, Charles. *On the Origin of Species*. New York: Athenum, 1972.

Darwin, Charles. *The Life and Letters of Charles Darwin*. Vol. 1. New York: D. Appleton, 1896.

Dewitt, Bryce S. "Quantum Gravity: the New Synthesis." In *General Relativity*. Edited by S.W. Hawking and W. Israel. Cambridge: Cambridge University Press, 1979.

Dewitt, Bryce S. "Quantum Mechanics and Reality." *Physics Today*, September 1970, pp. 30–35.

Dickerson, Richard E. "X-ray Analysis and Protein Structure." In *The Proteins,* Vol. II. Edited by H. Neurath. New York: Academic Press, 1964.

Dirac, P.A.M. "The Evolution of the Physicist's Picture of Nature." *Scientific American,* May 1963, pp. 45–53.

Dixon, Malcolm and Webb, Edwin C. *Enzymes.* 3d ed. New York: Academic Press, 1979.

Dobzhansky, Theodosius. "Darwinian Evolution and the Problem of Extraterrestrial Life." *Perspectives in Biology and Medicine.* Vol. 15, no. 2, Winter 1972, pp. 157–175.

Dobzhansky, Theodosius. "From Potentiality to Realization in Evolution." In *Mind in Nature.* Edited by J.B. Cobb, Jr. and D.R. Griffen. Washington, D.C.: University Press of America, 1978.

Dodson, Edward O. and Dodson, Peter. *Evolution, Process and Product.* New York: D. Van Nostrand Co., 1976.

Eddington, Arthur. *The Philosophy of Physical Science.* New York: Macmillan Co., 1939.

Edwards, Paul, ed. *The Encyclopedia of Philosophy.* Vol. 5. New York: Macmillan Publishing Co. and The Free Press, 1967.

Eigen, Manfred. "Selforganization of Matter and the Evolution of Biological Macromolecules." *Die Naturwissenschaften.* Vol. 10, October 1971, pp. 465–523.

Eigen, Manfred and Schuster, Peter. "The Hypercycle," Parts A, B, and C. *Die Naturwissenschaften.* Vol. 64, 1977, pp. 541–565; Vol. 65, 1978, pp. 7–41; Vol. 65, 1978, pp. 341–369.

Elliot, Alfred M. and Ray, Charles, Jr. *Biology.* 2d ed. New York: Meridith Pub. Co., 1965.

Fine, Terrence L. *Theories of Probability.* New York and London: Academic Press, 1973.

Fisher, Ronald. *The Genetical Theory of Natural Selection.* 2d ed. New York: Dover, 1958.

Fodor, Jerry A. "The Mind-Body Problem." *Scientific American,* January 1981, pp. 114–123.

French, A.P., ed. *Einstein: A Centenary Volume.* Cambridge, Mass.: Harvard University Press, 1979.

Freundlich, Yehudah. "Mind, Matter, and Physicists." *Foundations of Physics.* Vol. 2, no. 2/3, 1972, pp. 129–147.

Garey, A.S. "Superweak Interactions and the Biological Time Direction." *Origins of Life.* Vol. 9, 1978, pp. 1–5.

Gillespie, Neal C. *Charles Darwin and the Problem of Creation.* Chicago: University of Chicago Press, 1979.

Glaessner, M.F. "Biological Events and the Precambrian Time Scale." In *Adventures in Earth History.* Edited by P. Cloud. San Francisco: W.H. Freeman and Co., 1970.

Gnedenko, Boris V. *Theory of Probability.* 4th ed. Bronx, New York: Chelsea, 1968.

Goldschmidt, Richard. *The Material Basis of Evolution.* New Haven: Yale University Press, 1940.

Gosvāmī, Satsvarūpa Dāsa. *Readings in Vedic Literature.* Los Angeles: Bhaktivedanta Book Trust, 1977.

Gould, Stephen J. "Chance Riches." *Natural History,* November 1980, pp. 36–44.

Gould, Stephen J. "Hen's Teeth and Horse's Toes." *Natural History,* July 1980, pp. 24–28.

Gould, Stephen J. *The Panda's Thumb.* New York: W.W. Norton and Co., 1980.

Gould, Stephen J. and Eldridge, Niles. "Punctuated Equilibria: The Tempo and Mode of Evolution Reconsidered." *Paleobiology.* Vol. 3, 1977, pp. 115–151.

Grasse, Pierre-P. *Evolution of Living Organisms.* New York: Academic Press, 1977.

Hadamard, Jacques. *The Psychology of Invention in the Mathematical Field.* Princeton: Princeton University Press, 1949.

Harland, W.B., *et. al.*, eds. *The Fossil Record.* London: Geological Society of London, 1967.

Hawking, S.W. and Israel, W., eds. *General Relativity.* Cambridge: Cambridge University Press, 1979.

Heisenberg, Werner. *Physics and Beyond.* New York: Harper and Row, 1971.

Heisenberg, Werner. "The Representation of Nature in Contemporary Physics." *Daedalus.* Vol. 87, no. 3, 1958, pp. 95–108.

Helmholtz, Hermann Von. *Über die Erhaltung der Kraft.* Ostwald's Klassiker der Exakten Wissenschaften Nr. 1, 1847.

Hinkel, Peter C. and McCarty, Richard E. "How Cells Make ATP." *Scientific American,* March 1978, pp. 104–123.

Huffman, D.A. "A Method for the Construction of Minimum Redundancy Codes." *Proceedings of the I.R.E.* Vol. 40, September 1952, pp. 1098–1101.

Huxley, Julian. *Evolution in Action.* New York: Harper and Brothers, 1953.

Huxley, Thomas H. *Essays on Some Controverted Questions.* London: Macmillan and Co., 1892.

Jacob, K.; Jacob, Chinna; and Shrivastava, R.N. *Nature.* Vol. 172, no. 4369, 1953, pp. 166–167.

Jammer, Max. *The Philosophy of Quantum Mechanics.* New York: John Wiley and Sons, 1974.

Jauch, J.M. *Are Quanta Real?* Bloomington: Indiana University Press, 1973.

Jones, James P. "Recursive Undecidability—An Exposition." *American Mathematical Monthly,* September 1974, pp. 724–738.

Kavirāja, Kṛṣṇadāsa Gosvāmī. *Śrī Caitanya-caritāmṛta.* Bengali text, translation, and commentary by A.C. Bhaktivedanta Swami Prabhupāda. *Ādi-līlā* 3 vols., *Madhya-līlā* 9 vols., *Antya-līlā* 5 vols. Los Angeles: Bhaktivedanta Book Trust, 1974–1975.

Kepner, W.A.; Gregory, W.C.; and Porter, R.J. "The Manipulation of the Nematocysts of Chlorohydra by Microstomum." *Zoologisher Anzeiger.* Vol. 121, Jan.–June 1938, pp. 114–124.

Kleene, Stephen C. *Introduction to Metamathematics.* New York: Van Nostrand, 1952.

Kolmogorov, Andrei N. "Logical Basis for Information Theory and Probability Theory." *IEEE Transactions on Information Theory*. Vol. IT-14, no. 5, September 1968, pp. 662–664.

Layzer, David. "The Arrow of Time." *The Astrophysical Journal*. Vol. 206, 1 June 1976, pp. 559–569.

Lewin, R. "Evolutionary Theory Under Fire." *Science*. Vol. 210, 21 November 1980, pp. 883–887.

Macbeth, Norman. *Darwin Retried: An Appeal to Reason*. Boston: Gambit, 1971.

Mattuck, Richard D. and Walker, Evan H. "The Action of Consciousness on Matter: A Quantum Mechanical Theory of Psychokinesis." In *The Iceland Papers*. Edited by A. Puharich. Amherst, Wisconson: Essentia Research Associates, 1979.

Mayr, Ernst. "The Emergence of Evolutionary Novelties." In *Evolution After Darwin*. Vol. 1, *The Evolution of Life*. Edited by S. Tax. Chicago: University of Chicago Press, 1960.

McDougall, I.; Compston, W.; and Hawkes, D.D. *Nature*. Vol. 198, no. 4880, 1963, pp. 564–567.

Messiah, Albert. *Quantum Mechanics*. Vol. 2. Amsterdam: North-Holland Pub. Co., 1965.

Monod, Jacques. *Chance and Necessity*. New York: Alfred A. Knopf, 1971.

Mott, N.F. "The Wave Mechanics of α-Ray Tracks." *Proceedings of the Royal Society*, London. Vol. 126, 1929, pp. 79–84.

Nagel, Ernest. *The Structure of Science*. New York and Burlingame: Harcourt, Brace, and World, 1961.

Newton's Principia. Translated by Andrew Motte. New York: Daniel Adee, 1846.

Oparin, A.I. *The Origin of Life*. 2d ed. New York: Dover, 1953.

Orgel, Leslie E. *The Origins of Life*. New York: Wiley, 1973.

Poincaré, Henri. *The Foundations of Science*. Lancaster, Pa.: The Science Press, 1946.

Popper, Karl R. and Eccles, John C. *The Self and Its Brain*. New York: Springer-Verlag, 1977.

Prigogine, Ilya; Nicolis, Gregoire; and Babloyantz, Agnes. "Thermodynamics of Evolution." *Physics Today,* November 1972, pp. 23–28.

Rensberger, B. "Recent Studies Spark Revolution in Interpretation of Evolution." *The New York Times,* 4 November 1980, p. C3.

Rensch, Bernhard. *Evolution Above the Species Level.* New York: Columbia University Press, 1960.

Rosenfeld, Leon. "The Measuring Process in Quantum Mechanics." *Suppl. Progr. Theor. Phys.,* extra n. 1965, pp. 222–231.

Ruelle, David. "Strange Attractors." *Mathematical Intelligencer.* Vol. 2, no. 3, 1980, pp. 126–137.

Russell, Bertrand. "A Free Man's Worship" (1903). *In Mysticism and Logic, and Other Essays.* London: Allen and Unwin, 1963.

Satir, Peter. "How Cilia Move." *Scientific American,* October 1974, pp. 44–52.

Schrödinger, Erwin. *What is Life? and Mind and Matter.* Cambridge: Cambridge University Press, 1967.

Shannon, Claude E. "A Mathematical Theory of Communication." *Bell System Technical Journal.* Vol. 27, July 1948, pp. 379–423.

Sherman, Irwin W. and Sherman, Vilia G. *Biology: A Human Approach.* New York: Oxford University Press, 1975.

Shklovskii, Iosif S. and Sagan, Carl. *Intelligent Life in the Universe.* San Francisco: Holden-Day, 1966.

Simpson, George G. *This View of Life.* New York: Harcourt, Brace, and World, 1964.

Slater, John C. *Quantum Theory of Molecules and Solids.* Vol. 1. New York: McGraw Hill, 1963.

Smith, John Maynard. "Hypercycles and the Origin of Life." *Nature.* Vol. 280, 9 August 1979, pp. 445–446.

Smith, John Maynard. "The Limitations of Evolutionary Theory." In *The Encyclopedia of Ignorance,* edited by R. Duncan and M. Weston-Smith. New York: Pocket Books, 1978.

Snelling, N.J. *Nature.* Vol. 198, no. 4885, 1963, pp. 1079–1080.

Staehelin, L. Andrew and Hull, Barbara E. "Junctions Between Living Cells." *Scientific American,* May 1978, pp. 141–152.

Stainforth, R.M. *Nature.* Vol. 210, no. 5033, 1966, pp. 292–294.

Tax, Sol and Callender, Charles, eds. *Evolution After Darwin.* Vol. 3, *Issues in Evolution.* Chicago: University of Chicago Press, 1960.

Thakur, Bhakti Siddhanta Saraswati. *Shri Brahma-Samhita.* Madras, India: Sree Gaudiya Math, 1958.

Thompson, Richard. "A Measure of Shared Information in Classes of Patterns." *Pattern Recognition.* Vol. 12, no. 6, December 1980, pp. 369–379.

Tolman, Richard C. *The Principles of Statistical Mechanics.* Oxford: Claredon Press, 1938.

Valentine, James W. "The Evolution of Multicellular Plants and Animals." *Scientific American,* September, 1978, pp. 141–158.

Villee, Claude A. and Dethier, Vincent G. *Biological Principles and Processes.* Philadelphia, Pa.: W.B. Saunders Co., 1971.

von Neumann, John. *Mathematical Foundations of Quantum Mechanics.* Princeton: Princeton University Press, 1955.

von Neumann, John. *Theory of Self-Reproducing Automata.* Edited by Arthur Burkes. Urbana, Illinois: University of Illinois Press, 1966.

Wadia, Darashaw N. *The Geology of India.* 3d ed. London: Macmillan, 1953.

Watson, James D. *Molecular Biology of the Gene.* 3d ed. Menlo Park, California: W.A. Benjamin, 1977.

Weinberg, Steven. "Conceptual Foundations of the Unified Theory of Weak and Electromagnetic Interactions." *Science.* Vol. 210, 12 December 1980, pp. 1212–1218.

Weinberg, Steven. *The First Three Minutes.* New York: Bantum Books, 1977.

Weinberg, Steven. "The Forces of Nature." *American Scientist.* Vol. 65, March–April 1977, pp. 171–176.

Weisz, Paul B. *Elements of Biology.* New York: McGraw Hill Book Co., 1969.

Weizenbaum, Joseph. *Computer Power and Human Reason*. San Francisco: W.H. Freeman and Co., 1976.

Whitehead, Alfred N. *Process and Reality: An Essay in Cosmology*. Corrected edition. Edited by D.R. Griffin and D.W. Sherburne. New York: The Free Press, 1978.

Wigner, Eugene P. "Epistemological Perspective on Quantum Theory." In *Contemporary Research in the Foundations and Philosophy of Quantum Theory*. Edited by C.A. Hooker. Boston: Reidel Publishing Co., 1973.

Wigner, Eugene P. "On Hidden Variables and Quantum Mechanical Probabilities." *American Journal of Physics*. Vol. 38, no. 8, August 1970, pp. 1005–1009.

Wigner, Eugene P. "Physics and the Explanation of Life." *Foundations of Physics*. Vol. 1, no. 1, 1970, pp. 35–45.

Wigner, Eugene P. "Remarks on the Mind-Body Question." In *The Scientist Speculates*. Edited by I.J. Good. New York: Basic Books, 1962.

Wigner, Eugene P. "The Probability of the Existence of a Self Reproducing Unit." In *The Logic of Personal Knowledge*. London: Routledge and Kegan Paul, 1961.

Wigner, Eugene P. "Two Kinds of Reality." *The Monist*. Vol. 48, 1964, pp. 248–264.

Wilson, Edward O. *On Human Nature*. Cambridge: Harvard University Press, 1978.

Wilson, E. Grant. *The Mystery of Physical Life*. New York: Abelard Schuman, 1964.

Winston, Patrick H. *Artificial Intelligence*. Reading, Mass.: Addison-Wesley, 1977.

Winston, Patrick H. "The MIT Robot." In *Machine Intelligence 7*. Edited by B. Meltzer and D. Mitchie. New York: John Wiley and Sons, 1972.

Yockey, Hubert P. "A Calculation of the Probability of Spontaneous Biogenesis by Information Theory." *Journal of Theoretical Biology*. Vol. 67, 1977, pp. 377–398.

Yockey, Hubert P. "On the Information Content of Cytochrome c." *Journal of Theoretical Biology*. Vol. 67, 1977, pp. 345–376.

Zukav, Gary. *The Dancing Wu Li Masters*. New York: William Morrow and Co., 1979.

Index